The Complete Sybase Replication Server Quick Reference Guide

Versions 12.6, 15.0.1 & 15.1
2nd edition

Rob Verschoor

Sypron Publications

The Complete Sybase Replication Server Quick Reference Guide

Replication Server versions 12.6, 15.0.1 & 15.1
2nd edition

by Rob Verschoor

ISBN 90-806117-3-5

Published by:
Sypron B.V.
Het Wolfseind 24
3823 VS Amersfoort
The Netherlands
Internet **www.sypron.nl**
Email **sypron@sypron.nl**

Printed in The Netherlands

First edition : July 2004 (RS 12.0, 12.1, 12.5 & 12.6)
Second edition : June 2008 (RS 12.6, 15.0.1 & 15.1)

Contents

Foreword

Sybase Replication Server was designed as a versatile and powerful software product, and that goal has certainly been achieved. Unfortunately, it seems as if RepServer was never meant to be easy to use -- some of the RepServer syntax isn't easy to remember, and troubleshooting may require you to look for clues in a dozen different places. As a result, a DBA can quickly find him/herself at the wrong side of all that power and versatility.
To be fair, some of these issues can hardly be avoided: replication systems are never simple, and will quickly be an order of magnitude more complex than a single database. Nevertheless, many infrequently used commands and concepts of RepServer tend to slip your mind, especially when your replication system keeps running without any problems -- which, fortunately, is the case most of the time.
Invariably though, the moment comes when you need to take action, and that's when this book will be convenient: it contains all RepServer commands, RSSD procedures and ASE procedures you might need in practice. Apart from describing the basics of each command, I have also included some background information and practically useful tips, as well as a few handy RSSD queries for some of those things you sometimes need to figure out (well, at least I had to...).
When you're a RepServer DBA, there are those moments when you'll need all the help you can get -- this book will be your companion.

I'd like to thank Irfan Khan, Naveen Puttagunta, Heping Shang, Wanda Beck, Erik van Maasakkers, Alex Bruschke, Rutger van Veenendaal, Carel Cornelius, Richard Van Veen, Greg Carter, Lilei Chen and Chris Huston for answering many questions and providing valuable feedback. Also, big thanks to Simone, for her support and understanding while writing this book.

Rob Verschoor
Amersfoort, June 2008, 2nd edition

About this Quick Reference Guide

Replication Server versions covered in this edition
The information in this Quick Reference Guide applies to RepServer version 12.6 or later, a Unix/Linux environment, and an ASE-hosted RSSD, except where indicated otherwise. Also, most of the text assumes ASE-to-ASE replication for ASE version 12.0 or later, although most commands and features would apply just as well to non-ASE replication. The following RepServer versions are covered in this book:

- **12.6** - the base RepServer version used for this book.
- **15.0** - the main enhancements in this version are added support for routes with an embedded RSSD, support for ASE 15.0 features (including replication of encrypted ASE columns, without requiring decryption), increased disk partition size (1 Tb), improved GUI tools, and better integration with PowerDesigner.
- **15.0.1** - the most important new feature in this release is the ability to use prepared statements for replicate databases (➢p.34); performance also improved due to internal enhancements. The **rs_subcmp** utility was also improved.
- **15.1** - this version contains many new or enhanced features, such improved rs_ticket functionality, new syntax for request functions, usability enhancements for monitor counters, stable queue caching for better performance, and more.

Much of the information in this book is still valid for pre-12.6 RepServer versions, but this is not indicated explicitly.
Throughout this Quick Reference Guide, notations like '**(15.0.1)**' indicate new or changed functionality in the corresponding RepServer version (here, 15.0.1); likewise, '**(pre-15.0)**' marks functionality that existed until version 15.0, but not in 15.0 or later.
Unless indicated otherwise, all version numbers refer to RepServer. When versions of other products are involved, this is indicated explicitly, for example 'ASE 15.0.2 and RS 15.0.1'. Here, 'RS' indicates RepServer to avoid any confusion.

How complete is 'Complete'?
I have called this RepServer Quick Reference Guide 'Complete', because it covers almost all aspects of RepServer you may need in daily practice -- although any book about a software product as complex as RepServer must be incomplete by definition. Also, it is obvious that a 148-page booklet simply cannot contain the same amount of information as a bookshelf filled with full-size manuals -- no matter how small you

print. For practical reasons, the following topics have therefore been omitted:

- System design aspects are not covered (except for some basic data modelling aspects; ➢p.10). Although essential for any replication system, a quick reference guide is not the best place for discussing system design issues. See the *Replication Server Design Guide* (➢p.13) for details.
- Only some aspects of heterogeneous replication are covered, such as a selection of the commands for non-ASE RepAgents (➢p.23).
- Replication system recovery is not included, apart from mentioning it briefly (➢p.118). There is simply too much to say about this rather complex topic, and including a summary would only create a false impression of completeness. Instead, see the *Replication Server Administration Guide* and *Replication Server Troubleshooting Guide* (➢p.13).
- Some features are covered only partly, or not at all, for example LDAP, SSL, security mechanisms and High-Availability failover for the RSSD.
- Although most actions can also be performed through the Sybase Central plug-ins (➢35), this book is primarily focused on the actual RepServer commands and procedures, as executed manually through **isql**.

Note that this Quick Reference Guide is not a tutorial: the reader is expected to be familiar with the basic concepts of RepServer. Nevertheless, if you're new to RepServer, you may find it useful to read section 2 (➢p.9). Also, section 1 contains some starting points for common DBA tasks.

How to use this Quick Reference Guide

All information in this Quick Reference Guide is grouped by topic, such as 'Table repdefs' or 'Routes' (see the table of contents; ➢p.3). The index (➢p.136) contains all commands, functions, stored procedures, etc. in alphabetical order. Many references are included in the index more than once; for example, **rs_helppub** is also included as **helppub, rs_**.

Each command description includes the things you need most: the syntax, a short description of the functionality and parameters, and often an example. In addition, there is often a bit of background information and some practical tips. This information will usually be sufficient; when you need more details or background information, see one of the RepServer product manuals, like the *Replication Server Reference Manual* or the *Replication Server Administration Guide* (➢p.13).

Syntax conventions

The syntax notation follows commonly used conventions, and will usually be self-explanatory. Still, here are some guidelines:

- Literal text, such as command keywords, is printed in **bold**. Placeholders for variables or parameters are printed in *italic* - you should replace this with something. For example: **drop replication definition** *repdef_name*.
- Parentheses -'**(**' and '**)**'- and commas are part of the command itself. Square brackets -'[' and ']'-, curly brackets -'{' and '}'-, pipes -'|'-, and 3-dots -'...'- are never part of a command, but indicate optional parts of the command.
- In some cases, the syntax has been simplified for practical reasons, omitting non-essential parts for better readability. For example [**NULL** | *table_name*] is used, although [{ **NULL** | *table_name* }] would have been more formally correct.

Terminology and Acronyms

The following terminology and acronyms are used in this Quick Reference Guide:

RS, RepServer	Replication Server
RepAgent	Replication Agent
LTM	Log Transfer Manager (an old name for RepAgent)
DSI	Data Server Interface, an RS thread connecting to a replicate database
RSI	Replication Server Interface, an RS thread connecting to another RepServer for a route
RSM	Replication Server Manager, a program for monitoring components of a replication system
RCL	Replication Server Command Language; this acronym is used in the Sybase documentation, but not in this book
command	a RepServer language command (**alter connection**)
statement	an SQL language statement (**select**, **create table**)
repdef	replication definition
route	a one-way connection between two RepServers
dataserver	generic name for a database server, either ASE or non-ASE, containing or managing a database
primary data-server/	a dataserver/database containing primary data

database	
replicate data-server/ database	a dataserver/database containing replicate data
primary table/ procedure	a table/stored procedure, located in a primary database, which is the source of replicated data
replicate table/ procedure	a table/stored procedure, located in a replicate database, which is the target of replicated data
primary RepServer	a RepServer where repdefs are created
replicate RepServer	a RepServer where subscriptions are created; when no routes are used, this is the same as the primary RepServer
RSSD	Replication Server System Database
ERSSD	Embedded RSSD, hosted by ASA
primary RSSD	RSSD for a primary RepServer
replicate RSSD	RSSD for a replicate RepServer
.cfg file	the configuration file for a RepServer, typically named '*repserver_name*.**cfg**' (➢p.115)
warm standby pair	one active database and one standby database, synchronized by continuous replication, and related to a logical connection that can look like a single database
database replication	database repdefs and -subscriptions (➢p.43)
quiescing	stopping the data flow through a replication system to allow maintenance to be performed (➢p.116)
replication domain	one or more RepServers registered in the same ID server
heterogeneous replication	replication between different types of database, for example from ASE to Oracle
bi-directional replication	a replication architecture where a database is both a primary and a replicate database at the same time
system [stored] procedures	database-independent ASE stored procedures, starting with **sp_*** (**sp_setreptable**), and residing in the **sybsystemprocs** database
ASE	Adaptive Server Enterprise
ASA	Adaptive Server Anywhere, a.k.a. 'SQL Anywhere'
DDL	SQL Data Definition Language statements (**create table**, **create database**, etc.)
DML	SQL Data Manipulation Language statements (**select**, **insert**, **update**, **delete**, etc.)
LTL	Log Transfer Language; used for communication between RepAgents and RepServer
OQID	Origin Queue ID, a 36-byte identifier for each transaction
T-SQL	Transact-SQL, the SQL implementation by Sybase
bcp	an OS-utility to 'bulk copy' data from files to ASE tables and vice versa
OS	Operating System
a.k.a.	also known as
➢p.49 / ➢19.5	see page 49 / see section 19.5

Errata
Errata will be available on-line at **www.sypron.nl/repqr/errata.html**. Please email any errors or comments to **repqr@sypron.nl**.

Electronic Supplement
All RSSD queries appearing in this book, as well as some additional RSSD queries and handy RSSD procedures, are available electronically for owners of this book. To download a copy, go to **www.sypron.nl/repqr/supplement**.

Undocumented commands: warning & disclaimer
Most information in this Quick Reference Guide concerns documented and supported functionality. However, some useful undocumented or unsupported commands are included as well. Please note that using undocumented or unsupported commands may constitute a risk: such commands may have unexpected side effects, may cause irreversible damage to your databases or replication system and/or lead to loss of data. Use such commands entirely at your own risk, and do <u>not</u> contact Sybase Technical Support for assistance. When a command is not documented (and therefore not supported), this is indicated in the description.
In any case, neither the author, nor the publisher, nor Sybase Inc. (nor its subsidiaries), assume any responsibility for errors or omissions, nor do they accept any liabilities for damages resulting from the use of the information in this book.

Overview & General Concepts

1 Starting points for common RepServer DBA tasks

Task	Recommended action
Create a new RepServer	Use **rs_init** (➢p.98)
Start or stop a RepServer	See section 27 (p.98)
Determine the current status of a RepServer	Use RepServer commands like **admin who** (➢p.25)
Determine the RSSD for a RepServer	Run **admin rssd_name** and/or **sysadmin erssd**. See section 33 (➢p.109)
Run an RSSD stored procedure (like **rs_helprep**)	First, connect to the RSSD dataserver with **isql** (➢p.109); then run the RSSD procedure
Create a connection to a primary or replicate database	Use **rs_init** (➢p.98), or the Sybase Central plug-ins RSP (➢p.116) or RMP (➢p.115)
Set up publish-subscribe replication for tables or stored procedures	1. Create connections to a primary and a replicate database (see above) 2. Create a repdef (for a primary table or stored procedure; ➢p.36,39). Multiple repdefs can also be grouped in a publication (➢p.54) 3. Mark the primary table or stored procedure for replication (➢p.15) 4. Create a subscription to the repdef or publication (➢p.56)
Set up a warm standby	See section 19.3 (➢p.67)
Set up database replication	1. Create connections to a primary and replicate database (see above) 2. Create a database repdef (➢p.43) 3. Mark the database for replication (➢p.15) 4. Create one or more subscriptions to the database repdef (➢p.56)
Enable password encryption for a RepServer	Use **rs_init** (➢p.98)
Reverse-engineering of RepServer objects	Use the Sybase Central plug-in RSP (➢p.116)
Change configuration parameters	See section 24 (➢p.90)
Find out why replication isn't working	See section 43 (➢p.127)
Improve performance of your replication system	See section 40 (➢p.120)

If you need to create RepServers, database connections, warm standbys (etc.) regularly, it is recommended to create an **rs_init** resource file that can be used as a template. This allows you to run these common operations from the command line with **rs_init -r** instead of having to go through the interactive **rs_init** dialog every time. For more information on creating an **rs_init** resource file, see p.98.

2 RepServer basics

This section briefly describes some elementary aspects of RepServer:

- RepServer is Sybase's enterprise-level data replication product for log-based, publish-subscribe replication. RepServer provides best performance and functionality for ASE-to-ASE replication, but also supports heterogeneous replication (between different database types, like MS SQL Server, DB2 and Oracle).
- RepServer's unit of replication is a transaction (not just an individual row modification): either the entire transaction is successfully applied to the replicate database, or it isn't applied at all. Only committed transactions are replicated.
- RepServer replicates the effect of a DML statement (i.e. the changes to the data), not the DML statement itself. From the perspective of RepServer, it is not possible to tell from the transaction log whether two updated primary rows are the result of one or two DML statements.
- RepServer guarantees that replicated transactions will commit in the same order in the replicate database as they did in the primary database.
- RepServer can also replicate stored procedure executions, which are handled as if they're part of a primary transaction.

- Replication by RepServer is asynchronous: it takes a certain amount of time (though usually quite short) until a committed primary transaction has been applied to a replicate database. This time ('latency') may increase due to factors like heavy workload in RepServer or a dataserver, network interruptions, etc.
- RepServer is designed to recover automatically from temporary unavailability of databases, other RepServers and network connections.
- In a typical replication system, replicate data is expected to remain identical to the primary data. For this reason, replicate data should only be modified by RepServer, not by other users or applications.
- In ASE, creation of, and operations on, #temporary tables are not replicated. In ASE pre-15.0.1, operations in system databases (e.g. **master**, **tempdb**) cannot be replicated either (see page 47 for the solution in ASE 15.0.1, as well as for a workaround for ASE pre-15.0.1).
- Many RepServer commands for creating or dropping objects (subscriptions, routes, etc.) are asynchronous: the command returns immediately while RepServer executes it in the background. To determine whether a command has completed, examine the RepServer errorlog or use RSSD stored procedures.

2.1 Data model considerations for replication systems

A well-designed data model is important for every database application, but it's absolutely essential for a replication system. This section highlights some data modelling issues to bear in mind, but it is by no means complete: please consult the *Replication Server Design Guide* (➢p.13) for additional replication system design considerations.

Unique primary keys must be enforced
For replication to be practically useable, it is essential that each primary table has a unique primary key, which must be enforced by a unique index. Although RepServer itself does neither require nor verify this, unexpected things may happen when this uniqueness is not guaranteed.
Let's assume a primary table **t** exists with primary key column **pk**, but without a unique index; a corresponding table repdef exists as well. Two rows are inserted into this table, with **pk** = **100**; these inserts are correctly replicated to the replicate table.
Next, one of the two rows is deleted from the primary table (for example, with **set rowcount 1**, or by selecting on another column). This row deletion is replicated as the SQL statement **delete t where pk = 100**. When this statement is executed in the replicate database, both replicate rows are deleted. As a result, the primary and replicate tables are now out of sync. A similar effect can occur for updates on a primary row.

Be careful about updating multiple primary keys
Care should also be taken about updating the primary key (note that updating primary keys shouldn't normally be needed anyway in a proper data model). Let's assume the primary table **t** mentioned above has a unique index on **pk** and contains two rows with **pk** = **10** and **11**. The following update to the primary table may cause problems in the replicate: **update t set pk = pk + 1**. Depending on the existence of a unique index on the replicate table, both replicate rows may end up with the same value for **pk**, or the replicate update may fail.
The background of this problem is that this update hits two primary rows, and is therefore replicated as the following two SQL statements in the replicate database (executed in one transaction):

update t set pk = 11 where pk = 10
update t set pk = 12 where pk = 11

The order in which these statements are executed in the replicate database is determined by the order in which the rows in the primary table were updated (which should be considered unpredictable). If they're executed in the order shown without a unique index on the replicate table, both replicate rows will end up with **pk** = **12**; with a unique index, the transaction fails due to a duplicate key error. Only when these updates are executed in reverse order, they will execute correctly.
To avoid such problems, do not update multiple primary keys in a single statement.

Be careful about using float/real datatypes
The datatypes **float** and **real** should be used reluctantly in a replication system, especially when replicating between different database types and/or different hardware platforms. These datatypes have a machine-dependent representation, meaning they might be represented as different values on different replicate databases. This could be potentially problematic when all columns are included in the replicate SQL state-

ment, for example in a warm standby without using repdefs.
Due to their limited precision, **float** and **real** datatypes should never be part of a primary key in any database, irrespective of replication considerations.

Missing replicate rows may go unnoticed
Perhaps surprisingly, RepServer won't mind if a replicate row does not exist. A replicate **update** or **delete** statement referencing a non-existing replicate row simply ends successfully, affecting 0 rows. Since RepServer only checks the error status of the replicate SQL statement, nothing is found to be wrong in this situation. If needed, use function strings to implement checks for existing replicate rows.

Avoid SQL reserved words as identifiers
ASE allows using SQL reserved words as object names or column names by using the option **set quoted_identifier on**. This also allows unusual identifiers such as containing spaces, or consisting of spaces entirely. Such identifiers are likely to lead to syntax errors in replicate SQL statements in the replicate database. Although this may be worked around with customized function strings and/or renamed column names in repdefs, it is perhaps wiser to avoid such identifiers in the first place.

Ensure proper indexing in the replicate database
Indexes should exist in the replicate database for best query performance, especially for **update**, **delete** and **select** statements. Typically, these indexes are identical to those in the primary database, but variations are possible. When the replicate database is used for different purposes than the primary, for example for reporting, additional indexes may be created in the replicate. If it is guaranteed that only **insert** statements are replicated, then replicate performance might be improved by removing some indexes in the replicate. If the replicate database is a standby copy that may need to assume the role of primary database, the indexes (as well as the rest of the schema) will need to be identical to the primary.

2.2 *Why replication systems can be so difficult...*

Replication systems have a tendency to be complex, and to be difficult to manage and troubleshoot. This is mainly because the entire replication system is essentially one big database system where the different components can influence each other. For example, when the transaction log of a replicate database fills up, this will eventually be felt in the primary databases if no corrective action is taken. Since each component of a replication system is already complex by itself, this obviously applies even more to the system as a whole.
RepServer offers many great features, but some will significantly increase the complexity of a replication system. If it is important to keep your replication system simple, keep the following suggestions in mind (note that this is not intended to discourage the use of these features, but only to point out their impact on overall complexity):

- Replicate all columns of each primary table, and all rows (i.e. do not use a **where**-clause in subscriptions or articles). Also, keep identifiers and datatypes of all primary and replicate columns and parameters identical.
- Let all primary and replicate tables and procedures be owned by the same user, preferably **dbo** or the maintenance user. Don't use identically named tables with different owners.
- Use only one replication definition and one subscription per table.
- Don't use routes unless absolutely necessary. Each additional RepServer also introduces another RSSD and RepServer errorlog, requiring DBA attention.
- Use one-way replication, where each primary database contains only primary data, and no replicate data. Use bi-directional replication only if all issues and implications, including recoverability, are fully understood.
- Don't replicate stored procedures that modify tables that are also replicated themselves (➢p.49).
- Don't use customized function strings.
- Don't use request functions (➢p.41).

3 *Sybase data replication products*

Sybase has different products for data replication (also called 'data movement'). Except for RepServer and Replication Agent, they are not discussed further in this book:

- **Replication Server** - the main topic of this quick reference guide: Sybase's high-end replication product for heterogeneous, log-based, publish-subscribe replication. RepServer is based on the Sybase Open Server framework.

- **Replication Agent** and **Enterprise Connect Data Access** (ECDA; formerly known as DirectConnect, EnterpriseConnect, OmniConnect and Mainframe-Connect) are separate Sybase products required for heterogeneous replication (i.e. to/from non-ASE databases; ➢p.12).
- **ASE Replicator** - a free replication tool that provides log-based, publish-subscribe replication between ASE databases. ASE Replicator is included with ASE since version 12.5.0.1 at no additional cost. However, its functionality, performance and reliability are significantly less than RepServer's, making it generally unsuitable for large, high-volume or mission-critical systems.
  See **www.sypron.nl/aserep.html** for more information about ASE Replicator.
- **RepConnector** - a middleware component running in a J2EE-compliant application server, basically acting as a replicate database to RepServer. It converts replicate transactions to XML messages and delivers these to messaging products like Tibco, MQSeries, etc. RepConnector is sold as a separate product. For more information, see **www.sybase.com**.
- **Mirror Activator** - used in conjunction with third-party disk replication products (like EMC SRDF, Veritas Volume Replicator, Hitachi TrueCopy, and others), where the disk-level-replicated log devices are read by the MirrorActivator Replication Agent, which sends the primary transactions to RepServer. This combines the efficiency of disk-level replication with transactional replication and allows the replicated disk devices to be used by a replicate ASE server.
- **OpenSwitch** - though not a pure data replication product, OpenSwitch provides failover and load balancing capabilities for client connections to one or more ASE servers. OpenSwitch is often used in combination with a RepServer warm standby.
- **Mobilink** - a data synchronization product primarily found in combination with Sybase ASA (a.k.a. SQL Anywhere), though capable of bi-directional heterogeneous replication between ASE, Oracle, DB2, messaging products, and more. Mobilink can be seen as the successor to SQL Remote.
- **SQL Remote** - a message-based, publish-subscribe replication product primarily aimed at Sybase ASA (a.k.a. SQL Anywhere). However, SQL Remote could also be used to replicate to or from ASE, although performance and functionality are significantly less than with RepServer.
  As of ASE 12.5, SQLRemote is no longer supported for ASE. In previous ASE versions, SQLRemote was bundled with ASE and located in **$SYBASE/SQLRemote**.
- **PowerDesigner** - a modelling tool, providing -among many other things- graphical modelling for RepServer systems, known as the 'Information Liquidity Model' (use this term to search for a whitepaper at **sybase.com**).

4 Products required for heterogeneous replication

RepServer supports heterogeneous replication, i.e. replication between different types of primary and replicate databases (for example, from ASE to Oracle and IBM's DB2). The following Sybase products are required for heterogeneous replication:

- The RepServer product itself.
- ASE, in case ASE is used for the RSSD; when using ASA for the embedded RSSD, ASE is not needed.
- To replicate to or from a non-ASE database, the products Sybase Replication Agent and/or Sybase Enterprise Connect Data Access are required (see below). In turn, these products require one or more of the RepServer license options **REP_MSSQL**, **REP_UDB** (for DB2), **REP_ORACLE** or **REP_INFORMIX** (➢p.13).
- Sybase Replication Agent, a separate product, is required to use a non-ASE primary database. Sybase has RepAgents available for Oracle, Microsoft SQL Server, Informix and IBM's DB2. For more information about non-ASE RepAgents, ➢p.23.
  In principle, RepAgents could be written for any data source, based on the Log Transfer Language (LTL) specifications (for details see the *Replication Server Design Guide* and the *Heterogeneous Replication Guide*; ➢p.13). For example, a RepAgent has been implemented for Adabas (although not as an officially supported Sybase product).
- The Sybase Enterprise Connect Data Access connectivity product is required

when using a non-ASE replicate database. Product documentation can be found at **www.sypron.nl/repqr2/dc**.

Sybase provides connectivity products for the following databases:

- Oracle
- Microsoft SQL Server
- Informix
- Sybase ASA (SQL Anywhere)
- DB2 (for Unix, Windows, AS/400, MVS/OS/390)
- IMS

Note that this list may not be complete. Contact Sybase for full details.

- Additional products from the respective database vendors may also be required.

When replicating to a non-ASE replicate database, there are two ways to connect to the replicate database:

a. From RepServer, connect directly to the replicate non-ASE database through Enterprise Connect Data Access. This offers best overall performance, but can be more technically complex since datatype conversion issues may need to be addressed specifically.

b. In an ASE database, create proxy tables that map (through Enterprise Connect Data Access) to the replicate tables in the non-ASE database. From RepServer, connect to this ASE database and replicate into the proxy tables. This is technically simpler because the ASE proxy table mechanism handles all datatype conversion issues, but requires additional ASE licensing and incurs more overhead.

When using heterogeneous replication, datatype conversion issues must be addressed. RepServer supports datatype conversions between most database types through predefined function strings and datatype translations. See section 11.2 for additional information.

5 Licensable options & license keys

Starting with version 12.5, some RepServer features can only be used when an additional license is obtained from Sybase. This license comes with an encrypted key which must be entered in 'SySam' (the Sybase license manager, residing in the **$SYBASE/$SYBASE_SYSAM** directory). In pre-15.0, the pathname of the license file is contained in the environment variable **$LM_LICENSE_FILE**. To start/stop the license manager, use the OS-level command **lmutil** (in **$SYBASE_SYSAM/bin**; where a 'vendor name' is required, specify **SYBASE**).

The license manager must be running when RepServer is started; if not, it will still start, but all licensable options will be disabled. These options are:

- **REP_SERVER** - not an option by itself, but this license key is required when any of the other license keys below is installed.
- **(pre-15.0) REP_SSL** - enables SSL for encrypting all network traffic (➢p.94). In 15.0, this is included in the base **REP_SERVER** license.
- **REP_ORACLE** - required for replication to/from Oracle.
- **REP_MSSQL** - required for replication to/from Microsoft SQL Server.
- **REP_UDB** - required for replication to/from IBM's DB2.
- **REP_INFORMIX** - required for replication to/from Informix.

See the *Replication Server Installation Guide* (➢p.13) for more information about the SySam license manager.

6 RepServer documentation

All RepServer-related product manuals are available at **sybase.com**. Most documentation can be searched on-line and can also be downloaded as PDF documents:

RepServer	**www.sypron.nl/repqr2/rs**
ASE	**www.sypron.nl/repqr2/ase**
non-ASE RepAgents	**www.sypron.nl/repqr2/ra**
Enterprise Connect Data Access	**www.sypron.nl/repqr2/dc**
ASA/SQL Anywhere	**www.sypron.nl/repqr2/asa**

The most important RepServer manuals (see **www.sypron.nl/repqr2/rs**) are:

- *Replication Server Administration Guide* - the place to look when you require detailed information about a specific feature.

- *Replication Server Reference Manual* - describes individual RepServer commands, RSSD procedures and RSSD tables, and configuration of the ASE RepAgent (for non-ASE RepAgents, see **www.sypron.nl/repqr2/ra**).
- *Replication Server Heterogeneous Replication Guide* - describes how to replicate between different types of databases (for example from ASE to Oracle). Not needed if only ASE-to-ASE replication is used.
- *Replication Server Design Guide* - describes different architectures for replication systems.
- *Replication Server Troubleshooting Guide* - the name says it all...
- Lastly, a poster of the RSSD tables data model can be downloaded (in PDF format); see **www.sypron.nl/repqr2/rsstd**.

Here's an arbitrary selection of some other RepServer-related Internet resources:

The Sybase FAQ (the 'REP' section)	**www.isug.com/Sybase_FAQ**
RepServer tips & tools at **www.sybase.com**	see **www.sypron.nl/repqr2/x7**
Newsgroups at Sybase's own news server **forums.sybase.com**	**sybase.public.rep-server**, **sybase.public.rep-agent**, **sybase.public.mirr-activator**
RepServer information at Rob Verschoor's web site	**www.sypron.nl/rs_tips.html**

RepAgents & Primary Databases

7 Marking tables/procedures/databases for replication

To replicate primary data, it must be marked for replication first. Such a mark indicates to the RepAgent which data modifications and procedure executions it should pick up and forward to RepServer.
A repdef may be required to actually replicate the marked data (for example, with regular repdef-subscription replication), but a repdef is not always needed (for example, with a warm standby).
Section 7.1 describes how to mark primary data for replication in primary ASE databases; for non-ASE databases, ➢p.24.

When a primary table or stored procedure is marked for replication but no corresponding repdef exists, RepServer discards the data received from the RepAgent, and logs warning message 32020 (**'Table '*table_name*' is not defined'**; also for stored procedures) in the RepServer errorlog.

7.1 Primary ASE databases

The stored procedures in this section are executed in the primary ASE database. These procedures are created by **$SYBASE/$SYBASE_ASE/scripts/installmaster** (Windows: **instmstr**).

sp_setreptable [*table_name* [, { **true** | **false** } [, { **owner_on** | **owner_off** | **NULL** }
[**(ASE 15.0.1)** , **use_index**]]]]
(ASE procedure; for a non-ASE primary database, use **pdb_setreptable** (➢p.24)
Marks (**true**) or unmarks (**false**) a table for replication. With **owner_on**, the table owner is taken into account; this enables replication of multiple tables with the same name but with different owners. With **owner_off** (=default), the table owner is ignored. With only *table_name*, displays the current replication status for that table; without any parameters, lists all tables marked for replication in the current database.
sp_setreptable sets the replication status of all **text**, **image** and **rawobject** columns in the table to **always_replicate** (this can be changed with **sp_setrepcol**).
In some cases, primary data can be replicated without marking the table for replication, but by using the configuration parameter **rep_as_standby** instead (➢p.34).
In ASE 15.0.1, **use_index** creates a replication index (➢p.19) for every **text/image/rawobject** column in the table.
<u>*Warning:*</u> when the table has **text/image/rawobject** columns and contains many rows, **sp_setreptable** may take a long time. Read section 7.3 (➢p.18) first!
Example: **sp_setreptable MyTable, true**

sp_setreplicate [*table_name* [, { **true** | **false** }]]
(ASE procedure) Marks (**true**) or unmarks (**false**) a table for replication. Use **sp_setreptable** instead of **sp_setreplicate**, except for one reason: **sp_setreplicate** is faster than **sp_setreptable** because it sets the replication status of **text**, **image** and **rawobject** columns to **do_not_replicate** (also see section 7.3 on page 18). This status can be changed with **sp_setrepcol**.
Note: in old RepServer versions, **sp_setreplicate** was also used to mark stored procedures for replication. Although still supported, it is strongly recommended to use **sp_setrepproc** instead.
Example: **sp_setreplicate MyTable, true**

sp_setrepdefmode *table_name*, { **owner_on** | **owner_off** }
(ASE procedure) Enables (**owner_on**) or disables (**owner_off**) whether a table owner is taken into account for table replication (see **sp_setreptable**).
Example: **sp_setrepdefmode MyTable, owner_on**

sp_setrepcol *table_name* [, { *column_name* }]
[, { **do_not_replicate** | **always_replicate** | **replicate_if_changed** }
[**(ASE 15.0.1)** , **use_index**]]
(ASE procedure; for a non-ASE primary database, use **pdb_setrepcol** (➢p. 24))
Changes or displays the replication status for **text**, **image** or **rawobject** columns. With only *table_name*, displays the status for all such columns in the table; with also *column_name*, for only that column.
By specifying the third parameter, changes the replication status for the specified column; with **null** for the column name, changes the status for all **text/image/rawobject** columns in the table. Possible replication status values are:

- **always_replicate** - replicates the **text/image/rawobject** column when any column in the row is modified.

- **replicate_if_changed** - replicates the **text/image/rawobject** column only when the column itself is modified.
- **do_not_replicate** - does not replicate the **text/image/rawobject** column at all.

For **text**, **image**, or **rawobject** columns, these settings should correspond to those in the table repdef, or data will not be replicated successfully.
In ASE 15.0.1, **use_index** creates a replication index (➢p.19) on the column.
Warning: when the status of a **text/image/rawobject** column is changed from **do_not_replicate** to **always_replicate** or **replicate_if_changed**, and the table contains many rows, **sp_setrepcol** may take a long time. Read section 7.3 (➢p.18) first!
Example: **sp_setrepcol MyTable, MyImageCol, replicate_if_changed**

sp_setrepproc [*proc_name* [**,** { **'function'** | **'false'** } [**,** { **log_sproc** | **log_current** }]]]
(ASE procedure; for a non-ASE primary database, use **pdb_setrepproc** (➢p. 24))
Marks (**'function'**) or unmarks (**'false'**) a stored procedure for replication through a function repdef. With **log_sproc** (=default), the stored procedure execution is written to the transaction log of the database where the procedure actually exists, also if the procedure is executed from a different database; with **log_current**, it is logged in the database from where the procedure is executed.
With only *proc_name*, displays the current replication status for that procedure; without parameters, lists all procedures marked for replication in the current database.
Example: **sp_setrepproc MyProc, 'function'**

sp_setrepproc *proc_name* **,** { **'table'** | **'false'** } [**,** { **log_sproc** | **log_current** }]
(ASE procedure) Marks a stored procedure for replication through a table repdef (i.e. not a function repdef! -- see the appendix about *'Asynchronous Procedures'* in the *Replication Server Administration Guide*; ➢p.13). However, it is unlikely you'll need this, so use **sp_setrepproc**...**'function'** instead (see above).

sp_reptostandby *database_name* [**,** **'L1'** | **'all'** | **'none'** [**(ASE 15.0.1) , use_index**]]
(ASE procedure; for non-ASE databases, run **pdb_setreptable** (➢p.24) for all tables)
Marks (**'L1'** or **'all'**) or unmarks (**'none'**) all tables in a database for replication through a warm standby or through database replication; also marks the database for replication of certain DDL statements and ASE system stored procedures (see below for a list of supported DDL statements and system stored procedures):

- **'L1'** sets the DDL replication level to the current ASE version; when upgrading ASE, it remains at this level.
- **'all'** sets the DDL replication level to the current ASE version; when upgrading ASE, additional DDL replication features of the new ASE version are enabled automatically.
- **'none'** - unmarks the database for replication.

Notes:

- Replication of DML, DDL and system procedures may be affected with **set replication** for individual sessions (➢p.17). Also note that filter settings for a database repdef may disable some of this replication (➢p.44).
- Replication of stored procedures in the database is not affected by **sp_reptostandby**; these must be marked independently with **sp_setrepproc**.
- When an individual table in a marked database is also replicated through a table repdef (for example, to a replicate database outside the warm standby), that table must also be marked individually with **sp_setreptable**. As an alternative, the configuration parameter **rep_as_standby** can be used instead (➢p.34).
- **sp_reptostandby** sets the replication status of all **text**, **image** and **rawobject** columns in the database to **replicate_if_changed**; this cannot be changed with **sp_setrepcol**. Only when a table is also marked with **sp_setreptable**, the status of individual columns can be changed with **sp_setrepcol**.
  In ASE 15.0.1, **use_index** creates a replication index (➢p.19) for every **text/image/rawobject** column in the database.
  Warning: when the database contains tables with **text/image/rawobject** columns that also contain many rows, **sp_reptostandby** may take a long time to complete. Read section 7.3 (➢p.18) first!
  By enabling ASE traceflags **9130** and **3604** first, the progress of **sp_reptostandby** is displayed.

In ASE 12.0, the following T-SQL DDL statements and ASE system stored procedures are replicated when **'L1'** is specified:

alter table	**create default**	**create index**
create procedure	**create rule**	**create table**
create trigger	**create view**	**drop default**
drop index	**drop procedure**	**drop rule**
drop table	**drop trigger**	**drop view**
grant	**revoke**	
sp_addalias	**sp_addgroup**	**sp_addmessage**
sp_adduser	**sp_addtype**	**sp_bindefault**
sp_bindmsg	**sp_bindrule**	**sp_changegroup**
sp_chgattribute	**sp_commonkey**	**sp_config_rep_agent**
sp_dropalias	**sp_dropgroup**	**sp_dropkey**
sp_dropmessage	**sp_droptype**	**sp_dropuser**
sp_foreignkey	**sp_primarykey**	**sp_procxmode**
sp_recompile	**sp_rename**	**sp_setrepcol**
sp_setreplicate	**sp_setrepmode**	**sp_setrepproc**
sp_setreptable	**sp_unbindefault**	**sp_unbindmsg**
sp_unbindrule		

In ASE 12.5, these DDL statements and system procedures are also replicated:

create plan	**create schema**	**install java**
remove java		
sp_add_qpgroup	**sp_drop_qpgroup**	**sp_export_qpgroup**
sp_import_qpgroup	**sp_rename_qpgroup**	**sp_drop_all_qplans**

In ASE 12.5.4, these DDL statements and system procedures are also replicated (RS 12.6 ESD#5 is needed to replicate encrypted data):

create encryption key	**drop encryption key**	**alter encryption key**
sp_encryption (for **system_encr_passwd**)		

In ASE 15.0.1, a limited number of operations in the **master** database can be replicated (➢p.47). This concerns the following commands only ('regular' DML/DDL, and other **sp_*** stored procs will not be replicated for the master database):

create role	**drop role**	**alter role**
grant role	**revoke role**	**sp_role**
sp_addlogin	**sp_droplogin**	**sp_modifylogin**
sp_password	**(ASE 15.0.2) sp_passwordpolicy**	**sp_locklogin**
sp_defaultdb	**sp_defaultlanguage**	**sp_displaylevel**

For a database marked with **sp_reptostandby**, note that neither **update statistics** is replicated (but **sp_recompile** is), nor **reorg**, nor table creation by **select..into**, nor creation of **#**temporary tables. **truncate table** is not replicated as part of DDL replication, but can be replicated separately (➢p.63). Also note that DDL replication requires the ASE RepAgent to be configured with **'send warm standby xacts'** = **true** (➢p.21) to avoid errors in the replicate dataserver when DDL statements or ASE system stored procedures are executed in a transaction (like ASE error 2762).

set replication { **on** | **off** | **force_ddl** | **default** }
(ASE command) Executed in a primary ASE database, enables or disables replication of subsequent DML for the current session, as well as the DDL and ASE system stored procedures on page 17. This applies to a warm standby as well as to database replication. Note that filter settings for a database repdef may disable some of this replication (➢p.44). Possible settings:

- **on** (=default) - enables replication of DML, DDL and system procedures, but the precise effect depends on how primary data has been marked for replication:
  - For databases where **sp_reptostandy** is set to **'none'**, only DML is replicated, and only for tables marked with **sp_setreptable**.
  - For databases where **sp_reptostandby** is set to **'L1'** or **'all'**, DML, DDL and system procedures are replicated for the entire database.
- **default** - same as **on**.
- **off** - disables replication of all subsequent DML, DDL and system procedures for the current session, until overridden with **set replication on** or **set replication force_ddl**.
- **force_ddl** - enables replication of DDL and system procedures for the current session. In addition, DML is replicated depending on how primary data has been marked for replication:
  - For databases where **sp_reptostandy** is set to **'none'**, DML is replicated

only for tables marked with **sp_setreptable**.

– For databases where **sp_reptostandby** is set to **'L1'** or **'all'**, DML is replicated for the entire database.

Example:
set replication off
delete MyTable where MyKey = 123 -- deleted row(s) are not replicated
create table YourTable (YourCol int) -- **create table** is not replicated
set replication on
delete MyTable where MyKey = 456 -- deleted row(s) are replicated

7.2 Marking data for a warm standby or database repdef

Primary data can only be replicated if it has been marked for replication. For a warm standby or a database repdefs/subscriptions, this can be done in different ways:

- The active/primary database can be marked with **sp_reptostandby** (➢p.16), causing all tables in the database to be replicated to the standby/replicate database; any settings with **sp_setreptable** for individual tables are ignored. To replicate DDL and ASE system stored procedures, **sp_reptostandby** is required, as well as **'send warm standby xacts' = true** for the ASE RepAgent, (➢p.21).
- Primary tables in the active/primary database can be marked individually with **sp_setreptable** (➢p.15); if **sp_reptostandby** is not used, only the marked tables are replicated to the standby/replicate database.
- In pre-12.6, when a table is replicated to a database outside the warm standby, the table must be marked with **sp_setreptable** even if **sp_reptostandby** has already marked the database. In 12.6, the configuration parameter **rep_as_standby** (➢p.34) can be used instead.
- Primary stored procedures (i.e. non-system stored procedures) must be marked with **sp_setrepproc** (➢p.16) in order to be replicated to the standby/replicate database; this is independent of whether the active/primary database is marked with **sp_reptostandby**.

Table repdefs are not required for a warm standby or for a database repdef/subscription, since **sp_reptostandby** can be used which applies to all tables. Reasons to create table repdefs anyway are:

- Improving performance: with a repdef, only the **primary key** columns from the repdef are used in the **where**-clause of the replicate SQL statement, reducing the length of replicated messages and query optimization time; without repdefs, all columns are used for the **where**-clause (also see the **send standby** option; ➢p.48) In addition, minimal column replication (➢p.49) can be used for further improvements. No subscription to the table repdef is required.
- When the standby/replicate dataserver runs an older ASE version, repdefs may be required if that ASE version does not support the number of table columns used in the active database. For example, ASE 12.5+ allows 1024 columns per table while ASE 12.0 does not support more than 128 columns in a SQL **where**-clause. In this example, a repdef must be used for primary tables that have more than 128 columns, or replicate SQL statements will run into a syntax error in the replicate ASE server.
- When creating a table repdef for one of the above reasons, it is not necessary to mark the table with **sp_setreptable** if **sp_reptostandby** was already used.

7.3 Be careful when marking big text/image tables in ASE!

When a primary table contains **text/image/rawobject** columns, and the table contains many rows, a potentially serious problem may occur when marking such data for replication in ASE with **sp_setreptable**, **sp_reptostandby** or **sp_setrepcol**.
For technical reasons, the first page of each **text/image** page chain must be updated to enable future replication of the **text/image** data. One such update is required for each **text/image** column in each row. For large, multi-million row tables, this means that the transaction can take a long time, blocking other users who try to access the table (the update uses an exclusive table lock). In addition, the transaction may consume a lot of space in the transaction log. In production systems, it may therefore be practically impossible to mark such data for replication in a primary database.
This problem can occur in the following situations:

- When marking a database for replication with **sp_reptostandby** (➢p.16), and the database contains tables with **text/image** columns and many rows.

- When marking a table for replication with **sp_setreptable** (➢p.15), and the table has **text/image** columns and many rows.
- When changing the status of an individual **text/image** column with **sp_setrepcol** (➢p.15) from **do_not_replicate** to **always_replicate** or **replicate_if_changed**, when the table has many rows.

When marking a table for replication with **sp_setreplicate** (➢p.15), the problem does not occur since **sp_setreplicate** leaves **text/image** columns marked as **do_not_replicate**. However, if one of those columns needs to be replicated, it must still be marked with **sp_setrepcol**.

Solution in ASE 15.0.1: replication index

ASE 15.0.1 introduces the 'replication index' as a solution for this problem. This is a nonclustered index on the row pointer column to the **text/image** page chain, which is used internally for replicating changes to the **text/image** data. A replication index is created by specifying the **use_index** option with **sp_setreptable**, **sp_reptostandby** or **sp_setrepcol**.
Creating a replication index is much faster than the classic procedure described above; also, only a shared table lock is used while creating the replication index. A replication index is dropped automatically when unmarking the table/column for replication; it cannot be dropped with **drop index**.

Solution in ASE pre-15.0.1

If you're running ASE pre-15.0.1, an alternative solution to this problem has been published by Jeff Tallman of Sybase, in the form of the stored procedure **sp_setreptable_text** (which is a modified version of the standard **sp_setreptable**). Although this procedure is formally unsupported by Sybase, it works very well (though using a replication index in ASE 15.0.1 is preferred).
sp_setreptable_text completes quickly, independent of the size of a table, because existing **text/image** page chains are not modified. Newly inserted rows and updated rows will be replicated correctly; only minimally logged operations against existing **text/image** data is not replicated.
The stored procedure **sp_setreptable_text** can be downloaded from **www.sybase.com**. For the current location of this stored procedure, see **www.sypron.nl/repqr2/x1**.

Possible workaround in ASE pre-15.0.1

If **text/image** columns for large tables must be marked for replication without locking out users in the primary database, a possible workaround may be to create an empty table with identical schema, mark it for replication, and copy the rows in small transactions to the new table. Obviously, this may bring problems of its own.

7.4 ASE secondary truncation point vs. RSSD locater

In a primary ASE database, a so-called 'secondary truncation point' is maintained in the transaction log (this is also called the 'LTM truncation point'; for non-ASE RepAgents, the 'LTM locator' is a similar concept). This point marks how far log records have been delivered to RepServer by the RepAgent, and is essential for replication: without a secondary truncation point, a RepAgent will not start. The transaction log will never be truncated beyond the secondary truncation point, since this would cause unprocessed log records to be lost.
The secondary truncation point in the primary transaction log is actually derived from a similar value, called a 'locater', stored in the RSSD table **rs_locater**. When RepServer determines that all log records for a log page have been received and processed (and stored in the stable queues), it updates the RSSD table **rs_locater** for the primary database to mark that log page as processed. The RepAgent regularly requests the current locater value from RepServer, and updates the position of the secondary truncation point in the transaction log accordingly.

(In case you're wondering: the primary truncation point -though not usually called by that name- is the point until where the log can be truncated with **dump transaction**; this corresponds to the start of the oldest open transaction. The secondary truncation point can never be ahead of the primary truncation point.)

The secondary truncation point in the primary ASE database is managed with the **dbcc** commands below.

dbcc gettrunc

(ASE command) Displays information about the secondary truncation point in the transaction log of the current ASE database. **dbcc gettrunc** returns these columns:

- **'secondary trunc page'** - the page in the transaction log where the secondary truncation point currently resides, depending on the following column.

- **'secondary trunc state'** - if **1**, the secondary truncation point is valid (= active); if **0**, no secondary truncation point is currently maintained.
- **'db rep stat'** - an integer consisting of status bits (see the documentation)
- **'generation id'** - the database generation ID
- **'database id'** - the database ID
- **'database name'** - the database name
- **'ltl version'** - the log transfer language (LTL) version used by the RepAgent

dbcc settrunc ('ltm', 'ignore' | 'valid')
dbcc settrunc ('ltm', 'begin' | 'end')
dbcc settrunc ('ltm', 'pageid', *page_no* **)**
(ASE command) With **'ignore'**, the secondary truncation point in the transaction log of the current database is deactivated (also known as disabled or removed). ***Warning:*** ***this is a drastic, last-resort option that will stop all replication from this database, and may cause transactions to be lost. Don't do this unless you fully understand the implications!***
With **'valid'**, the secondary truncation point is re-established. The RSSD procedure **rs_zeroltm** (see below) should be run before restarting the RepAgent.
With **'begin'** or **'end'**, the secondary truncation point is moved to the start or end of the transaction log, respectively. With **'pageid'**, sets the secondary truncation point to the specified page; this should be done only in special troubleshooting procedures.
To execute this **dbcc settrunc**, RepAgent must not be running in this database.

dbcc dbrepair (*database_name*, **'ltmignore')**
(ASE command)Deactivates the secondary truncation point in the specified database. This can be used instead of **dbcc settrunc** when the database is not accessible.

dbcc settrunc ('ltm', 'gen_id', *db_generation_no* **)**
(ASE command) Sets the database generation number for the current database. See section 41 (➢p.125) for more information.

admin get_generation, *dataserver*, *database*
(RepServer command) Returns the current database generation number for the specified primary database. See section 41 (➢p.125) for more information.

rs_zeroltm *primary_dataserver*, *primary_database*
(RSSD procedure) Resets the locater for the specified primary database in the RSSD table **rs_locater**. Before running **rs_zeroltm**, the RepAgent should be stopped. When the RepAgent is restarted after running **rs_zeroltm**, it sends the current secondary truncation point in the transaction log to RepServer, which stores it in **rs_locater**.
rs_zeroltm should be used when the secondary truncation point in the primary transaction log, or the primary database's generation number, has been changed explicitly by the DBA (with **dbcc settrunc**). After running **rs_zeroltm**, the RSSD table **rs_locater** is resynchronized with the transaction log when the RepAgent is restarted.

7.5 Primary non-ASE databases

In non-ASE primary databases, data is marked for replication with a heterogeneous RepAgent, using RepAgent commands like **pdb_setreptable**. See section 8.3(➢p.23).

8 Replication Agents

A replication agent ('RepAgent') is the component that picks up the primary transactions to be replicated from the primary database, and sends these to RepServer.

8.1 ASE RepAgent configuration

In ASE 11.5+, RepAgents are threads inside ASE (for ASE pre-11.5, an external RepAgent, called 'LTM' (Log Transfer Manager; an old name for RepAgent) must be used instead. LTMs are not covered in this book; see the RepServer documentation).
The ASE procedures in this section should be executed in the primary ASE database.
When RepServer has no connection for a particular database, but the ASE RepAgent tries to connect anyway, the ASE RepAgent will not start and ASE error 9261 will appear in the ASE errorlog ('aborting due to an unrecoverable communications or Replication Server error'). To resolve this, either create a database connection in RepServer (see section 13; ➢p.29), or disable the ASE RepAgent.

sp_configure 'enable rep agent threads' {, **1** | **0** }
(ASE procedure) Enables (**1**) or disables (**0**; = default) internal RepAgent threads in ASE (dynamic).

sp_help_rep_agent [*database_name* | **NULL** [, *filter*]]
(ASE procedure) Displays information about all RepAgent threads in this ASE server, or only for the specified *database_name*. *filter* (**'recovery'**, **'config'**, **'process'**, **'scan'**, **'security'** or **'all'**) limits the output to specific aspects.
To show which RepAgents are running, run **sp_help_rep_agent null, process**. To list the databases where a RepAgent is configured, run **sp_config_rep_agent**.

sp_start_rep_agent *database_name* [, **'recovery'** [, '*connect_dataserver*', '*connect_database*' [, '*repserver_name*', '*repserver_username*', '*repserver_password*']]]
(ASE procedure) Starts the RepAgent thread for *database_name* (the secondary truncation point must be valid). For normal operations, only *database_name* is specified. To start the RepAgent in recovery mode, **'recovery'** must be specified; the other options can be specified as well -- see **sp_config_rep_agent**.
Once started, the RepAgent is automatically started after an ASE restart.

sp_stop_rep_agent *database_name* [, **'nowait'**]
(ASE procedure) Stops the RepAgent thread for the specified database; **'nowait'** stops immediately. Once stopped, the RepAgent is not automatically started after an ASE restart.

sp_config_rep_agent [*database_name* [, *option*, *value* [, *...more values...*]]]
(ASE procedure) Without parameters, lists the databases where a RepAgent is configured. With only *database_name*, displays all configuration settings for the RepAgent in that database. With *option*, displays the current setting for that option and database; with also *value*, modifies the setting. Most changes take effect once the RepAgent is restarted.
RepAgent config settings are stored in the **sysattributes** table in *database_name*.

Examples: **sp_config_rep_agent prod_db, 'retry timeout', '20'**
sp_config_rep_agent prod_db, 'send warm standby xacts', true

option and *value* can be one of the following (note that is sufficient to specify a unique substring for *option*; also note that numeric values must be quoted):

- **'enable'**, '*repserver_name*', '*repserver_username*', '*repserver_password*' - configures the RepAgent for connecting to the specified RepServer with the specified username and password; also sets the secondary truncation point to valid in the database. *repserver_name* must be defined in the **interfaces** file used by this ASE server.
- **'disable'** [, **'preserve secondary truncpt'**] - removes the RepAgent configuration for this database. With **'preserve secondary truncpt'**, leaves the secondary truncation point unchanged; otherwise (=default), it is disabled.
- **'rs servername'**, '*repserver_name*' - the name of the RepServer to connect to.
- **'rs username'**, '*repserver_username*' - the RepServer username to be used for connecting to the RepServer.
- **'rs password'**, '*repserver_password*' - the password to be used for connecting to the RepServer.
- **'send maint xacts to replicate'**, { **true** | **false** } - if **true** (default = **false**), sends maintenance user transactions to RepServer.
- **'send warm standby xacts'**, { **true** | **false** } - if **true** (default = **false**), enables replication of DDL statements and certain system stored procedures, for a database marked with **sp_reptostandby** (➢p.16). Without this option, DDL statements and ASE system stored procedures are executed inside a transaction in the replicate database, which usually leads to an error in the DSI (like ASE error 2762).
- **'scan batch size'**, '*no_of_log_records*' - the maximum number of log records sent to RepServer in a single batch (default = **1000**).
- **'scan timeout'**, '*no_of_seconds*' - the number of seconds before again requesting a new secondary truncating point from RepServer (default = **15**).
- **'retry timeout'**, '*no_of_seconds*' - when there is no connection with RepServer, the number of seconds before retrying to connect (default = **60**).
- **'fade timeout'**, '*no_of_seconds*' - when no log records are available, the number of seconds before RepAgent disconnects from RepServer (default = **30**).

- **'skip ltl errors',** { **true** | **false** } - if **true** (default = **false**, except during recovery), RepAgent ignores LTL errors returned by RepServer.
- **'batch ltl',** { **true** | **false** } - if **true** (=default), LTL commands are sent to RepServer in batches; if false, they are sent one by one.
- **'connect dataserver',** '*dataserver_name*' - when RepAgent is started in recovery mode to scan the log of a database dump (and/or log dumps) that were restored into a different database, specifies the name of the original dataserver.
- **'connect database',** '*database_name*' - same as **'connect dataserver'**, but for the database name.
- **'skip unsupported features',** { **true** | **false** } - if **true** (default=**false**), RepAgent skips log records for features not supported by an older version of RepServer.
- **'ha failover',** { **true** | **false** } - if **true** (=default), RepAgent starts automatically after an ASE failover (when using the ASE High Availability feature (ASE_HA)).
- **(ASE 12.5) 'send buffer size',** { **'2k'** | **'4k'** | **'8k'** | **'16k'** } - the network packet size (Kbytes) used when connecting to RepServer.
- **(ASE 12.5) 'short ltl keywords',** { **true** | **false** } - if **true** (default = **false**), RepAgent sends shortened LTL to RepServer for better performance.
- **(ASE 12.5) 'priority',** '*value*' - sets the priority for a RepAgent thread. Possible values are **0**..**6** (lower value = higher priority; default = **5**), but only **4**..**6** are formally supported by Sybase (3 is also possible but lower values have no effect).
- **(ASE 12.5.4 ESD#8) 'bind to engine',** '*engine_number*' - binds the RepAgent to the specified ASE engine. By default, the RepAgent is affinitied to the ASE engine with the least amount of network I/O at the moment the RepAgent starts. NB: this option was not yet available in ASE 15 when this book went to press.
- **(ASE 12.5) 'schema cache growth factor',** '*value*' - when set to a higher value (**1**..**10**; default = **1**), RepAgent caches the schema of replicated tables and/or procedures for a longer time (allows better performance when many schema changes occur in the primary database, but require more memory).
- **(ASE 12.5) 'send structured oqids',** { **true** | **false** } - if **true** (default = **false**), RepAgent sends compressed OQID data to RepServer for better performance.
- **(ASE 12.5) 'data limits filter mode',** { **'off'** | **'stop'** | **'skip'** | **'truncate'** } - defines how RepAgent handles log records that use the extended column/parameter limits of ASE 12.5+: if **'off'** (=default), sends all log records to RepServer; if **'stop'**, RepAgent shuts down; if **'skip'**, RepAgent skips such log records; if **'truncate'**, truncates any data beyond the ASE pre-12.5 limit before sending it.
- **'security mechanism',** '*mechanism_name*' - specifies the name of the security mechanism to use for connections to RepServer (default = none/blank).
- **'unified login' / 'mutual authentication' / 'msg confidentiality' / 'msg integrity' / 'msg replay detection' / 'msg origin check' / 'msg out of sequence check',** { **true** | **false** } - when a security mechanism is used (see previous bullet), these options can specify (when **true**; default = **false**) specific network security features to be used, similar to those described on page 95.
- **'traceon',** '*traceflag*' / **'traceoff'**, '*traceflag*' - (undocumented) enables or disables a RepAgent traceflag (see below)
- **'trace log file',** '*pathname*' - (undocumented) directs all output for RepAgent traceflags to the specified file.

(ASE 12.5.0.3) sp_sysmon '*hh:mm:ss*', **'repagent'**
(ASE procedure) Displays RepAgent statistics for the specified interval.

8.2 ASE RepAgent traceflags (undocumented)

Some undocumented traceflags exist for ASE RepAgents, as listed in the table below. Note: RepAgent traceflags are not formally supported by Sybase. It should also be noted that these traceflags are unlikely to produce much useful information for a DBA.

To enable a RepAgent traceflag, use the **traceon** option of **sp_config_rep_agent** in the primary ASE database. To disable, use **traceoff**.
Example: **sp_config_rep_agent my_db, 'trace log file', '/tmp/my_db.trace'**
sp_config_rep_agent my_db, 'traceon', '9201'

To determine whether a particular traceflag is currently enabled, run **sp_config_rep_agent** *db_name*, **'traceon'** (or look for the line **'trace flags'** in the output of **sp_config_rep_agent** *db_name*). A bit will be set for each enabled traceflag according to the table below.

RepAgent traceflag	Bit value	Information logged to trace file
9200	1	some RepAgent configuration information
9201	2	LTL data sent to RepServer
9202	4	changes to the secondary truncation point
9203	8	information about log records
9204	16	information about internal allocations
9205	32	information about transactions found in the transaction log
9206	64	information about RepAgent running in recovery mode
9208	256	information about the schema cache
9210	1024	information about RepAgent waking up
9211	2048	information about log records for updates
9212	4096	information about log records for updates
9217	131072	**(ASE 12.5.3)** Allows RepAgent to continue after encountering an inconsistent log record, as indicated by ASE error 9289. With traceflag 9217, message 9290 is logged instead.

8.3 Non-ASE RepAgents

Sybase Replication Agent is the product name for the collective RepAgents for non-ASE primary databases, such as Oracle, Informix, DB2 (Unix/Windows) and MS SQL Server. These are also known as 'heterogeneous RepAgents', 'LAN RepAgents', or abbreviated as 'RAX'. This section briefly describes some aspects of version 12.5 of these RepAgents. For full details, see the *Replication Agent Administration Guide* (**www.sypron.nl/repqr2/ra**). Sybase also offers a RepAgent for DB2/mainframe, but this is not covered in this book.
The RepAgents for Oracle, Informix and MS SQLServer are based on triggers in the primary database which create a 'pseudo-transaction log' (also called 'shadow table'); the DB2 RepAgent accesses the DB2 transaction log directly. Non-ASE RepAgents do not support some functionality offered by ASE RepAgents, such as DDL replication (for DB2, neither procedure replication).
Non-ASE RepAgents are Java-based and require the Java Run-time Environment (JRE). Connections to the primary database and RepServer require JDBC and jConnect, respectively. Non-ASE RepAgents are individual OS processes and may run on a different host than the primary database or RepServer.

Sybase Replication Agent is installed in **$SYBASE/RAX-15_0** (for RA 15.0). For each non-ASE primary database, a separate RepAgent instance must be created with the tools **administrator** or **ra_admin**. An instance is essentially an independent application with its own installation directory tree (**$SYBASE/RAX-***xx_y***/***instance_name***/**...).
To manage and configure non-ASE RepAgents, use the GUI tool **administrator** (Windows:**administrator.bat**) or the command-line tool **ra_admin** (Windows: **ra_admin.bat**). These are located in **$SYBASE/ RAX-***xx_y***/bin**.
Mirror Activator will be installed in **$SYBASE/MA-15_0** (for MA 15.0).

ra -i*instance_name* [**-admin | -replicate**]   (Windows: **ra.bat**)
Starts a RepAgent instance in 'Admin' or 'Replicating' state (default = **-admin**).

ra_admin [*options*]
Creates and manages RepAgent instances. *options* can be:

-b	returns the pathname of the RepAgent base directory
-c *instance_name*	creates a new instance with this name
-p *port_number*	(with **-c**) the port number for the new RepAgent to listen on
-t *database_type*	(with **-c**) the database type: **ibmudb**, **informix**, **mssql**, **oracle**
-f *old_instance_name*	(with **-c**) copies the new instance from an existing instance
-d *instance_name*	deletes the specified instance
-l	lists all known RepAgent instances
-v *instance_name*	verifies the specified instance

Non-ASE RepAgent commands
After a RepAgent instance is started with **ra**, use **isql** to connect to it (initial username = **sa**; no password). From **isql**, RepAgent commands can then be executed. A selection of these commands is described below in brief. See the *Replication Agent Administration Guide* (**www.sypron.nl/repqr2/ra**) for a full list, and full details.

ra_help [*repagent_command*]
Returns help information for RepAgent commands.

ra_version / **ra_version_all**
Returns version information about the RepAgent, RepServer and primary database.

log_system_name
Displays the location of the RepAgent errorlog file

pdb_setreptable [**all** | *table_name*] [,] [*replicate_table_name* ,] [**mark** [, **owner**] | **unmark** [, **force**] | **enable** | **disable**]
Marks or unmarks one or more primary tables for replication.

pdb_setrepproc [**all** | *proc_name*] [,] [**mark** | **unmark** [, **force**] | **enable** | **disable**]
Marks or unmarks one or more primary stored procedures for replication(not for DB2).

pdb_setrepcol [**all** | *table_name* [, *column_name*]] [,] [**enable** | **disable** [, **force**]]
Enables or disables replication of LOB columns.

pdb_gen_id [*db_generation_no*]
Displays or updates the database generation number for the primary database.

ra_locator [**update** | **zero**]
Returns or clears (**zero**) the current LTM locator (similar to the ASE secondary truncation point), or gets (**updates**) a new value from RepServer.

pdb_truncate_xlog
Truncates the RepAgent transaction log (but not beyond the LTM locator).

ra_config [*repagent_parameter* [, *value*]]
Displays or modifies a config parameter setting. See the *Replication Agent Administration Guide* for a full list of parameters.
ra_set_login *username*, *password*
Changes the username and password for connecting to RepAgent (default=**sa**/none).

ra_dump [**database,** | **transaction,**] *database_name*, *dump_label*
Places a dump marker in the RepAgent log (for use with 'coordinated dumps').

suspend / **quiesce** / **resume**
Changes the RepAgent state between 'Admin' and 'Replicating'.

ra_status
Returns the current RepAgent status.

shutdown [**immediate**]
Shuts down RepAgent.

test_connection [**RS** | **PDS**]
With **RS**, tests the connection to RepServer and the RSSD; with **PDS**, tests the connection to the primary database. Without parameters, tests all connections.

trace [*traceflag*, { **true** | **false** }]
(Undocumented) Lists all active traceflags or enables/disables a traceflag. Some traceflags: **RACONTRC** (traces connections and query execution); **RACONTRCSQL** (traces SQL statements); **LATRCSQL** (LTL-related SQL sent to primary database).

Core Replication Functionality

9 RepServer syntax basics

The RepServer command language is quite similar to ASE T-SQL from a technical point of view. Some remarks:

- RepServer keywords are case-insensitive. For identifiers, this depends on the sort order used by RepServer; the installation default is case-sensitive.
- Identifiers (names of databases, repdefs, etc.) can be up to 30 bytes long in pre-RS 15.0; in RS 15.0, names of tables, columns, stored procedures, repdefs, functions, function strings, publications and articles can be 255 bytes. Parameters in function repdefs can be 30 bytes (255 in RS 15.0) after the leading '@'.
If desired, spaces and other characters can be included by enclosing an identifier in double quotes (i.e. **create replication definition " $#%@*"**...). Trailing spaces are automatically removed.
- User-defined identifiers cannot start with **'rs_'**. This prefix is reserved for RepServer system identifiers.
- Although not recommended, it is allowed to use RepServer keywords as identifiers by enclosing the identifier in double quotes (i.e. **create replication definition "my replication definition"** ...).
- The RSSD does not contain a list of reserved words for the RepServer command language. A full list of reserved words can be found in chapter 2 of the *Replication Server Reference Manual* (➢p.13).
- Comment syntax is identical to ASE T-SQL. Two styles are supported:
  /* a comment between delimiters */
  -- a comment until the end of this line
- Like T-SQL, a backslash '\' can be used as a line continuation character for long character strings.
- Special syntax considerations apply to the specification of language templates for function strings (➢p.79).
- When entering a RepServer command with a syntax error, the resulting error messages (usually errors 2056 or 16022) aren't always clear. Common syntax errors include incorrectly specifying or omitting quotes, or omitting a materialization clause with some forms of **create subscription**.

10 Getting RepServer status information

The following commands provide overall RepServer status information. Additional status information can be obtained with RSSD procedures like **rs_helproute**.
In pre-15.0.1, the actual name of a RepServer (which is not necessarily identical to the name used in **interfaces** files) can only be found with the RSSD query:

select charvalue from rs_config where optionname='oserver'

or with:

rs_configure oserver (never use **rs_configure** to change any settings!)

Only in 15.0.1 or later, it is possible to find the RepServer name from RS itself with the following command: **admin config, oserver** .
Renaming a RepServer is a non-supported operation; see page 133.

admin who [**, no_trunc**]
Displays all RepServer threads and their status. Without doubt, **admin who** is the most frequently used RepServer command. The undocumented parameter **no_trunc** displays some columns in a longer format.

admin who_is_up / admin who_is_down
Displays the RepServer threads that are running and not running, respectively.

admin version
Displays the full RepServer version ID.

admin disk_space
Displays the state and amount of used space for all disk partitions in this RepServer.

admin health
Displays RepServer status information. **Mode** is usually NORMAL, but can also indicate it's doing recovery, rebuilding queues or running in standalone mode. **Quiesce**

indicates whether RepServer is quiesced (➢p.116). **Status** is HEALTHY when all threads are running, otherwise SUSPECT.

admin logical_status [, *logical_dataserver*, *logical_database*]
Displays the status of logical connections (i.e. warm standby); ➢p.71.

admin rssd_name
Displays the name of database and dataserver for the RSSD; ➢p.109.

admin log_name
Displays the pathname of the current RepServer errorlog file. This was either specified during RepServer startup, or later modified by **admin set_log_name**.

admin set_log_name, '*logfile_name***'**
Closes the current RepServer errorlog file and continues in the specified new file.

admin echo, '*character_string***'** [**(15.0) , with_log**]
Echoes the specified string; this can be used to check if RepServer is running. With **with_log**, the string is also written to the RepServer errorlog file.

admin pid
Displays the process ID of the RepServer OS process.

admin time
Displays the current system time at the RepServer host.

admin cwd
(Undocumented) Displays the directory where RepServer was started. When a relative pathname is specified for the RepServer errorlog (with **admin set_log_name**) or for a dump file (with **sysadmin dump_file**), the path is relative to this startup directory.

11 Datatypes, datatype classes & -translations

For a table or function repdef, the datatype of each column and parameter must be specified. The following native RepServer datatypes are available, corresponding to most datatypes in primary and replicate databases (certainly for ASE and MS SQL Server). Additional datatypes can be defined for non-ASE databases (➢section 11.2).

RepServer native datatype	Remarks
int, **smallint**	4-byte and 2-byte integer, respectively (signed)
tinyint	1-byte integer (unsigned only)
(15.0) unsigned int, **smallint**	4-byte and 2-byte integer, respectively (unsigned)
(15.0) [**unsigned**] **bigint**	8-byte integer (signed or unsigned)
numeric, **decimal**, **identity**	1-38 numeric digits; don't specify precision or scale
identity	for replicating ASE identity columns (➢p.52)
float, **real**	8-byte and 4-byte floating-point number, respectively; machine-dependent
datetime, **smalldatetime**	8-byte and 4-byte date+time
date	date without time
time	time without date
money, **smallmoney**	8-byte and 4-byte numeric (5-digit precision)
char(*n***)**, **varchar(***n***)**	$n \leq 255$ for RS pre-12.5 or ASE pre-12.5
unichar(*n***)**, **univarchar(***n***)**	dataservers must support Unicode
binary(*n***)**, **varbinary(***n***)**	$n \leq 255$ for RS pre-12.5 or ASE pre-12.5
bit	replicate data values are in hexadecimal; for numeric format, use **tinyint** instead
rs_address	used for bitmap subscriptions (➢p.63); primary datatype is typically a 4-byte integer
text, **image**	size of the actual data is not limited by RepServer
(15.0) unitext	like **text**, but encoded in UTF-16
rawobject	use for off-row stored Java objects; handled as **image** by RepServer
rawobject in row	use for serialized, in-row stored Java objects; handled as **varbinary(255)** by RepServer
(ASE 15.0.2, RS 15.1) timestamp	for replicating ASE **timestamp** columns (see below)
(15.1) opaque	for replicating (non-ASE) datatypes currently not supported by RepServer

Notes:

- The datatypes **text**, **image**, **rawobject** [**in row**] cannott be used for parameters, primary key columns or searchable columns/parameters in repdefs.
- The datatype **rs_address** cannot be used for primary key columns in repdefs.
- Especially for [**var**]**char**, **uni**[**var**]**char** and [**var**]**binary**, the length of the datatype declared in a repdef should be at least as long as in the primary database. When the repdef datatype is too short for actual primary data, the distributor associated with the primary database will shut down. When this happens, the repdef datatype must either be corrected (with **alter replication definition**...**alter columns**) or the incoming data must be skipped when resuming the distributor (➢p.29).
- In pre-RS 15.1/pre-ASE 15.0.2, columns with ASE **timestamp** datatype (a special datatype; not related to clock time) cannot be replicated exactly: although replication involving such columns will work, the replicate values will be different from the primary values since ASE **timestamp** columns are automatically assigned a value by the ASE server. Also, a warning is written to the RepServer errorlog for each replicated **insert** or **update**. Should it be required to replicate primary **timestamp** column values in, use **varbinary(8)** for the column's datatype in both the repdef and the replicate table.
  In RS 15.1/ASE 15.0.2, ASE **timestamp** columns can be replicated exactly. In table repdefs, use the **timestamp** datatype; for a warm standby and for database repdefs/subscriptions when no repdefs are used, the behaviour depends on the config setting **send_timestamp_to_standby** (➢p.35).

11.1 Specifying datatypes in a repdef

When creating a table repdef or function repdef, a datatype must be specified for each column or parameter (except when a column has already been defined in an earlier repdef: its datatype may then be omitted in subsequent repdefs; if specified anyway, it must be identical for all repdefs).
For a column, two datatypes are distinguished:

- The declared datatype, which is the datatype RepServer receives from the RepAgent. This must always be specified, unless it was already specified in a different repdef for this table.
- The published datatype; before RepServer forwards primary data through the replication system, it converts the data from its declared datatype to a published datatype: this is the format in which primary data becomes available for subscriptions. A published datatype can be specified for each column with the **map to** clause in **create/alter replication definition**. If no **map to** clause is specified for a column, its published datatype is the same as the declared datatype.

Examples: **create replication definition MyTable with primary at PROD.prod_db**
(MyCol int, YourCol datetime map to rs_oracle_datetime)
primary key(MyCol)

create replication definition MyTable2 with primary at DB2.prod_db
(MyCol int, YourCol rs_db2_date map to datetime)
primary key(MyCol)

Notes:

- The RSSD procedures (**rs_***) display only the declared datatype for a column. To determine the published datatype, either query the RSSD table **rs_columns** directly (➢p.28), or use the RSP plugin for Sybase Central (➢p.116).
- For parameters in a function repdef, no **map to** clause can be specified, so the published datatype is the same as the declared datatype.

admin translate, *value***,** *source_datatype***,** *target_datatype*
Converts *value* from the specified source datatype to the target datatype. Both datatypes must either be native RepServer datatypes (➢p.26), or exist in the RSSD table **rs_datatype**.
This command can be used for testing/troubleshooting data conversion issues in heterogeneous replication systems.
Example: **admin translate, '01-Jan-2004 12:34:56.123',**
datetime, rs_oracle_datetime

11.2 Datatype classes and datatype translations

Note: when replicating from ASE to ASE only, this section can be ignored.

A 'datatype class' is a group of datatype definitions, representing different datatype

formats used by different databases such as ASE, Oracle, DB2, etc. Datatype definitions are also referred to as 'user-defined datatypes' (UDDs) in the RepServer documentation; note that this is unrelated to the ASE concept of user-defined datatypes (as created with **sp_addtype**).
RepServer datatype definitions can be used to define 'datatype translations'; these are needed when the primary and replicate database are of a different type (for example, when replicating from a primary Oracle database to replicate ASE and DB2 databases). For most datatypes, RepAgent and RepServer perform the necessary conversion automatically; for some datatypes, like date/time data, the translation can be defined explicitly.
This datatype conversion can be done on two levels:

- For an individual primary column (or parameter) in a repdef. For each column (or parameter), a datatype must be specified. By adding the **map to** *datatype* clause to the column declaration in the repdef (see above), all incoming values for that column will be translated to the specified datatype before being replicated further through the replication system.
  The official RepServer documentation calls this 'column-level translations'.
- For all data replicated to a replicate database. By creating datatype classes and datatype translations through the predefined SQL scripts mentioned below, a set of datatype translations is attached to a function string class. For a replicate database using that function string class, all data values replicated to that database are converted by the DSI according to those translations (only for those datatypes for which a translation has been defined).
  The official RepServer documentation calls this 'class-level translations'.

The two types of translations can be mixed. Column-level translations (**map to** in the repdef) are applied before class-level translations (performed by the DSI).

To initialize datatype classes, datatype definitions and datatype translations for heterogeneous replication, certain predefined SQL scripts, located in the **$SYBASE/$SYBASE_REP/scripts** directory, must be executed in the RSSD.
For example, when replicating from a primary ASE database to a replicate Oracle database, the scripts **hds_oracle_funcstrings.sql**, **hds_oracle_udds.sql** and **hds_clt_ase_to_oracle.sql** should be run (you may need to edit some of these scripts with the actual name of your RSSD database).
In addition, some further setup steps are required. See the *Replication Server Configuration Guide* (➢p.13), chapter *Installing and Implementing Heterogeneous Datatype Support* for full details.

11.3 RSSD tables - datatypes

Datatype classes are stored in the RSSD table **rs_classes**, with **rs_classes.classtype** = **'D'**. For each datatype class, the RSSD table **rs_datatype** contains datatype definitions for that class.
The RSSD table **rs_translation** contains datatype translations for a particular function string class (the so-called 'class-level translations'). The RSSD table **rs_columns** contains the datatype conversions specified in the repdef with **map to** (the so-called 'column-level translations'), in columns **declared_dtid** (the declared datatype) and **publ_dtid** (the published datatype).
The RSSD **rs_*** procedures do not display any information about datatype translations. Instead, query the RSSD tables directly.
(Note: the exact relationship between datatype classes and function string classes remains unclear; in fact, there may not even be a direct relationship - the RepServer documentation just doesn't contain much information about this topic.)

By default, no datatype classes are defined in the RSSD tables **rs_classes** and **rs_datatype** (except for the standard class **rs_rs_dt_class**). Other datatype classes, like **rs_oracle_dt_class**, exist as an empty class by default: a row exists in **rs_classes**, but no corresponding rows exist in **rs_datatype**. The SQL scripts in **$SYBASE/$SYBASE_REP/scripts** insert rows into these RSSD tables, thus creating the datatype definitions and translations for these classes.
In principle, it should be possible to create your own datatype classes and corresponding translations. Because no RepServer commands exist for this purpose, it would require manually inserting rows into the RSSD tables **rs_classes**, **rs_datatype** and **rs_translation**. Unfortunately, exactly how to define such rows is mostly undocumented, but the SQL scripts mentioned above, and the RSSD table descriptions in the *Replication Server Reference Manual* (➢p.13), may be a source of inspiration. Creating your own datatype classes and -translations is probably not officially supported by Sybase.

12 Connections to RepAgents

resume distributor *dataserver.database* [**skip transaction**]
Resumes a suspended distributor (DIST thread) for a connection to a primary database. The distributor matches incoming primary transactions against repdefs and subscriptions, writing replicated transactions from the inbound queue into outbound queues. There is one DIST thread for each inbound queue.
skip transaction deletes the first transaction from the inbound queue; this may be needed when the distributor shuts down due to invalid incoming data (for example, when incoming primary data is incompatible with the corresponding repdef datatype). The skipped transaction is written into the RSSD exceptions log tables (➢p.85), and can then be viewed with the RSSD procedure **rs_helpexception** (but note that **resume connection** (instead of **resume distributor**) is displayed as the source of the logged transaction. Nevertheless, these transactions can be recognized because the column **'Dest Site'** in the output is displayed as **'.'** (i.e. just a dot)).

suspend distributor *dataserver.database*
Suspends the distributor (DIST thread) for a connection to a primary database. In pre-15.1, a suspended distributor is not maintained over a RepServer reboot. To disable the distributor permanently (like for a warm standby under certain conditions), use **alter logical connection**...**set distribution off** (➢p.66).

suspend log transfer from { *dataserver.database* | **all** }
Disconnects a RepAgent for a primary database (with **all**, for all primary databases) from RepServer and prevents the RepAgent from reconnecting. This is the first step in quiescing the replication system (➢p.116); use **admin quiesce_check** to test whether this RepServer is quiesced after suspending the RepAgents.

resume log transfer from { *dataserver.database* | **all** }
Allows RepAgents to connect to the RepServer again.

admin who, dist
Displays status information and some statistics for the distributor threads for primary databases in this RepServer.

allow connections
A troubleshooting command (➢p.118), allowing RepServer to accept connections only from RepAgents started in recovery mode.

13 Connections to primary/replicate databases

Database connections are typically created with the **rs_init** utility (➢p.98). When a connection is created manually with **create connection**, this also requires running the SQL script **$SYBASE/$SYBASE_REP/scripts/rs_install_replicate.sql** (Windows: **rsinsrep.sql**), and for a primary database, also **rs_install_primary.sql** (Windows: **rsinspri.sql**), creating dataserver logins and database users. In addition, for a primary database, the secondary truncation point is enabled and the RepAgent is configured. **rs_init** performs all of these steps in one operation.
From the perspective of RepServer, a connection always represents at least a replicate database. When **log transfer** is set to on with **create/alter connection**, the connection is also for a primary database.

create connection to *dataserver.database*
  set error class [**to**] *error_class_name*
  set function string class [**to**] *function_class_name*
  [**set username** [**to**] *maintuser_name*
    set password [**to**] *maintuser_password*]
  [**set** *database_config_parameter* [**to**] **'***value***'** [...*more* **set** *clauses*...]] ➢p.32
  [**set** *security_config_parameter* [**to**] **'***value***'** [...*more* **set** *clauses*...]] ➢p.94
  [**with** { **log transfer on, dsi_suspended** }]
  [**as active for** *logical_dataserver.logical_database* |
    as standby for *logical_dataserver.logical_database* [**use dump marker**]]
Creates a connection to the specified database, which is now controlled by the current RepServer. Typically executed by the **rs_init** utility.
Example: **create connection to PROD.sales_db**
  set error class to rs_sqlserver_error_class
  set function string class to rs_sqlserver_function_class
  set username to sales_db_maint
  set password to no_discounts_today
  set dsi_num_threads to '5'

Notes:

- *maintuser_name* and *maintuser_password* specify the maintenance user for this database; this will be stored in the RSSD table **rs_maintusers**. These can be omitted only when network-based security (Kerberos, DCE) is used. Note that a maintenance user must be specified even for a primary-only database.
- For ASE databases, the default error class and function string class are **rs_sqlserver_error_class** and **rs_sqlserver_function_class**. These classes can be changed with **alter connection**. For function string classes for non-ASE databases, see page 72.
- For *database_config_parameter*, see page 32; for *security_config_parameter*, see the **msg_*** and **id_msg_*** parameters on page 94.
  Multiple parameters can be specified in one **create connection** command.
- **with log transfer on** creates a **REP AGENT** thread for this database in RepServer; this makes sense only for primary databases where a RepAgent actually exists.
- **with dsi_suspended** leaves the DSI to the database in a suspended state. This could be used when the database will only act as a primary database, no redundant DSI connection into that dataserver is desired, and no request functions (➢p.41) are delivered to this database.
- **as active for** and **as standby for** apply to a warm standby only (➢p.65).
- **use dump marker** can only be used when creating the connection for the standby database in a warm standby (➢p.66).
- When creating connections to non-ASE databases, see the sample scripts in **$SYBASE/$SYBASE_REP/scripts** for recommended connection settings (e.g. **hds_oracle_connection_sample.sql** for an Oracle database).

alter connection to *dataserver.database*
{ **set error class** [**to**] *error_class_name* |
set function string class [**to**] *function_class_name* |
set password [**to**] *maintuser_password* |
set *database_config_parameter* [**to**] '*value*' | ➢p.32
set *security_config_parameter* [**to**] '*value*' | ➢p.94
set security_services [**to**] **'default'** |
set log transfer [**to**] { **on** | **off** } }

Modifies an attribute for the specified database connection. The change takes effect once the connection is resumed (it is good practice to suspend the connection before changing a parameter). Unlike **create connection**, **alter connection** can set only one attribute at a time.

Examples: **alter connection to PROD.sales_db set dump_load to 'on'**
alter connection to PROD.sales_db set password to 'buynowpaylater'

Most options are similar to **create connection**; however, note the following:

- **set password** changes the password for the maintenance user in the RSSD table **rs_maintusers**.
  Only for an embedded RSSD, the dataserver login password in ASA and the corresponding password in the **.cfg** file are changed as well (➢p.111). In a classic ASE RSSD, the password in the **.cfg** file and the ASE dataserver password for the RSSD primary user must be updated separately by the DBA.
- **set security_services to 'default'** resets all network security features for this connection to their RepServer-wide defaults (➢p. 94).
- **set log transfer off** disallows the RepAgent for the primary database to connect to RepServer; this also removes the corresponding REP AGENT thread from RepServer; **set log transfer on** does the reverse. Do not use quotes around **on** and **off**! (note: removing the REP AGENT thread makes sense only when the database will not be used as a primary anymore).
- The maintenance user's password can be changed with **alter connection**, but the maintenance user itself cannot. A workaround is described on page 134.
- Changing the password for the RSSD maintenance user with **alter connection** modifes the password in the RSSD table **rs_maintusers** but does not modify the password in the RepServer's **.cfg** file. Again, see page 134.

drop connection to *dataserver.database*
Removes the connection to the (primary or replicate) database from the RepServer. Dropping a connection only modifies data in the RSSD; it does not affect primary or replicated data. Repdefs and/or subscriptions associated with the connection must have been dropped first.

sysadmin dropdb, *dataserver*, *database*
Removes a database from the ID Server. This is a troubleshooting command; use only when **drop connection** fails.

configure connection ...
Identical to **alter connection**.

resume connection to *dataserver.database*
[**skip** [**(15.1)** *N*] **transaction** | **execute transaction**]
Resumes a suspended connection (DSI thread) to a replicate database. With **skip transaction**, the first transaction in the outbound queue is not applied to the replicated database but written into the RSSD exceptions log tables (➢p.85); the logged transaction can be viewed with the RSSD procedure **rs_helpexception**. In 15.1, **skip** *N* **transaction** does the same but skips the first *N* transactions in the queue.
Warning: skipping transactions should be used only as a last resort, since it may result in differences between the primary and replicate database.
The option **execute transaction** should only be used when error 5152 occurs in the RepServer errorlog (**'There is a system transaction whose state is not known. DSI will be shut down'**).

suspend connection to *dataserver.database* [**with nowait**]
Suspends a connection (DSI thread) to a replicate database. By default, the DSI tries to complete replicate transactions currently being applied; **with nowait** suspends the DSI immediately.

13.1 RSSD tables - database connections

Each database connection is stored in the RSSD table **rs_databases**, with columns **ltype** = **ptype** = **'P'**.

The following tables are not located in the RSSD, but in the primary and/or replicate databases (these tables may also exist in the RSSD, but only because the RSSD is considered to be a primary and/or replicate database as well):

rs_lastcommit
Contains information about the last committed replicate transaction from each primary database. **rs_lastcommit** exists in each replicate (and primary) database, along with the stored procedures **rs_update_lastcommit** and **rs_get_lastcommit**, which RepServer uses to access **rs_lastcommit**.

rs_threads
Applies only when parallel DSI is used for a connection to a replicate database. **rs_threads** is used to perform transaction serialization between parallel DSI threads. With **dsi_commit_control** = **'on'** (➢p.97), a more efficient RepServer-algorithm is used instead of **rs_threads**.
rs_threads exists in each replicate (and primary) database.

(15.1) rs_ticket_history
In replicate databases only, contains replicated 'tickets' (➢p.132) .

rs_info
Applies only to non-ASE replicate databases. Contains the character set and sort order used by the non-ASE replicate database. **rs_info** is created by scripts like **hds_oracle_setup_for_replicate.sql** (located in **$SYBASE/$SYBASE_REP/scripts**).

13.2 Getting information about database connections

rs_helpdb [*dataserver*, *database*]
(RSSD procedure) Displays a list of all databases known in this RSSD. With a dataserver/database name, displays only that database.

rs_helprepdb [*replicate_dataserver*, *replicate_database*]
(RSSD procedure) Without any parameters, displays a list of all replicate databases with subscriptions to primary data in the current RepServer (either table/function/database repdefs or publications). When no route is involved, this is the list of all replicate databases in this RepServer. With a dataserver/database name, displays that database only when such subscriptions exist. To display the actual repdefs, publications or subscriptions, use **rs_helprep/rs_helpsub**, **rs_helppub/rs_helppubsub** or **rs_helpdbrep/rs_helpdbsub**.

admin show_connections
Displays the current status of database connections (as well as outgoing routes) from this RepServer.

admin who, dsi
Displays some (but not all) connection-specific parameter settings, as well as various statistics for each connection.

13.3 Configuration parameters for database connections

The configuration parameters on the following pages apply to database connections. They can be modified (one parameter at a time) with **configure replication server** to set RepServer-wide defaults; when specified with **create connection** or **alter connection**, these server-wide defaults are overridden for the specified connection.
Examples: **alter connection to PROD.sales_db set dump_load to 'on'**
configure replication server set db_packet_size to '16384'

Notes:

- All parameter values, including integers, must be specified as quoted strings.
- Except for **disk_affinity**, all parameters are stored in the RSSD table **rs_config**, and changes take effect once the connection is resumed (it is good practice to suspend the connection before changing a parameter). For details about parameter storage in **rs_config**, see page 91.
- In pre-15.0.1, there is no system-supplied procedure to display all non-default configuration parameter settings for a connection (some, but not all, connection-specific settings are displayed by **admin who, dsi**). Instead, use the RSSD procedure **rs_helpcfg_db** (included in the electronic supplement to this book; ➢p.8). In 15.0.1, **admin config** can also be used (➢p.90).
- The network security configuration parameters named **msg_***, as described on page 94, can also be defined for a route.
- Configuration parameters for parallel DSI are described on page 96.

List of configuration parameters for database connections:

- **disk_affinity** - when set to the name of a disk partition, tries to allocate disk space for the queues for this connection on that partition (➢p.101). When **'off'** (=default), space is allocated on the next free segment in the current (or next) partition.
- **batch** - when **'on'** (=default), multiple SQL statements can be sent to the replicate database in a single command batch; when **'off'**, each SQL statement is sent to the replicate database individually.
- **batch_begin** - when **'on'** (=default), **begin transaction** can be in the same batch as DML and other SQL statements.
- **command_retry** - the maximum number of times (default=**3**) a SQL statement is retried by the DSI connection when it encounters a dataserver error that has an action of **retry_stop** or **retry_log** assigned to it (➢p.83).
- **dsi_cmd_batch_size** - the maximum number of bytes (default=**8192**) that can be put into a single command batch.
- **dsi_cmd_separator** - the character used to separate different SQL statements in a command batch; it is also used to replace single semicolons in function string language templates (➢p.79). Default = newline character ('**\n**'; ASCII: **0A**).
- **db_packet_size** - the maximum network packet size (in bytes; default=**512**) for the DSI connection. Sybase recommends setting this parameter to **16384**; on slower networks, it should not be set lower than **2048**. Note that the corresponding dataserver must be configured to support this network packet size.
- **dsi_charset_convert** - defines character set conversion handling for the DSI connection. When **'on'** (=default), performs all necessary conversions; for unconvertible characters, the DSI is shut down; **'allow'** is identical to **'on'**, but unconvertible characters are applied anyway; **'off'** performs no conversion at all. During subscription materialization, **'off'** behaves as **'allow'**.
- **dsi_exec_request_sproc** - enables (**'on'**, =default) or disables (**'off'**) delivery of request stored procedures (a.k.a. request functions; ➢p.41) for a database connection.

- **dsi_fadeout_time** - the number of seconds of idle time (default=**600**) before a DSI connection is closed. When set to **-1**, it will never be closed.
- **dsi_max_xacts_in_group** - specifies the maximum number of transactions from the same primary database in a 'group' (default=**20**; maximum=**100**). A group is applied to the replicate database as a single transaction to help improve performance.
- **dsi_xact_group_size** - specifies the maximum size (in bytes; default=**65536;** no maximum) for a grouped transaction (see **dsi_max_xacts_in_group** above). When set to **-1**, transactions are not grouped.
- **dsi_keep_triggers** - when **'off'** (=default for warm standby databases), all triggers in the replicate ASE database are disabled for the DSI session (with the ASE statement **set triggers off**); when **'on'** (=default for regular (=non-warm-standby) databases), triggers will work normally for the DSI.
  Note: combining triggers and replication can be tricky. If a replicated primary table has a trigger that modifies a non-replicated primary table, then the trigger should be active on the replicate side too. However, if a trigger on a replicated primary table modifies another replicated primary table, the trigger should probably not be active on the replicate side (the latter is the reason why, in a warm standby database, triggers are disabled by default).
- **dsi_max_cmds_to_log** - when a transaction is logged into the RSSD exceptions log tables (➢p.85), specifies the maximum number of statements that will be logged. Default = **-1**, meaning everything is logged.
- **dsi_max_text_to_log** - when a transaction is logged into the RSSD exceptions log tables (➢p.85), this specifies the maximum number of bytes to be logged for each **rs_writetext** function. Default = **-1**, meaning everything is logged.
- **dsi_replication** - default = **'off'** for a standby database in a warm standby, and **'on'** otherwise.
  When **'on'**, log records for modifications applied to the replicate database by the DSI (by the maintenance user) are marked as 'replicated', allowing these modifications to be picked up by a RepAgent (which must be configured to pick up maintenance user transactions). This is needed in some cases, for example when a warm standby pair (i.e. a logical connection) also acts as a replicate database for subscriptions. When **'off'**, log records for DSI transactions are marked as 'not replicated' (with the ASE statement **set replication off**). When using database repdefs in a setup where a replicate database may later be changed to a primary database, **dsi_replication** should be **'off'** for that replicate database to avoid earlier DSI-applied replicate transactions from being replicated again when the replicate database is changed to a primary database.
- **(15.0) dsi_replication_ddl** - when **'off'** (=default), transactions for replicated DDL are marked again for replication in the replicate database. When **'on'**, these DDL transactions are not marked for replication (the DSI executes **set replication off/on** before/after the DDL command). This requires that the maintenance user in the replicate dataserver has been granted **set session authorization** (or **set proxy**).
- **dsi_sql_data_style** - formats datatypes for compatibility with DB2 (**'db2'**), Lotus Notes (**'notes'**), Sybase ASA/SQL Anywhere (**'watcom'**) or Sybase SQL Remote (**'sqlremote'**). For connections to ASE databases, use **''** (=an empty string; =default) or **'sql'**.
- **dsi_sqt_max_cache_size** - maximum amount of memory (in bytes) for the SQT cache for the DSI connection (i.e. outbound queue). Default = **0**, meaning that the current value of the server-wide parameter **sqt_max_cache_size** is used.
- **(12.6 ESD#7) dist_sqt_max_cache_size** - maximum amount of memory (in bytes) for the SQT cache for the distributor (i.e. inbound queue). Default = **0**, meaning that the current value of the server-wide parameter **sqt_max_cache_size** is used. Unlike the DSI SQT cache, it is much less common to have to enlarge the DIST SQT cache.
- **dsi_text_convert_multiplier** - a **float** value indicating whether the volume of **text** data in the replicate database must expand (set to > **1.0**) or shrink (set to < **1.0**) as a result of character set conversion. Default = **1**.
- **dump_load** - when set to **'on'**, coordinated dumps (➢p.117) are enabled for the replicate database; when **'off'** (=default), they are disabled.
- **save_interval** - the number of minutes (default=**0**) messages in the DSI queue are saved after being applied successfully to the replicate database. Increasing

this setting improves recoverability (through **sysadmin restore_dsi_saved_segments**), but requires additional disk space. The current setting is displayed by **admin who, sqm** (in the column **Save_Int:Seg**).

- **exec_cmds_per_timeslice** - the maximum number of LTL commands the RepAgent Executor thread (i.e. the REP AGENT thread inside RepServer, not the RepAgent outside RepServer) can process before it must yield the CPU. Possible values are **1** to **2147483648**; default = **5**.
- **exec_sqm_write_request_limit** - the amount of memory (in bytes) for the RepAgent Executor thread to buffer messages waiting to be written to the inbound queue. In 15.0.1, possible values are **16384** to **2147483647**; default = **1048576**. In pre-15.0.1, possible values are **16384** (=default) to **983040**.
- **sub_sqm_write_request_limit** - the amount of memory (in bytes) for subscription (de)materialization threads for buffering messages not yet written to the outbound queue. In 15.0.1, possible values are **16384** to **2147483647**; default = **1048576**. In pre-15.0.1, possible values are **16384** to **983040**; default = **32768**.
- **md_sqm_write_request_limit** - the amount of memory (in bytes) for the Distributor (DIST) thread for buffering messages not yet written to the outbound queue. In 15.0.1, possible values are **16384** to **2147483647**; default = **1048576**. In pre-15.0.1, possible values are **16384** to **983040**; default = **100000**.
- **(pre-12.1) md_source_memory_pool** - in 12.1, this parameter has been superseded by **md_sqm_write_request_limit**.
- **rep_as_standby** - this applies to a primary database connection or a logical connection. When **'on'**, table subscriptions can be created for table repdefs in a primary database that has been marked with **sp_reptostandby**, without the need to mark these primary tables with **sp_setreptable**. This requires the ASE RepAgent to have the option **'send warm standby xacts'** enabled. When set to **'off'** (=default), a primary table must have been marked explicitly with **sp_setreptable**.
- **dsi_rs_ticket_report** - when **'on'** (default = **'off'** in pre-15.1, **'on'** in 15.1), the **rs_ticket_report** function gets delivered to the replicate database (➢p.132).
- **(15.0) dist_stop_unsupported_cmd** - determines how to handle replicated commands for new features that are not supported by older RepServer versions. When **'off'** (=default), the distributor (DIST thread) skips the newer commands if they would be sent to RepServers with an incompatible older version. When **'on'**, the distributor is suspended when such a command is encountered; to resolve, either skip the transaction or set this parameter to **'off'**.
- **(15.0) dsi_isolation_level** - defines the ANSI transaction isolation level used for the replicate dataserver. Possible values are **'0'**, **'1'**, **'2'**, **'3'** or **'default'**. When set to **'default'** (=default), the DSI does not set a specific isolation level, thus using the replicate dataserver's own default isolation level. Replaces **isolation_level_3** in **dsi_serialization_method** in 15.0.
- **(15.0) use_batch_markers** - for replicate dataservers that require additional SQL for command batching, when **'on'** (default = **'off'**) the functions **rs_batch_start** and **rs_batch_end** will be executed to allow batching of replicate SQL commands. This is intended for non-ASE dataservers.
- **(15.0.1) dynamic_sql** - when **'on'** (default = **'off'**), allows prepared statements (sometimes known as 'dynamic SQL') to be used when applying replicate SQL statements to the replicate dataserver (in 15.0.1, this is supported for ASE and DB2; in 15.1, also for Oracle, MS SQL and UDB).
  This feature improves DSI performance since the query plan is cached for prepared statements, thus reducing optimizer overhead in the replicate dataserver. This setting applies only to replicate **insert**, **update** or **delete** statements that do not involve **text/image/raw object** columns and that refer to 255 columns at most. For **update/delete**, the **where**-clause cannot contain **NULL** values. Prepared statements are not used for SQL resulting from custom function strings. In some cases, it is required that the column order in repdefs is the same as in the table, or prepared statements will not be used.
  In ASE, prepared statements are implemented as light-weight processes (LWPs). Existing LWPs are visible through the MDA table monCachedProcedures, with ObjectID < 0. Ensure the ASE parameter **'number of open objects'** is set high enough to accommodate all LWPs.
  admin stats, dsi has counters on usage of prepared statements (**DSIEDsqlPrepared**, **DSIEDsqlExecuted**).
  For a connection, this setting takes effect immediately, without suspending/resuming the connection. For the RepServer-wide setting, connection

suspend/resume is required.
In 15.1, use of prepared statements can be switched off for individual repdefs, either for all DSIs (with **alter replication definition**...**without dynamic sql**), or for a specific DSI (with **set dynamic_sql off** ; ➢p.38). Disabling the DSI-specific config setting described above disables all prepared statements for this DSI, irrespective of any repdef-level settings.

- **(15.0.1) dynamic_sql_cache_size** - defines how many prepared statements can be used by the DSI (**1**..**65535**; default = **100**); set this to the number of tables being replicated through this DSI. The max. number of prepared statements for the DSI is 3 * **dynamic_sql_cache_size**.
For a connection, this setting takes immediate effect, without suspending/resuming the connection. For the RepServer-wide setting, suspend/resume is required.

- **(15.0.1) dynamic_sql_cache_management** - defines what happens when all prepared statements (as defined by **dynamic_sql_cache_size**) are in use and subsequent SQL statements do not match existing prepared statements. When **'mru'**, the oldest prepared statements are removed and reused. When **'fixed'** (=default), subsequent SQL statements are executed as normal SQL language statements instead of as prepared statements.
For a connection, this setting takes immediate effect, without suspending/resuming the connection. For the RepServer-wide setting, suspend/resume is required.

- **(RS 15.1, ASE 15.0.2) send_timestamp_to_standby** - in ASE 15.0.2, it is possible to replicate the actual values of ASE timestamp columns (➢p.27). For a warm standby and for database repdefs/subscriptions, where no table repdef exists for a replicated table containing a timestamp column, this config setting determines whether the actual timestamp value from the primary row is replicated (**'on'**) or whether the timestamp value in the replicate row is assigned by the replicate dataserver (**'off'**, = default).
When using a repdef that includes the timestamp column with the **timestamp** datatype, the actual primary timestamp value is always replicated when using ASE 15.0.2.

- **(15.1) dsi_alt_writetext** - only relevant when EnterpriseConnect/DirectConnect 15.0 ESD#2 is used to access the replicate database. When **'dcany'**, Repserver sends primary key values along when text/image-type data needs to be updated, allowing better performance. When **'off'** (=default), RepServer sends a text pointer instead.

14 Replication definitions

14.1 Summary

A replication definition (further abbreviated as 'repdef') marks primary data that can be replicated. As such, a repdef represents the 'publish' part of 'publish-subscribe' replication. There are three types of repdefs:

- Table repdefs (created with **create replication definition**), for replicating SQL DML statements; see below.

- Function repdefs (created with **create function replication definition**) for replicating the execution of a stored procedure; ➢p.39. This is often referred to as 'function replication', and sometimes as 'applied functions'.

- Database repdefs (created with **create database replication definition**) for replicating an entire database (or parts of it); ➢p.43. A database repdef is similar to a warm standby, although there are some important differences.

Repdefs are typically used in combination with subscriptions (the other part of 'publish-subscribe'). Exceptions are a warm standby (➢p.65), database repdefs (➢p.43) and request functions in pre-15.1 (➢p.41; in pre-15.1, repdefs can be used without subscriptions for request functions).
Repdefs may also be grouped into publications (➢p.54).
For table and function repdefs, the DBA must ensure a repdef name is unique across all RepServers with routes between them, since RepServer cannot always verify this constraint itself. The same applies for database repdef names. Although not recommended, a database repdef may have the same name as a table or function repdef.
It is good practice to include a type-identifying tag such as **'_rdf'** in each repdef name, to distinguish it from other objects such as publications or articles. Note that this will require **with all tables named** to be specified for table repdefs (see below).

All commands in the following sections are executed at the primary RepServer, except **set autocorrection** and **set dynamic_sql**, which are executed in the replicate RepServer.

14.2 Table repdefs

create replication definition *table_repdef_name*
with primary at *dataserver.database*
[**with all tables named** [*owner_name.*]*table_name* |
[**with primary table named** [*owner_name.*]*table_name*]
[**with replicate table named** [*owner_name.*]*table_name*]]
(*column_name* [**as** *replicate_colname*] *datatype* [[**not**] **null**] [**map to** *datatype*]
[**,** *...more columns...*] **)**
primary key (*column_name* [**,** *...more columns...*] **)**
[**searchable columns (** *column_name* [**,** *...more columns...*] **)**]
[**send standby** [{ **all** | **replication definition** } **columns**]]
[**replicate** { **minimal** | **all** } **columns**]
[**replicate_if_changed (** *column_name* [**,** *...more columns...*] **)**]
[**always_replicate (** *column_name* [[**,** *...more columns...*] **)**]
[**(15.1)** { **with** | **without** } **dynamic sql**]

Creates a repdef for a primary table in the specified primary database. Multiple repdefs may be created for the same primary table; see the *Replication Server Reference Manual* (➢p.13) for a full description of the precise effects. All repdefs for a table can be displayed with the RSSD procedure **rs_helpreptable**.

To actually replicate primary data, the primary table must also have been marked for replication with the ASE procedure **sp_setreptable** (➢p.15); alternatively, the configuration parameter **rep_as_standby** can be used instead (➢p.34).

Examples: **create replication definition Accounts** -- table name is also 'Accounts'
with primary at PROD.cust_db
(AccountNo int, Balance numeric) primary key (AccountNo)

create replication definition Accounts_rdf -- table name is 'Accounts'
with primary at PROD.cust_db
with all tables named Accounts
(AccountNo int, Balance numeric) primary key (AccountNo)

Notes:

- Table names: by default, *table_repdef_name* is assumed to be identical to the name of both the primary and the replicate table. **with all tables named** specifies a different name for both tables; **with primary/replicate table named** specifies a different name for the primary and replicate table, respectively. **with all tables named** and **with primary/replicate table named** are mutually exclusive. These clauses must also be used to specify a non-default table owner.
  Note that **create replication definition** does not verify the existence, schema or permissions of neither the primary nor the replicate table.
  When specifying the table owner, single or double quotes may optionally be used, but make sure the **.** character is not inside the quotes (i.e. **'***owner***'.'***table***'** or **"***owner***"."***table***"**, but not **"***owner.table***"**).

- Column names: by default, column names are assumed to be identical in the primary and replicate table. If not, **as** *replicate_colname* specifies the name in the replicate table as it will be used in SQL statements in the replicate database.

- The primary *dataserver.database* can be either a normal database connection or a logical connection (i.e. a warm standby pair).

- Datatypes: the *datatype* for a column is mandatory except when that column was already declared in another repdef for the same primary table. **null** or **not null** (=default) can be specified for **text**, **image**, or **rawobject** columns only, and must match the nullability of the column in the primary and replicate database. **numeric** and **decimal** columns must be specified without precision or scale. **map to** specifies a datatype conversion for the column. See page 26 for more information about RepServer datatypes and the **map to** clause.

- **primary key**: the columns listed in the **primary key** clause typically reflect the table's actual primary key. These **primary key** columns will be part of the **where**-clause of SQL **update** and **delete** statements executed in the replicate database. It is therefore recommended that an index on these columns exists in the replicate database when many updates or deletes are replicated, although this is neither verified nor enforced by RepServer. The **primary key** clause has no effect on the primary database.
  In a warm standby or database repdef, and with multiple repdefs for a table, the union of all **primary key** columns for all repdefs for this table is used as the primary key, depending on the **send standby** option (➢p.48).

Note: if no primary key or unique set of columns can be determined for a table, it is unlikely that such a table should be replicated at all (➢p.10).

- **searchable columns** specifies the columns that can be referenced in the **where**-clause of **create/define subscription** and **create article**.
- **send standby** affects which columns are replicated and which columns are considered to be the primary key; this applies only to a warm standby or when database replication is combined with table repdefs. See page 48 for more information about **send standby**.
  Specifying a **send standby** option automatically disables any active **send standby** option for other repdefs for this table.
- **replicate all columns** replicates all table columns to the replicate database. To improve performance, **replicate minimal columns** replicates only those columns whose values have really been changed (i.e. a column that is updated to its current value will not be replicated). **replicate all columns** is the default for regular (non-warm standby) replication; in a warm standby, **replicate minimal columns** is enabled by default.
  For more information about minimal column replication, see page 49.
- **replicate_if_changed** and **always_replicate** can be used for **text**, **image** and **rawobject** columns only, and specify how the column should be replicated. These settings should match those by **sp_setrepcol** (➢p.15) in the primary database. When no status is specified explicitly, it is set to **always_replicate** if the column does not occur in another repdef; if it does, the status is set to the existing repdef. See page 51 for details about **text/image/rawobject** replication.
- In 15.1, **without dynamic sql** disables use of prepared statements (➢p.34) for this repdef for all replicate databases. Default is **with dynamic sql**, enabling prepared statements. When enabled, it can be disabled for a specific replicate database with **set dynamic_sql off** (➢p.38).
  Note that using prepared statements requires that the **dynamic_sql** option has been enabled for the replicate database with **alter connection** (➢p.34).
  The current setting for a repdef can be checked with the RSSD procedure **rs_helprep** in the primary RSSD.

alter replication definition *table_repdef_name alter_clause*
Modifies an existing repdef. *alter_clause* can be one of the clauses listed below. These clauses are largely similar to **create replication definition** above; see there for more information. After modifying a repdef, it is a good idea to wait a short period (e.g. 30-60 seconds) before resuming DML statements against the corresponding primary table.
For *alter_clause*, the possibilities are listed below. Note that different clauses cannot be combined in a single command.

- **with replicate table named** [*owner_name*.]*table_name*
  Renames the replicate table. The primary table cannot be renamed.
- **add** *column_name* [**as** *replicate_colname*] *datatype* [[**not**] **null**] [**map to** *datatype*] [**,** *...more columns...*]
  Adds one or more columns to the repdef. Note that columns cannot be dropped from a repdef.
- **alter columns with** *column_name* **as** *replicate_colname* [**,** *...more columns...*]
  Renames the replicate column name for a primary column. The primary column itself cannot be renamed.
- **alter columns with** *column_name datatype* [[**not**] **null**] [**map to** *datatype*] [**,** *...more columns...*]
  Changes the datatype of a column. See page 26 for more information about RepServer datatypes and the **map to** clause.
- { **add** | **drop** } **primary key** *column_name* [**,** *...more columns...*]
  Adds or drops one or more **primary key** columns.
- { **add** | **drop** } **searchable columns** *column_name* [**,** *...more columns...*]
  Adds or drops one or more **searchable columns**.
- **send standby** [**off** | { **all** | **replication definition** } **columns**]
  Modifies the **send standby** status of the repdef (➢p.48). **send standby off** removes any **send standby** setting for this repdef.
- **replicate** { **minimal** | **all** } **columns**
  Modifies minimal column replication setting for this repdef.
- { **always_replicate** | **replicate_if_changed** } *column_name* [**,** *...more columns...*]
  Changes the replication status to either **replicate_if_changed** or **al-**

ways_replicate for one or more **text**, **image** and **rawobject** columns. When the modified columns also occur in other repdefs, their status is changed in those repdefs as well. See page 51 for more details about **text/image** replication.

- **(15.1)** { **with** | **without** } **dynamic sql**
  Enables/disables use of prepared statements for this repdef for all replicate databases. See **create replication definition**.

Examples: **alter replication definition Accounts alter columns with Balance int**
alter replication definition Accounts add primary key Balance

drop replication definition *table_repdef_name*
Drops a repdef, including its repdef-specific functions and corresponding function strings. No subscriptions or articles should exist for this repdef. When an article still exists for the repdef, use the RSSD query on page 55 to determine the corresponding articles and publication. When a subscription still exists, use **rs_helprep** to determine the subscription.

(15.1) set dynamic_sql { **on** | **off** } **for** *table_repdef_name*
with replicate at *dataserver.database*
Executed in the replicate RepServer, enables (**on**, =default situation) or disables (**off**) use of prepared statements (➢p.34) for this table repdef for the specified replicate database. The current setting can be checked with the RSSD procedures **rs_helpsub** (for repdef subscriptions) or **rs_helppubsub** (for publication subscriptions), both in the replicate RSSD.
Using prepared statements requires that the dynamic sql option has been enabled for the repdef for all replicate databases with **create/alter replication definition** (➢p.37) as well as for the specified replicate database with **alter connection** (➢p.34). When the repdef-level setting (➢p.37) is **off**, **set dynamic_sql on** does not override this.

set autocorrection { **on** | **off** } **for** *table_repdef_name*
with replicate at *dataserver.database*
Executed in the replicate RepServer, enables (**on**) or disables (**off**, =default situation) autocorrection for this table repdef for the specified replicate database.
The purpose of autocorrection is to prevent errors during subscription materialization due to missing or duplicate rows in the replicate table. When autocorrection is enabled, RepServer converts each primary **insert** or **update** to a **delete** followed by an **insert** in the replicate database. This avoids errors due to missing or duplicate rows, but the additional queries will cost some performance.
Autocorrection only has an effect when a subscription exists for the table repdef (although it can already be enabled when no subscription exists).
Autocorrection cannot be enabled when **replicate minimal columns** is enabled for a repdef. If autocorrection is already enabled when **replicate minimal columns** is enabled, primary inserts and updates are replicated normally but without autocorrection; corresponding warning messages are written to the RepServer errorlog.
Autocorrection requires that all **text**, **image** and **rawobject** columns in the repdef to be marked as **always_replicate**.
Autocorrection settings are stored in the RSSD table **rs_repobjs** in the replicate RSSD. The current autocorrection status is displayed by **sp_helpsub** (in the '**A/C**' column) and by **sp_helppubsub**.
Notes:

- Although autocorrection can be enabled at any moment, it is normally used only during non-atomic materialization (i.e. enable autocorrection <u>before</u> running **create subscription**...**without holdlock**). Once subscription materialization is complete and the subscription status is 'Valid', disable autocorrection to improve performance.
- When RI constraints are used in the replicate database, autocorrection may not be possible because these constraints may interfere with the SQL **delete** statements generated by autocorrection.
- When using custom function strings, ensure correct replicate SQL statements will be generated before enabling autocorrection.
- In ASE, instead of using autocorrection, it may also be possible -and more efficient- to use a unique index with **ignore_dup_key.**
- Although pointless, autocorrection can also be enabled for a function repdef; however, this has no effect.
- Autocorrection cannot be enabled for a database repdef , nor for a warm standby, even when table repdefs are created (because autocorrection only works when a subscription exists for the table repdef).

14.3 Schema changes for replicated tables

When changing the schema of a replicated primary table (i.e. using **alter table** to add or drop a column, or modify a column's datatype), care needs to be taken to avoid jeopardising the stream of replicated transactions. In short, problems may occur when modifying the schema of the primary table while earlier transactions for that table (based on the old schema) are still in the RepServer queues, waiting to be applied to the replicate database; it is possible that such transactions cannot correctly be applied to the replicate anymore.
To avoid such problems, follow these steps to modify the schema of a primary table:

1. Ensure no users or applications perform any DML on the primary table-to-be-modified anymore (perhaps, even on the entire primary database). From a replication perspective, read-only activity may continue.
2. Ensure all transactions for the primary table have been applied to all replicate databases. This can be verified by performing an **insert** or **update** statement on the primary table and waiting until it arrives at the replicate databases (presumably, another DML statement should then be run to undo this insert or update). The **rs_ticket** feature (➢p.132) can also be used to verify this.
3. Quiesce the replication system (➢p.116).
4. Run **alter table** to make the desired schema change for the primary table (and probably also for the replicate table).
5. Change the table repdef to reflect the primary table's schema change (with **alter replication definition**), and wait until the changes have reached all replicate RSSDs (if any). Possible changes can include:
   - When a primary table's column is added: add that column to the repdef columns, primary key columns and/or searchable columns.
   - When a primary table's column is dropped: drop that column from the primary key columns and searchable columns. The column does not need to be removed from the table repdef itself (this is in fact only possible by dropping and recreating the repdef).
   - When the datatype of a primary table's column is modified: change the column's declared datatype (possibly also its published datatype); ➢p.27.
6. If any of the added, dropped or modified primary columns are referenced in the **where**-clause of a subscription or article, additional action is needed: such a subscription must be dropped (**without purge**) and recreated (**without materialization**); an article must also be dropped and recreated, and its publication must be refreshed (i.e. run **validate publication** and **create subscription**...**for new articles**; ➢p.60).
7. DML activity on the primary table by users and applications can now be resumed (however, it is recommended to perform some DML statements first to test if everything works correctly!)

Further details about schema changes can be found in the *Replication Server Administration Guide* (➢p.13).

14.4 Function repdefs (stored procedure replication)

With a function repdef, the execution of a stored procedure in a primary database is replicated, along with the actual parameter values (if any) supplied to the procedure. In the replicate database, a replicate stored procedure will be executed with the same parameter values as in the primary database. Note that the replicate stored procedure is not required to be identical to the primary procedure: it may perform a completely different function. Note that a replicate stored procedure is always executed inside a transaction. This means that it may not be possible to use DDL statements (e.g. **select**...**into**) in the stored procedure.
When a primary stored procedure updates a primary table that is itself replicated, be aware of the precise effects; see page 49 for details.
Stored procedures can be replicated in two different ways: applied functions (the 'normal' function repdefs) and request functions. See page 41 for more details.

(15.1) create applied function replication definition *function_repdef_name*
with primary at *dataserver.database*
[**with all functions named** *procedure_name* |
  [**with primary function named** *procedure_name*]
  [**with replicate function named** *procedure_name*]]
([*@parameter datatype* [,...*more parameters*...]] **)**
[**searchable parameters (** *@parameter* [,...*more parameters*...] **)**]
[**send standby** { **all** | **replication definition** } **parameters**]

create function replication definition *function_repdef_name*
with primary at *dataserver.database*
[**deliver as** *replicate_procedure_name*]
([*@parameter datatype* [,...*more parameters*...]] **)**
[**searchable parameters (** *@parameter* [,...*more parameters*...] **)**]
[**send standby** { **all** | **replication definition** } **parameters**]

Creates a function repdef for a primary stored procedure in the specified database. For a stored procedure to be replicated, it must have been marked for replication with **sp_setrepproc** *procedure_name*, **function** (➢p.16) in the primary database.
The syntax with **create function replication definition** is still supported in 15.1, though **create applied function replication definition** is recommended.
Examples: **create function replication definition p_AddOrder with primary at PROD.cust_db (@p_order_no int, @p_customer int, @p_amount int)**

(15.1) create applied function replication definition p_AddOrder2
with primary at PROD.cust_db
with primary function named p_AddOrder
with replicate function named p_AddOrder_replicate
(@p_order_no int, @p_customer int, @p_amount int)

Notes:

- Procedure/repdef names: in pre-15.1, with **create function replication definition**, the repdef name must be identical to the name of the primary stored procedure. Consequently, there can be only one function repdef for a primary procedure. By default, the primary procedure name is also the name of the replicate stored procedure, unless overridden with **deliver as**.
  In 15.1, with **create applied function replication definition**, the name of the function repdef can be chosen freely, and the names of the primary and replicate stored procedures specified independently. Consequently, there can be multiple function repdefs for a primary procedure. **with all functions named** specifies the name of the primary and replicate stored procedures; **with primary/replicate function named** specify the corresponding procedure names individually. If no procedure names are specified, the primary and replicate stored proc names will be assumed to be identical to the function repdef name. Note that **with all functions named** and **with primary/replicate function named** are mutually exclusive.
- Note that **create** [**applied**] **function replication definition** does not verify the existence, parameters or execution permissions of neither the primary nor the replicate procedure.
- The primary *dataserver.database* can be either a normal database connection or a logical connection (i.e. a warm standby pair).
- Parameters: the '**( )**' parentheses are required even if the procedure has no parameters. Ensure all listed parameter names are identical to the actual parameter names in the primary and replicate stored procedure; this is not verified by **create** [**applied**] **function replication definition**. The order in which the parameters are declared does not matter.
  Note that parameters cannot be renamed for the replicate procedure (as is possible for replicate column names in a table repdef).
- Datatypes: the *datatype* for a parameter is mandatory; **text**, **image**, or **rawobject** are not allowed for parameters. **numeric** and **decimal** parameters must be specified without precision or scale. See page 26 for more information about RepServer datatypes.
  Unlike columns in a table repdef, **map to** cannot be specified for parameters.
- **searchable parameters** specifies the parameters that can be referenced in the **where**-clause of **create/define subscription** and **create article**.
- **send standby all parameters** and **send standby replication definition parameters** affect which parameters are replicated; this applies only to a warm standby or when database replication is combined with function repdefs (see **send standby** on page 48).

Subscriptions to function repdefs must use **create subscription**...**without materialization**. Alternatively, the -more complex- bulk materialization sequence (i.e. **define/activate/validate subscription**; ➢p.57) can also be used.

(15.1) alter applied function replication definition *function_repdef_name*
with replicate function named *replicate_procedure_name* |
add @*parameter datatype* [**,** ...*more parameters*...] |
add searchable parameters @*parameter* [,...*more parameters*...] |
send standby { **all** | **replication definition** } **parameters** }

alter function replication definition *function_repdef_name*
{ **deliver as** *replicate_procedure_name* |
add @*parameter datatype* [**,** ...*more parameters*...] |
add searchable parameters @*parameter* [,...*more parameters*...] |
send standby { **all** | **replication definition** } **parameters** }

Modifies an existing function repdef. The clauses are similar to **create** [**applied**] **function replication definition** above; see there for more information. Note that **alter applied**... can only be used for function repdefs that were created with **create applied**...

Examples: **alter function replication definition p_AddOrder**
deliver as p_AddOrder_New

Notes:

- **(15.1) with replicate function named** *replicate_procedure_name*
  Changes the name of the replicate stored procedure.
- **deliver as** *replicate_procedure_name*
  Changes the name of the replicate stored procedure.
- **add @***parameter datatype* [**,** ...*more parameters*...]
  Adds one or more procedure parameters. Note that parameters cannot be dropped or renamed.
- **add searchable parameters @***parameter* [**,** ...*more parameters*...]
  Adds one or more **searchable parameters**; note that they cannot be dropped.
- **send standby** { **all** | **replication definition** } **parameters**
  Modifies the **send standby** status of this function repdef (➢p.48).

drop [**function**] **replication definition** *function_repdef_name*
Drops a function repdef, its user-defined function and the corresponding function string. No subscriptions or articles should exist for this repdef.

14.5 Applied functions & Request functions

There are two flavours of stored procedure replication (a.k.a. 'function replication'), know as 'applied functions' and 'request functions'.
Applied functions are the 'normal' way of replicating stored procedures: by creating a function repdef and a corresponding subscription, the execution of a stored procedure in a primary database is replicated to the replicate database where a replicate stored procedure is executed (➢14.4, p.39).
In contrast, the so-called request functions (a.k.a. 'request stored procedures') work somewhat differently, and in a way that may well appear strange (partly because the notions of primary and replicate sometimes seem to be the opposite of how things usually work). This also requires a function repdef, but in pre-15.1, no subscription is involved; however, when using the 15.1 syntax, a subscription is required.
Another difference is that applied functions are executed at the replicate dataserver by the maintenance user, while request functions are executed by the same user who originally executed the primary stored procedure.
The rest of this section discusses request functions only.

(15.1) create request function replication definition *function_repdef_name*
with primary at *dataserver.database*
with primary function named *procedure_name*
with replicate function named *procedure_name*
([**@***parameter datatype* [,...*more parameters*...]] **)**
[**searchable parameters (@***parameter* [,...*more parameters*...] **)**]
[**send standby** { **all** | **replication definition** } **parameters**]

(15.1) alter request function replication definition *function_repdef_name*
{ **with replicate function named** *replicate_procedure_name* |
add @*parameter datatype* [**,** ...*more parameters*...] |
add searchable parameters @*parameter* [,...*more parameters*...] |
send standby { **all** | **replication definition** } **parameters** }
The 15.1 syntax; this approach requires a subscription to be created to this function repdef.

create function replication definition *function_repdef_name*
with primary at *dataserver.database*
[**deliver as** *replicate_procedure_name*]
([*@parameter datatype* [,...*more parameters*...]] **)**
[**searchable parameters (** *@parameter* [,...*more parameters*...] **)**]
[**send standby** { **all** | **replication definition** } **parameters**]
The classic, pre-15.1 syntax; this requires no subscription. This syntax is still supported in 15.1, but **create request function replication definition** (above) is recommended since the 15.1 semantics are easier to understand.

Setting up a request function
To create a request function, follow these steps (admittedly, it is confusing that the concepts of primary and replicate database are interchanged in pre-15.1 and 15.1):

1. Ensure the username and password with which the stored procedure **ReqTest_request** (below) will be executed, exists in both the replicate and primary dataserver.
   Also, when using routes, ensure a route exists from the primary RepServer to the replicate RepServer, and another route in the opposite direction.
2. In the primary database (here, named **PrimDB**), create a stored procedure named **ReqTest_request**, and mark it for replication with **sp_setrepproc ReqTest_request, function**. This procedure is typically a 'dummy', not performing any action at all, and is just called with actual parameter values. A RepAgent must be running in this database.
3. In the replicate database (here, named **RepDB**), create a stored procedure named **ReqTest_replicate** (don't mark this procedure for replication, or it won't work; see the notes below). This procedure will typically perform the actual data modifications.
4. Create the following function repdef, depending on the RS version:

   In 15.1 -- execute in the RepServer which manages **PrimDB**:
   create request function replication definition my_request_repdef
   with primary at *primary_dataserver*.**PrimDB**
   with primary function named ReqTest_request
   with replicate function named ReqTest_replicate
   (*@param datatype*, ...**)**

   In pre-15.1 -- execute in the RepServer which manages **RepDB**:
   create function replication definition ReqTest_request
   with primary at *replicate_dataserver*.**RepDB**
   deliver as ReqTest_replicate (*@param datatype*, ...**)**
5. In 15.1 only, create a subscription to the request function repdef created in the previous step (execute in the RepServer which manages **RepDB**):

   create subscription my_request_sub for my_request_repdef
   with replicate at *replicate_dataserver*.**RepDB**
   without materialization

   In pre-15.1, no subscription is created.
6. Now, when executing the dummy procedure **PrimDB..ReqTest_request**, the final effect will be that **ReqTest_replicate** is executed by RepServer in primary database **RepDB**.

The underlying idea is that **RepDB..ReqTest_replicate** makes the required data changes to database **RepDB** based on the parameter values supplied in the original execution of **PrimDB..ReqTest_request**. In the bigger picture, **RepDB** would act as a centralised primary database and its data modifications would be replicated through normal table replication (not included in the above steps) back to database **PrimDB**. Then, the user who originally executed **PrimDB..ReqTest_request** will finally see that execution take effect when the actual data changes arrive in **PrimDB** through normal table replication (again, not included here).
See the *Replication Server Design Guide* for more information about replication system architectures.
Notes:

- It is essential that **ReqTest_replicate** is not marked for replication, since the effect described in section 14.12 (➢p.49) would cause its updates to the database tables in the central database not to be replicated further.
- Behind the scenes, RepServer connects to the replicate dataserver in order to execute **ReqTest_replicate**. For this connection, it uses the login and password of the session that originally executed **ReqTest_request**. This implies that the

same login name and password must exist in the primary and replicate dataservers (this is similar to the issues with 'subscription users'; ➢p.108).

- To allow request functions, the connection-specific configuration parameter **dsi_exec_request_sproc** must be set to **on** (=default) for the connection to the database where the procedure is replicated to (in this example, **RepDB**). When set to **off**, error 5158 will appear in the RepServer errorlog when executing **ReqTest_request**.

Request functions may seem a strange mechanism, especially in pre-15.1, and the apparent reversal of the concepts of primary and replicate database can indeed be confusing. In pre-15.1, the part that remains especially unusual is that no subscription is required for the first replication step (see the *Replication Server Administration Guide* for more details); this is the main reason why the more explicit syntax, requiring a subscription, is recommended to be used in 15.1.

14.6 Database repdefs

With a database repdef, an entire primary database can be replicated with just a single repdef and a single subscription, and marking the primary database with **sp_reptostandby** (in the simplest case; ➢7.2, p.18).
The replicated primary data can include DDL statements, executions of primary stored procedures and ASE system stored procedures. In addition, replication of specific tables, (system) procedure executions and transactions by specific users or with specific transaction names can also be included or excluded explicitly through so-called repdef 'filters' (see below).
In many ways, the functionality of a database repdefs and -subscriptions is similar to a warm standby. However, unlike a warm standby, a primary database can also be replicated to multiple replicate databases (by creating multiple subscriptions for a database repdef). For this reason, database repdefs/subscriptions are also referred to as 'Multiple Site Availability' (MSA). The name 'Multiple Warm Standby' is sometimes used as well, but this is somewhat misleading: database repdefs/-subscriptions do not support the automatic active/standby switchover that is so characteristic for a warm standby. However, a similar procedure is possible, as described in 14.7 (➢p.46).
A brief comparison of database repdefs and warm standby is on page 47.

create database replication definition *db_repdef_name*
with primary at *dataserver.database*
[[**not**] **replicate ddl**]
[[**not**] **replicate tables** [**in (** [*owner_name.*]*table_name* [**,** *...more tables...*] **)**]]
[[**not**] **replicate functions** [**in (** [*owner_name.*]*proc_name* [**,** *...more procs...*] **)**]]
[[**not**] **replicate system procedures**
[**in (** [*owner_name.*]*proc_name* [**,** *...more procs...*] **)**]]
[[**not**] **replicate transactions** [**in (** [*owner_name.*]*tran_name* [**,** *...more names...*] **)**]]
Creates a database repdef for the specified primary database. Multiple repdefs can be created for the same primary database. The repdef name can be chosen freely, but must be unique among database repdefs in the replication system.
For the various options, the defaults are **not replicate ddl**, **replicate tables**, **replicate functions**, **not replicate system procedures** and **replicate transactions**; these can be overridden or refined as described below.
Example: **create database replication definition prod_db_rdf**
with primary at PROD.prod_db
replicate ddl
replicate functions (p_AddNewOrder)
not replicate tables (temptab, guest.*)

Determining exactly which data is replicated through a database repdef depends on how data is marked for replication and on the properties of the database repdef.
First, anything marked for replication in the primary database will be picked up by the RepAgent (see 7.2, p.18, for full details on marking data for replication):

- If the database has been marked with **sp_reptostandby**, DML on all tables is replicated (a special case is when the ASE **master** database is replicated; for details, ➢p.47). Note that **sp_reptostandby** does not replicate stored procedures in the database: these must still be marked explicitly with **sp_setrepproc**. Apart from **sp_reptostandby**, replicating DDL and ASE system procedures also requires that the **replicate ddl** and **replicate system procedures** clauses, respectively, be enabled in the database repdef (see below); also, the ASE RepAgent must have option **'send warm standby xacts'** enabled (➢p.21) to avoid errors in the replicate dataserver when DDL statements and ASE system stored procedures are executed in a transaction (like ASE error 2762).

- If **sp_reptostandby** is not used, DML on all tables marked for replication with **sp_setreptable**, and all stored procedure executions marked for replication with **sp_setrepproc**, are replicated. DDL and ASE system stored procs will not be replicated irrespective of what is specified for the database repdef.
- Note that replication of DDL and ASE system procedures can be disabled with **set replication off** for individual sessions (➢p.17).

Next, the replicated data is subject to 4 'filters' of the database repdef. These filters (the [**not**] **replicate**... clauses) allow lists of tables, (system) procedure executions and transactions to be specified that will, or will not, be replicated. For tables and (system) procedures, a list of object names can be optionally specified; for transactions, a list of usernames or transaction names can be specified. Each name is in the format of [*owner_name*][**.**][*name*], where each part can also be * (meaning all) or **' '** (meaning none).
The database repdef filters are specified as follows:

- Filter for replication of DDL statements from the primary database:
  - **not replicate ddl** - no DDL is replicated at all, even when it has been enabled by **sp_reptostandby** or **set replication** (➢p.17). This is the default for DDL replication.
  - **replicate ddl** - replicates DDL in this database. A list of replicated DDL statements in ASE is on page 17 (note that DDL replication for non-ASE primary databases is not supported). Also note that the maintenance user for the replicate database must have sufficient permissions for executing the replicate DDL statements.

- Filter for replication of DML statements against tables in the primary database:
  - **replicate tables** - replicates DML against all primary tables that have been marked for replication with **sp_setreptable** or **sp_reptostandby**. This is the default for table replication.
  - **not replicate tables** - replicates no DML against any primary tables, even when these tables have been marked for replication with **sp_setreptable** or **sp_reptostandby**.
  - [**not**] **replicate tables in (***list-of-tables***)** - without **not**, replicates DML against the specified primary tables only, provided they have been marked for replication with **sp_setreptable** or **sp_reptostandby**. With **not**, replicates DML against all tables except those listed.
- Filter for replication of a certain set of stored procedure executions in the primary database (note that this applies to user-created stored procedures, and is independent of any options for <u>system</u> stored procedure replication, as described in the next bullet):
  - **replicate functions** - replicates all user-created stored procedures that have been marked for replication with **sp_setrepproc**. This is the default for stored procedure replication.
  - **not replicate functions** - replicates no user-created stored procedures at all, even when they have been marked for replication with **sp_setrepproc**.
  - [**not**] **replicate functions in (***list-of-stored-procs***)** - without **not**, replicates only the specified user-created stored procedures, provided they have been marked for replication with **sp_setrepproc**. With **not**, replicates all marked stored procedures except those listed.

- Filter for replication of ASE system stored procedure executions in the primary database (i.e. the Sybase-supplied **sp_*** stored procedures listed in the table on page 17; this is independent of any options for user-created stored procedure replication, as described in the previous bullet):
  - **not replicate system procedures** - replicates no ASE system stored procedures at all, even when it has been enabled by **sp_reptostandby** or **set replication** (➢p.17). This is the default for replicating system stored procedures.
  - **replicate system procedures** - replicates all ASE system stored procs.
  - [**not**] **replicate system procedures in (***list-of-stored-procs***)** - without **not**, replicates only the specified system stored procedures. With **not**, replicates all system stored procedures except those specified.

  When the name of the replicate database is different from the primary database, it is recommended to exclude those system procedures which require the database name as a parameter, such as **sp_config_rep_agent**.

- Filter for replication of transactions of any kind (DML, DDL, [system] stored procedure executions), executed by specific users or for specifically named transactions:
  - **replicate transactions** - replicates all transactions. This is the default.
  - **not replicate transactions** - replicates no transactions at all, irrespective of any other **replicate** options for this repdef.
  - [**not**] **replicate transactions in (***list-of-names***)** - without **not**, replicates transactions only when executed by the specified users or when the transactions have the specified transaction names. With **not**, replicates all transaction except those by the specified users or with the specified transaction names.

Notes:

- A subscription for a database repdef must be created with either **create subscription**...**without materialization** (➢p.59) or **define subscription** (➢p.61; optionally with the **use dump marker** clause to perform dump/load materialization). Multiple subscriptions, for different replicate databases, can be created for a database repdef.
- **rs_helpdbrep** (➢p.51) displays the current filter settings for a database repdef.
- For a database repdef, the primary *dataserver.database* can be either a normal database connection or a logical connection (i.e. a warm standby pair). The same applies for the replicate database.
- Unlike a warm standby, automatic changeover of a primary and a replicate database is not possible with database repdefs. Nevertheless, the DBA may perform such a switchover manually by creating repdefs and subscriptions as needed. In this case, the configuration parameter **dsi_replication** (➢p.33) should be **'off'** for each replicate database that may be changed to a primary later (this is to avoid earlier DSI-applied transactions from being replicated again when the replicate database is changed to a primary).
- For a database repdef, only class-specific function strings (like **rs_begin**; ➢section 20.10) can be customized for the function string class used by the DSI. Repdef-specific function strings (like **rs_insert**; ➢sections 20.8, 20.9) can be customized only for the function string class used by the DSI, if a table or function repdef with the **send standby** clause exists in the primary database. Otherwise, database repdefs use function strings from the **rs_default_function_class**, which cannot be customized.
- Replication of the ASE **truncate table** statement is disabled by default for a database repdef (but note that it was incorrectly enabled by default in early versions of 12.6). In **create/define subscription**, **subscribe to truncate table** can be specified to enable replication of this statement. To modify this setting, drop and recreate database subscription. The current setting is displayed by the RSSD procedure **rs_helpdbsub**.
  When a table repdef and -subscription exist for a table in the replicated database, the **send truncate table** setting for the table subscription overrides the setting for the database repdef.
- It is possible to mix database repdefs and table or functions repdefs; ➢p.50.
- Database repdefs cannot use autocorrection (this can only be used for table repdefs with a subscription; ➢p.38).

alter database replication definition *db_repdef_name*
with primary at *dataserver.database*
{ [[**not**] **replicate ddl**] |
[[**not**] **replicate tables** [**in (** [*owner_name.*]*table_name* [, *...more tables...*] **)**]] |
[[**not**] **replicate functions** [**in (** [*owner_name.*]*proc_name* [, *...more procs...*] **)**]]|
[[**not**] **replicate system procedures**
[**in (** [*owner_name.*]*proc_name* [, *...more procs...*] **)**]] |
[[**not**] **replicate transactions**
[**in (** [*owner_name.*]*tran_name* [, *...more names...*] **)**]] }
[**with dsi_suspended**]

Modifies a database repdef, replacing one filter in a command. This modification takes effect immediately. **with dsi_suspended** will suspend the DSI. See **create database replication definition** for a description of each filter.

Example: **alter database replication definition prod_db_rdf**
with primary at PROD.prod_db
not replicate ddl

drop database replication definition *db_repdef_name*
with primary at *dataserver.database*
Drops the specified database repdef. No subscriptions should exist for the repdef.

14.7 Switching primary/replicate with database repdefs/subs

Database repdefs and -subscriptions do not provide a feature for switching the primary and replicate databases in a single operation, like the **switch active** command for a warm standby. However, the DBA can perform a manual switchover as described below (assuming, of course, that such a switch makes sense in the overall design of the replication system).
Let's assume we have a database DB-A which is currently replicated to database DB-B with a database repdef and -subscription. In addition:

- Both databases have been marked for replication identically, and have log transfer enabled.
- A database repdef exists for both databases, a subscription exists only to the repdef for DB-A, with the replicate at DB-B.
- **dsi_replication** (➢p.33) must be set to **'off'** for both DSIs to DB-A and DB-B.

Reversing the direction of replication (i.e. from DB-B to DB-A) can be achieved with the following steps:

1. Enable the secondary truncation point in DB-B and set it to the end of the log (**rs_zeroltm**, **dbcc settrunc**). This marks the point that client applications can switch over to DB-B with the guarantee that their new transactions in DB-B will be replicated to DB-A later; however, note that some older transactions from DB-A may not yet have arrived in DB-B until step 4 below.
2. Ensure that all client applications disconnect from the DB-A, and do not reconnect. They should reconnect to DB-B instead.
3. Wait for the RepAgent in DB-A to reach the end of the log, then stop the RepAgent in DB-A (optionally, before stopping the RepAgent, insert a marker transaction, like **rs_ticket** or an insert into a dummy table first, to mark the last transaction to be replicated)
4. Wait until all transactions from DB-A have arrived at DB-B (for example, by checking for the arrival of the marker transaction from the previous step). This marks the point where all transactions from DB-A have arrived in DB-B.
   Then, disable the secondary truncation point in DB-A (though this can also be done later).
5. Drop the existing subscription to the database repdef for DB-A, with the replicate at DB-B, without purge.
6. (Optional) When you are switching the direction of replication because there is something wrong with DB-A, suspend the DSI to DB-A. Then, while starting the procedure to fix DB-A, proceed with the following steps.
7. Create a subscription to the database repdef for DB-B, with the replicate at DB-A, without materialization.
8. Start the RepAgent in DB-B. Replication now starts flowing from DB-B to DB-A, in the opposite way as before. If the connection to DB-A was suspended in step 6 above, the replicated transactions will accumulate in the outbound queue for DB-A.
9. (Optional) If the DSI to DB-A was suspended in step 6 above, resume it once DB-A is fixed. The accumulated transactions will now be applied to DB-A.

Variations are possible, for example when the primary database must always be replicated to multiple replicate databases.

The setup above, with database repdefs, gives the DBA more control over the effective switchover moment than a warm standby. For a warm standby, there is a period of time during **switch active** which the DBA cannot control, during which transactions applied in the standby-but-soon-active database will not be replicated (this is before the 'enable marker' gets written into the transaction log; ➢p.68). With the above setup, this period can be completely eliminated by allowing applications to switch to DB-B after step 1 above.
This setup also offers a choice of switchover moments: switching after step 1 is best for applications where it is most important that new transactions are never lost (i.e. will always be replicated). Switching after step 4 can be done for applications where a consistent view of the database is essential (i.e. all updates from DB-A have arrived in DB-B).

As with a warm standby, client applications will not switch to the new primary database automatically: this must be arranged outside RepServer. See 19.5 (➢p.69) for a common solution.

14.8 Warm standby vs. Database repdefs/subscriptions

Here is a brief comparison of the main differences between a warm standby and database repdefs:

Warm standby	**Database repdef & -subscription**
Supports replication of DDL, DML, stored procedures & system stored procedures.	Also supported. Filters can be configured in the database repdef to include/exclude replication of DDL, specific tables, stored procedures and transactions.
All-or-nothing: cannot filter primary data to be replicated (except by selectively marking primary tables or stored procedure for replication)	
Only 1 replicate database (the standby database).	Multiple replicate databases are possible.
The active and standby databases can be switched over automatically in a single operation.	No automatic primary/replicate switchover. A manual switchover can be performed by swapping the primary and replicate databases as described in 14.7 (➢p.46).
The active and standby databases can behave as a single database (a logical connection) for the purpose of creating table/function repdefs and subscriptions.	No equivalent. (note that both the primary as well as the replicate database for a database repdef/subscription can actually be a logical connection)
No subscriptions are used; table/function repdefs are optional.	Requires a database repdef and -subscription; table/function repdefs are optional.
The active and standby databases must be controlled by the same RepServer: routes cannot be used.	Routes can be used as for any other repdef and subscription.
Supports only ASE databases.	Supports also non-ASE databases (although DDL replication and some aspects of filtering may not always be supported).
Requires multiple setup steps, typically through the **rs_init** utility.	Less setup steps; **rs_init** is not needed.
No supported method for customizing function strings for the standby connection (➢p.70).	Class-specific function strings can be customized for the replicate database. When using table/function repdefs with **send standby**, repdef-specific function strings can also be customized.

14.9 Replicating data in the ASE 'master' database

In a warm standby, or in setup with database repdefs/subscriptions where the replicate and primary may be switched around, it is important that certain data in the ASE **master** database is kept in sync between the active and standby/replicate ASE dataserver. For example, password changes and newly added logins and roles should be sync'd to avoid problems when the active and standby are switched. Also, the mapping between **syslogins** and **sysusers** (**suid** ↔ **uid**) should be identical in the ASE servers containing the active and standby databases. If not, this can lead to permission problems when initializing the standby with a database dump from the active database.
Historically, it was not possible to replicate anything from the ASE **master** database, but as of ASE 15.0.1, this has changed.

Master database replication in ASE 15.0.1

In ASE 15.0.1, a limited number of operations in the ASE **master** database can be replicated. This concerns the following commands only ('regular' DML/DDL, and other **sp_*** stored procs will not be replicated from the **master** database):

create role	**drop role**	**alter role**
grant role	**revoke role**	**sp_role**
sp_addlogin	**sp_droplogin**	**sp_modifylogin**
sp_password	**(ASE 15.0.2) sp_passwordpolicy**	**sp_locklogin**
sp_defaultdb	**sp_defaultlanguage**	**sp_displaylevel**

Both the primary and replicate **master** database must be in ASE 15.0.1 (or later). This works with any RepServer version of 12.0 (or later).

Notes:

- Connections to the primary and replicate **master** databases must be created with **rs_init** as for any other database.
- An ASE RepAgent will be running in the primary **master** database, so its transaction log may need to be enlarged to ensure it does not fill up.
- The primary **master** database must be marked for replication with **sp_reptostandby 'master', 'all'**.
- The ASE RepAgent in the primary **master** database must be configured with **'send warm standby xacts' = true** (➢p.21)
- The **master** database can be replicated either as a warm standby, or as a database replication definition and corresponding subscription.
- When using a database repdef for the ASE **master** database, the repdef properties **replicate dll** and **replicate system procedures** must both be enabled (or the DDL commands and **sp_*** calls above, respectively, will not be replicated).
- Materialization of the replicate **master** database should be done manually.
- Replication of the **master** database does not replicate the actual **suid/srid** values for new logins and roles. Rather, it relies on identical contents for **syslogins** and **syssrvroles** on both sides so that the algorithms will pick the same values for new logins or roles.
- Since passwords for logins and roles are replicated as ciphertext, cross-platform synchronization is not supported (though it may actually work in some cases).
- Ensure that the **sp_*** procedures listed above are executed from within the **master** database if they are to be replicated.

Workaround in ASE pre-15.0.1

In ASE pre-15.0.1, common solutions for synchronizing data in the **master** database are to modify system stored procedures like **sp_addlogin** and **sp_password** to simulate replication of their execution. Such a mechanism must be set up by the DBA. For example, a system stored procedure can execute its counterpart in the replicate dataserver as an RPC. Alterntively, the modified stored procedure can write a row to a normally replicated user table in a user database which executes the corresponding system stored procedure on the replicate side (with a customized function string; see page 82 for an example).

14.10 'send standby' option in repdefs

send standby can be specified as an option in table repdefs (**send standby all columns**; **send standby replication definition columns**) and function repdefs (**send standby all parameters**; **send standby replication definition parameters**). This option applies only to a warm standby as well as when database replication is combined with table or function repdefs.
The absence or presence of **send standby** affects how primary data is replicated:

- Replicated columns: for a table repdef without a **send standby** option, or with only **send standby** (which is identical to **send standby all columns**), all columns of the primary table are replicated. With **send standby replication definition columns**, only the columns declared in the repdef are replicated.
- Primary key columns: for a table repdef with a **send standby** option (no matter which one), only the **primary key** columns of this repdef are used in the **where**-clause of replicate SQL **update/delete** statements. Without a **send standby** option, the union of all **primary key** columns for all repdefs for this table is used in the **where**-clause (Completeness note 1: without a repdef, all table columns are used in the **where**-clause of replicate SQL statements. Completeness note 2: when multiple repdefs exist for a table, only one repdef can have a **send standby** option enabled at a time).
- Replicated parameters: for a function repdef without a **send standby** option, or with only **send standby** (which is identical to **send standby all parameters**), all parameters of the primary stored procedure are replicated. With **send standby replication definition parameters**, only the parameters declared in the repdef are replicated.

For a warm standby only, the **send standby** options in the repdefs can be overridden by the configuration parameter **send_standby_repdef_cols** for the logical connection (➢p.69).
The current **send standby** setting for a repdef is displayed by the RSSD procedure **rs_helprep** (under '**Used by Standby**').

14.11 Replicating minimal columns

'Minimal column replication' is a repdef-specific feature to improve performance for table repdefs. Minimal column replication applies to primary **update** and **delete** statements only.
For normal replication, all columns for a modified row are replicated by default, including columns that have not changed. In contrast, minimal column replication only replicates those columns whose values have really been changed, in addition to the primary key columns. Especially for tables with many and/or long columns, minimal column replication can improve performance in the DSI (due to more efficient replicate update statements), over the network and in the stable queues (due to the replicated messages being shorter).
Minimal column replication is an attribute of a table repdef, specified either as **replicate all columns** (disabled; all columns are replicated) or **replicate minimal columns** (enabled).
Minimal column replication is disabled for regular replication (i.e. non-warm standby) by default. In a warm standby, it is enabled by default, but can be overridden with the configuration parameter **replicate_minimal_columns** (➢p.69).
Database repdefs do not support minimal column replication directly, but it can be used by mixing table repdefs with database repdefs. (➢p.50).
Notes:

- The current setting for minimal column replication for a repdef is displayed by the RSSD procedure **rs_helprep** (in the '**Send Min Cols.**' column).
- When replicating minimal columns, pay attention to triggers. When running an update like **update MyTable set Col=Col where MyKey=1** in the primary database, an update trigger on **MyTable** will be fired. Since this update is not replicated when using minimal column replication, the corresponding replicate trigger will not be fired. This could potentially lead to differences between the primary and replicate databases.
  On the other hand, without minimal column replication, all columns are updated in the **set** clause of the replicate **update** statement, even though they may not have been updated in the primary database. As a result, replicate update triggers that check specifically for modified columns may perform unnecessary or unwanted actions. Minimal column replication could solve this.
- Replicating minimal columns has some limitations:
  - It cannot be combined with **autocorrection** (➢p.38).
  - Non-atomic materialization cannot be used (➢p.56).
  - It cannot be combined with custom function strings for most repdef-specific functions. Only for **rs_insert**, **rs_update** and **rs_delete**, custom function strings can be created, albeit with some limitations for the latter two (➢p.81).

14.12 Mixing table replication and procedure replication

When mixing table replication and procedure replication, be aware of the precise effects. Since stored procedure replication overrides table replication, this combination may produce results that are different from what you perhaps expected.

When a primary stored procedure is marked for replication, and modifies a primary table that is also marked for replication, the rows modified by the stored procedure are not replicated. Instead, only the procedure execution is replicated, but not its effects in terms of row modifications. When a subscription for the table repdef exists, this means it will not receive any DML performed by the replicated stored procedure.
For this scenario to occur, the procedure must have been marked for replication with **sp_setrepproc**, and either the table with **sp_setreptable**, or the entire database with **sp_reptostandby** (for a warm standby or a database repdef). A function repdef may exist for the primary stored procedure, but this is not required.
As an example, assume the following table and stored procedure:

create table MyTable (a int)
create procedure MyProc @p int as insert MyTable values (@p)

Let's assume **MyTable** and **MyProc** are both marked for replication in the primary database, and repdefs and subscriptions exist for **MyTable** and **MyProc**. When the following primary transactions are executed, they are replicated as follows:

Primary transaction:	**Replicated through:**
insert MyTable values (100)	Table repdef for **MyTable**
exec MyProc 101	Function repdef for **MyProc** (<u>not</u> through the table repdef!)
insert MyTable values (102)	Table repdef for **MyTable**

As a result, when a subscription for the table repdef for **MyTable** exists, it will only receive the inserts for rows 100 and 102. The replicate table is now different from the primary table, which contains rows 100, 101 and 102. To keep the replicate table consistent with the primary table, a subscription for **MyProc**, and a replicate procedure inserting into the replicate **MyTable**, should also exist.

Mixing stored procedure replication and table replication as described above has some useful applications. For example, when large transactions with many row modifications occur in the primary database, it may be inefficient to replicate these through table replication. Instead, it may be faster to let a primary stored procedure perform the primary row modifications, and replicate the stored procedure. In the replicate database, the replicate procedure should then perform the same row modifications. This is functionally identical to table replication, but greatly reduces the amount of data that RepServer must process.

14.13 Mixing database repdefs and table/function repdefs

When database repdefs and table/function repdefs are mixed, the table/function repdefs override the database repdef: data for table/function repdefs is replicated according to those repdefs, and not to the database repdef (note that this mix makes the replication system more complex).
The main points are described below; however, it is recommended to consult the *Replication Server Administration Guide* (➢p.13), chapter *Managing Replicated Objects Using Multi-Site Availability*, for full details on the effects of mixing database repdefs with table/function repdefs.

When the primary database has been marked for replication with **sp_reptostandby** (➢p.16), in pre-12.6, individual tables must be marked explicitly with **sp_setreptable** in order to be replicated through a table repdef. In 12.6, with the configuration parameter **rep_as_standby** set to **'on'** (➢p.34), explicit marking with **sp_setreptable** is no longer necessary (this also applies when a warm standby is mixed with table repdefs in 12.6), though still allowed.

Table repdefs and function repdefs may be created in a database that is replicated through a database repdef for a number of reasons, as described below (note that no subscriptions are needed for these table or function repdefs). For most of these purposes, the repdef should include the **send standby** clause (see the *Replication Server Administration Guide* for full details; ➢p.13).

- Improve performance: a table repdef produces a smaller **where**-clause for replicate **update/delete** statements based on the **primary key** clause. With only a database repdef, all columns are used in the replicate **where**-clause. No subscription to the table repdef is required.
- For tables with many columns, a table repdef may be required if there is a limit to the number of predicates that the replicate dataserver can support in the SQL **where**-clause. With a repdef, only the repdef **primary key** columns are used.
- For customizing repdef-specific function strings; see page 45 for more info.
- A database subscription cannot have a **where**-clause. If such functionality is required, a subscription to a table repdef or function repdef must be used.
- Table and function repdefs have certain features not directly supported by database repdefs, like minimal column replication, different names for the primary/replicate table or replicate procedure, changing the datatype of primary columns or parameters, and **replicate_if_changed** for **text/image** columns. By using table or function repdefs, this functionality can still be used in database replication.

14.14 RSSD tables - repdefs

Tables and function repdefs are stored in the RSSD table **rs_objects**. For table repdefs, **rs_objects.objtype** = **'R'**; for function repdefs,**rs_objects.objtype** = **'F'**.
Database repdefs are stored in the RSSD table **rs_dbreps**; inclusion/exclusion lists for database repdef filters are stored in the RSSD table **rs_dbsubsets**.
Autocorrection settings for table repdefs are stored in the RSSD table **rs_repobjs** in the replicate RSSD.
When a RepServer has an outgoing route, the RSSD tables **rs_objects, rs_dbreps** and **rs_dbsubsets** are replicated to the destination RSSD.

14.15 Getting information about repdefs

To determine if a table repdef exists for a particular primary table, use the RSSD

procedure **rs_helpreptable**.
To determine if a function repdef exists for a particular primary stored procedure, use the RSSD procedure **rs_helprep** (since a function repdef always has the same name as its primary stored procedure).
To determine if a database repdef exists for a particular primary database, use the RSSD procedure **rs_helpdbrep**.
To find all repdefs for a particular primary database, use one of the RSSD queries from the electronic supplement to this book (➢p.8).

rs_helprep [*repdef_name*]
(RSSD procedure) Without parameter, displays a list of the table repdefs and function repdefs in the current RSSD. With *repdef_name*, displays details about that repdef. If no exact match is found, **'%'** is added to *repdef_name*, and then used as a wildcard.
rs_helpreptable *primary_database*, *table_name*
rs_helpreptable *primary_database*, *table_owner*, *table_name*
(RSSD procedure) Displays a list of all repdefs created for the specified primary table in the specified primary database. Specify *table_owner* only to match an owner that was explicitly specified in **create replication definition**.
Note that this information is taken from the RSSD table **rs_objects**; the existence of the table is not verified. Also note that a dataserver name cannot be specified.

rs_helprepdb [*replicate_dataserver*, *replicate_database*]
(RSSD procedure) Without any parameters, displays a list of all replicate databases with subscriptions to primary data in the current RepServer (either table/function/database repdefs or publications). When no route is involved, this is the list of all replicate databases in this RepServer. With a dataserver/database name, displays that database only when such subscriptions exist. To display the actual repdefs, publications or subscriptions, use **rs_helprep**/**rs_helpsub**, **rs_helppub**/**rs_helppubsub** or **rs_helpdbrep**/**rs_helpdbsub**.

rs_helpdbrep [*db_repdef_name* [, *primary_dataserver* [, *primary_database*]]]
(RSSD procedure) Without any parameters, displays all database repdefs in the current RSSD. The parameters behave as a filter and may be specified independently. All parameters may contain wildcard characters; default = **'%'**. When the parameters match exactly one database repdef, details for that repdef (in-/exclusion lists, subscriptions) are displayed.

15 Replicating text/image/rawobject columns

For replication of **text**, **image** or **rawobject** columns, some issues must be considered that do not apply to other datatypes. Since the data volume of **text**, **image** or **rawobject** columns can be potentially huge, RepServer supports additional replication options for these datatypes to avoid overloading the replication system by replicating unnecessary **text/image/rawobject** data. Each **text**, **image** or **rawobject** column has one of the following replication statuses:

- **always_replicate** - replicates the **text/image/rawobject** column when any column in the row is modified.
- **replicate_if_changed** - replicates the **text/image/rawobject** column only when the column itself is modified.
- **do_not_replicate** - does not replicate the **text/image/rawobject** column at all.

This replication status is set in two places. First, in the primary ASE database, the column status for each **text/image/rawobject** column is set with **sp_setreptable**, **sp_setreplicate** or **sp_setrepcol**; this determines which log records are picked up by the RepAgent. Second, the table repdef also defines a replication status for each **text/image/rawobject** column in the repdef. For successful replication, it is important that this status in the primary database and the repdef are identical (see below).

Column replication status in the primary database
In the primary database, the column replication status is set as follows:

- When marking a table with **sp_setreptable**, the replication status of all **text**, **image** and **rawobject** columns in the table is set to **always_replicate**; this can be changed with **sp_setrepcol**.
- When marking a table with **sp_setreplicate**, the replication status of all **text**, **image** and **rawobject** columns in the table is set to **do_not_replicate**; this can be changed with **sp_setrepcol**.
- **sp_setrepcol** sets the replication status of a particular **text**, **image** or **rawobject** column to **replicate_if_changed**, **always_replicate** or **do_not_replicate**.

- When marking a database with **sp_reptostandby**, the replication status of all **text**, **image** and **rawobject** columns in the database is set to **replicate_if_changed**; this cannot be changed with **sp_setrepcol**. Only when a table is also marked with **sp_setreptable**, the status of individual columns can be changed with **sp_setrepcol**.

The current replication status for each column can be displayed with **sp_setrepcol**.
Warning: for tables with **text/image/rawobject** columns containing many rows, marking the primary data for replication may take a long time. Read section 7.3 (➢p.18) first!

Column replication status in the repdef
The column replication status in the repdef is defined by **create/alter replication definition** with the clauses **replicate_if_changed** and **always_replicate** (=default). When a **text/image/rawobject** column occurs in multiple repdefs, its replication status is always identical for all repdefs. When creating a repdef with an explicitly specified column status, the column status must match the status for existing repdefs; by default it is set to the status in those existing repdefs. When the column status is changed with **alter replication definition**, it is changed automatically for all repdefs in which the column occurs.
Note that the status **do_not_replicate**, which is possible in the primary database, does not exist for a repdef column. If a column is marked as **do_not_replicate**, it should not occur in any repdefs.
The current repdef settings for **text/image/rawobject** columns are not displayed by the RSSD **rs_*** procedures. Instead, use one of the RSSD queries from the electronic supplement to this book (➢p.8).

Column replication status in primary database vs. repdef
As mentioned earlier, the column replication status of **text/image/rawobject** columns must be identical in the primary database and in the repdef. Specifically, the following situations will cause the DSI to shut down with an error message number:

- The column is marked as **do_not_replicate** in the primary database, but the column also appears in a repdef. Solution: change the column status in the primary database or recreate the repdef (and all its subscriptions) without the column.
- The column is marked as **replicate_if_changed** in the primary database, but as **always_replicate** in the repdef. Solution: change the column status either in the primary database or in the repdef.

When the column is marked as **always_replicate** in the primary database, but as **replicate_if_changed** in the repdef, this does not cause any problems.

Notes:

- When creating a subscription with **create subscription**, all **text/image/rawobject** columns longer than 32Kb are truncated automatically. To avoid this, use bulk materialization.
- In the primary table, do not use T-SQL keywords as column names for **text/image/rawobject** columns. Some of these, like **parameter**, may be used as a column name in T-SQL, but this will cause errors in the DSI.
- Each **text/image/rawobject** column has its own set of function strings for the functions **rs_datarow_for_writetext**, **rs_writetext**, **rs_get_textptr** and **rs_textptr_init**. In these cases, the **create/alter function string** commands must include the column name, like this:
  create function string *table_repdef_name*.*function_name*;*column_name*
  for *function_class_name ...*

16 Replicating identity columns

In Sybase ASE, an identity column is a numeric column with a special feature: the ASE server automatically assigns a sequential number to the column for each inserted row. An identity column in a Sybase ASE primary database can be replicated as any other column, but inserts and updates have some special aspects, as described below (there are no issues with deletes).
In a warm standby or with a database repdef, a primary table with an identity column will automatically be replicated correctly (using **set identity_insert**).
In Sybase ASE pre-12.5.3, identity columns must have the **numeric** datatype; in ASE 12.5.3, **int**, **smallint**, **tinyint** datatypes are also allowed; in ASE 15, **bigint** is allowed,a s well as **unsigned int/smallint/bigint**.
Primary identity columns in MS-SQLServer can be replicated in almost the same way

as ASE identity columns; see the *Replication Server Heterogeneous Replication Guide* for more information (➢p.13).

16.1 Replicating identity column inserts

In a table repdef, the datatype for a primary identity column can be specified either as **numeric**, **int**, **bigint**, etc. or as **identity**, depending on the datatype of the corresponding column in the replicate table:

- When the column datatype in the repdef is specified as **identity**, each insert into the replicate table will be enclosed by the SQL statements **set identity_insert** *table_name* **on** and **set identity_insert** *table_name* **off**. This datatype must be used when the corresponding column in the replicate table is an identity column.
- When the column datatype in the repdef is specified as **numeric/int/bigint/**etc., each insert into the replicate table is performed normally (i.e. without **set identity_insert**). This should be used when the corresponding column in the replicate table is not an identity column, but a regular **numeric/int/bigint/**etc. column. This datatype should also be used when replicating an ASE identity column to a non-ASE replicate database.

When replicating an identity column to multiple replicates with different column datatypes or to non-ASE databases, it may be necessary to create multiple repdefs: one with a datatype of **identity** for replicate identity columns in ASE databases, and another with a datatype of **numeric/int/bigint/**etc., for replicate numeric columns or non-ASE databases.

Examples:

In ASE: **create table PrimTab (ID numeric identity, MyCol char(10))**

In RS: **create replication definition PrimTab with primary at PROD.prim_db (ID identity, MyCol char(10)) primary key (ID)**

In RS: **create replication definition PrimTab2 with primary at PROD.prim_db with all tables named PrimTab (ID numeric, MyCol char(10)) primary key (ID)**

Notes:

- For a replicate table with an identity column, it is essential that the maintenance user is at least object owner of the replicate table, because this permission is required to execute **set identity_insert**. In practice, this is often solved by making the maintenance user an alias to **dbo**, or granting it **sa_role**.
- When using customized function strings for a repdef involving an identity column, the SQL statements **set identity_insert** *table_name* **on**/**off** must be included in the customized function string for **rs_insert**. Likewise, **set identity_update** *table_name* **on**/**off** should be included for **rs_update** (provided ASE 12.5.0.3+ is used).
- When using identity columns in ASE, always define the **identity_gap** setting (with **sp_chgattribute**) for all permanent tables with an identity column. This will help to avoid so-called 'identity gaps' that may occur as a result of a **shutdown with nowait** of ASE, ASE server crashes, or loading a database dump (for example, when initializing the standby database in a warm standby). See **www.sypron.nl/idgaps.html** for more information.

16.2 Replicating identity column updates

Identity columns are automatically assigned a value by the ASE server and are not normally expected to be updated. Nevertheless, in ASE 12.5.0.3+, an identity column can be updated by preceding the update with the SQL statement **set identity_update** *table_name* **on** (and setting it **off** again afterwards); this statement behaves similar to **set identity_insert**. To replicate such updates to identity columns, RepServer 12.6+ is required when the replicate column is also an identity column and the repdef datatype is **identity**. When the replicate column is a regular **numeric** column and the repdef datatype is also **numeric**, RepServer pre-12.6 also replicates these updates.

In ASE pre-12.5.0.3, updating an identity column is not possible (unless undocumented/unsupported tricks are used, which may require using similar tricks in the DSI). See my book 'Tips, Tricks & Recipes for ASE' (**www.sypron.nl/ttr**) for details.

16.3 Common problems when replicating identity columns

The following problems occur frequently when replicating identity columns, and cause the DSI to be suspended while these messages are written to the RepServer errorlog:

Error message:

Message from server: Message: 10354, State 1, Severity 14 -- 'Permission

denied. You must be either the system administrator (SA), the database administrator (dbo), or the owner of this object to perform this operation.

This error indicates that the maintenance user does not have sufficient privileges to run **set identity_insert** on the replicate table.
Solution: either recreate the table under the maintenance user to make it object owner, or make the maintenance user an alias to **dbo**, or grant **sa_role** to the maintenance user.

Error message:

Message from server: Message: 584, State 1, Severity 16 -- 'Explicit value specified for identity field in table '*your_table_name*' when 'SET IDENTITY_INSERT' is OFF.

This error indicates that the column datatype in the repdef is declared as **numeric** (or **int**, **smallint**, etc) instead of **identity**, and the column in the replicate table is an identity column. Solution: alter the repdef to correct the datatype as **identity**.

Error message:

Message from server: Message: 11065, State1, Severity 10 -- "SET IDENTITY_INSERT' is ON for table '*your_table_name*'.

This is not an error, but an informational message which is just not expected by RepServer. This message is generated only by ASE 12.5.0.3.
Solution: just ignore this error code in the DSI: **assign action ignore for** *error_class_name* **to 11065** (➢p.83; for ASE, *error_class_name* is usually **rs_sqlserver_error_class**).

17 Publications & Articles

A publication is a collection of table repdefs and/or function repdefs (named 'articles') for which a single subscription can be created. This is functionally equivalent to subscribing to each individual repdef, but it's less work for a DBA. When a repdef is included in a publication, it is still possible to subscribe to the individual repdef directly. All commands in this section are executed at the primary RepServer.

create publication *pub_name* **with primary at** *dataserver.database*
Creates an empty publication, without any articles. A repdef is included in a publication with **create article**.
A publication can include only repdefs for the same primary *dataserver.database* as the publication itself. A publication must be created in the same primary RepServer as the repdefs it will include. The publication name can be chosen freely, but must be unique in this RepServer. It is good practice to include a type-identifying tag such as **'_pub'** in the name.
Example: **create publication SalesData_pub with primary at PROD.prod_db**

drop publication *pub_name* **with primary at** *dataserver.database* [**drop_repdef**]
Drops the publication and all of its articles. No subscriptions should exist for the publication. Without **drop_repdef** (=default), the repdefs for the articles are not affected. With **drop_repdef**, also drops the repdefs for the articles, provided these repdefs are not used by other publications or subscriptions; repdefs that are still in use are not dropped, but their articles are -- no error message is displayed, however.
Example: **drop publication SalesData_pub**
with primary at PROD.prod_db drop_repdef

validate publication *pub_name* **with primary at** *dataserver.database*
Sets the status of the publication to 'Valid' (provided it is not empty), allowing new subscriptions to be created for this publication (when creating a subscription for a non-validated publication, the following error message is raised: **'Publication** *pub_name* **for** *dataserver.database* **is invalid.'**).
After an article is added to, or dropped from, a publication, the publication status is always 'Invalid' (this does not affect ongoing replication or existing subscriptions), requiring **validate publication** to be run. The current status of a publication can be displayed with **check publication** or **rs_helppub**.
Example: **validate publication SalesData_pub with primary at PROD.prod_db**

check publication *pub_name* **with primary at** *dataserver.database*
Displays the status of a publication and the number of articles it contains.
Example: **check publication SalesData_pub with primary at PROD.prod_db**

create article *article_name*
for *pub_name* **with primary at** *dataserver.database*
with replication definition { *table_repdef_name* | *function_repdef_name* }
[**where** *condition* [**and** *condition*] [**and** *...more conditions...*]
[**or where** *condition* [**and** *condition*] [**and** *...more conditions...*]
[**or** *...more where-clauses...*]]]
condition: { *column_name* | *@parameter_name* } { **<** | **>** | **>=** | **<=** | **=** | **&** } *value*
Creates an article for the specified table repdef or function repdef, thus adding it to the specified publication. A database repdef cannot be an article. The article name can be chosen freely, but must be unique in the publication. It is good practice to include a type-identifying tag such as **'_art'** in the name.
A **where**-clause consists of one or more conditions. Each condition limits the values of columns or parameters that will be replicated through this article. The *column_name* or *@parameter_name* in a condition must have been declared in the **searchable columns** or **searchable parameters** clauses in the corresponding repdef. *value* is a constant, and cannot include a column name or an expression.
Note that, unlike in SQL, the **or** keyword is not part of the **where**-clause, but joins different **where**-clauses. Also, the **where** keyword must be repeated for each **where**-clause. The **&** operator applies to bitmap subscriptions (➢p.63).
create article automatically invalidates the publication. New subscriptions cannot be created until the publication is validated with **validate publication**.
When a subscription already exists for this publication, no data will be replicated for the new article until the subscription is 'refreshed' with **create/define subscription ...for new articles**.
Example: **create article MyTab_art for MyData_pub**
with primary at PROD.prod_db with replication definition MyTab
where Col1 > 0 and Col2 = 'OK' or where Col3 >= 1 and Col4 = '??'

drop article *article_name*
for *pub_name* **with primary at** *dataserver.database* [**drop_repdef**]
Drops the specified article from the publication. No subscriptions should exist for the article. The subscription for an individual article can be dropped with **drop subscription...for article**.
With **drop_repdef**, also drops the repdef for this article, provided it is not used by other publications or subscriptions. When the repdef is still in use, it is not dropped but the article is; no error message is displayed, however.
drop article automatically invalidates the publication. New subscriptions cannot be created until the publication is validated with **validate publication**.
Example: **drop article MyTab_art for MyData_pub**
with primary at PROD.prod_db

17.1 Getting information about publications and articles

rs_helppub [*pub_name* [, *primary_dataserver* [, *primary_database* [, *article_name*]]]]
(RSSD procedure) Without any parameters, displays a list of all publications known in this RSSD. The parameters behave as a filter and can be specified independently. When the supplied parameter values match only a single publication, its articles and subscriptions (if any) are displayed as well. To display information about a specific article (incl. its **where**-clause) , specify: **rs_helppub null, null, null,** *article_name*

rs_helppubsub [*sub_name* [, *pub_name* [, *primary_dataserver* [, *primary_database* [, *replicate_dataserver* [, *replicate_database*]]]]]]
(RSSD procedure) Without any parameters, displays a list of all publication subscriptions in this RSSD. The parameters behave as a filter and can be specified independently.
For subscriptions across a route, **'Unknown'** may be displayed by **rs_helppubsub**. This does not indicate an error, but means that the value cannot be determined because it is stored in a different RSSD than where **rs_helppubsub** is executed.
Use **rs_helppub** to display all subscriptions for a particular publication or article. Use **check subscription** to display the current status of a particular subscription.

To find the publication for which a particular repdef is an article (for example, you may need this when you're not allowed to drop a repdef), run this query in the RSSD:
select Repdef=o.objname, Article=a.articlename, Publication=p.pubname
from rs_objects o, rs_articles a, rs_publications p
where o.objid = a.objid and a.pubid = p.pubid
and o.objname = '*repdef_name***'**

17.2 RSSD tables - publications and articles

Publications are stored in the RSSD table **rs_publications**. Articles are stored in the

RSSD table **rs_articles**. Article **where**-clauses are stored in the RSSD tables **rs_whereclauses** and **rs_rules**.

18 Subscriptions

Subscriptions to repdefs or publications can be created in a number of different ways, depending on the materialization method used:

- In its simplest form, a subscription is created with **create subscription**. By default, this command uses (non)atomic materialization; with the **without materialization** clause, no materialization is performed at all.
- Alternatively, the sequence of **define subscription**, **activate subscription**, **validate subscription** must be used for bulk (a.k.a. manual) materialization.

The different materialization methods, and the concept of materialization itself, are described below.

Terminology note: A subscription is created to a repdef or publication defined in a *primary* RepServer. By definition, the RepServer in which the subscription is created, is referred to as the *replicate* RepServer. Even when the primary and replicate RepServer are actually the same -when there are no routes- this terminology is still used.

18.1 Subscription materialization methods

Materialization is an operation performed by RepServer (or by the DBA) as part of creating a subscription. The purpose of materialization is to initialize the replicate table with all data from the primary table matching the subscription **where**-clause, if any (since the typical reason for having a replication system is to keep primary and replicate data identical).
The following materialization methods exist. With the exception of bulk materialization, all methods correspond to the **create subscription** command (➢p.59).

- No materialization - **create subscription**...**without materialization**. This is the fastest variation, where simply no materialization takes place at all.
  Use when: This method can be used when the replicate table does not need to be initialized, and for subscriptions to function repdefs (either directly or in a publication) and database repdefs. It can also be used if all update activity on the primary data can be suspended, so that the DBA can make a copy of the primary data (e.g. with **bcp** or database dump) to be loaded into the replicate.
- Atomic materialization - **create subscription**. This is the default method, used when no further materialization options are specified (i.e. in absence of **without holdlock**, **incrementally**, or **without materialization**).
  Atomic materialization guarantees that the replicate data exactly matches the primary data once the subscription is created: DML statements trying to modify primary data will be blocked until materialization is complete -- which is why this method is called 'atomic'. Technically, the subscription data is selected from the primary table with the SQL **holdlock** option (i.e. using a shared table lock for the duration of the SQL **select** operation), and inserted it into the replicate table in a single transaction.
  Use when: This method should preferably be used only when the amount of subscription data is relatively small (at most a few Mb's). For larger volumes of subscription data, this method can take a long time, while potentially blocking other users in the primary and replicate databases. In addition, the stable devices and the transaction log of the replicate database must be large enough to hold the total volume of materialization data.
- Incremental atomic materialization - **create subscription**...**incrementally**.
  Almost identical to atomic materialization, but inserts data into the replicate table in multiple transactions with a small number of inserted rows (typically, some multiple of 10 rows). This method avoids a single long-running transaction in the replicate database and requires less stable queue space. For the primary table, a shared table lock is still used, just as with atomic materialization.
  Use when: This method can be used when the **insert** transaction into the replicate table is too large or takes too long.
- Non-atomic materialization - **create subscription**...**without holdlock**. Similar to incremental atomic materialization, but the SQL **holdlock** is not used while selecting the subscription data from the primary table. Since primary data can therefore be modified while materialization is taking place, it is recommended to enable autocorrection to avoid errors due to duplicate or missing replicate data (➢p.38). Like incremental atomic materialization, data is inserted into the replicate table in multiple transactions with a small number of inserted rows.

Use when: This method can be used when the SQL **select**-with-**holdlock** from the primary table causes unacceptable blocking for users or applications who need to modify the primary table. It cannot be used for repdefs with **replicate minimal columns**.

➢ Note: Atomic, incremental atomic, non-atomic and no materialization are sometimes collectively referred to as 'automatic materialization' since all necessary materialization actions are performed automatically by **create subscription**. This contrasts with 'bulk' (or 'manual') materialization where the DBA must perform materialization explicitly (see below).

➢ Note: When using automatic materialization, and multiple subscriptions are created with overlapping **where**-clauses, a primary row is replicated to a replicate table only once.

- Bulk materialization - **define/activate/validate subscription**. This type of materialization must be performed explicitly by the DBA, for example by loading data into the replicate table with **bcp**. Bulk materialization is also known as 'manual' materialization.
  With bulk materialization, the challenge is to ensure that the replicate data remains in sync with the primary data, and no transactions are lost during subscription creation. This can be achieved in a number of ways; see the *Replication Server Administration Guide* (➢p.13) for full details. The simplest variation requires updates to the primary data to be suspended temporarily:

  1. Suspend all updates to the primary data; when the subscription is created over a route, run **admin quiesce_force_rsi** in all RepServers in the route.
  2. Extract the materialization data from the primary database, for example by making a database dump or doing a **bcp**-out of a table.
     In RS 12.6 and ASE 12.5.1, the ASE statement **quiesce database**...**to** *manifest_file* may also be used to copy the primary database on device level; with the ASE **mount** statement, the copied database is added to the replicate dataserver (see the *Replication Server Administration Guide* (➢p.13) for details).
  3. Run **define subscription** (& check subscription status = 'Defined')
  4. Run **activate subscription**...[**with suspension**] (& check status = 'Active'). Optionally, suspend the DSI to the replicate database with the option **with suspension**.
  5. When a database dump was made, load the dump into the replicate database. When data was copied to file(s) with **bcp**-out, copy these into the replicate table with **bcp**-in.
  6. Updates to the primary data can now be resumed.
  7. Run **validate subscription** (& check status = 'Valid')
  8. If the replicate DSI was suspended in step 3, resume the DSI.

  After steps 3, 4 and 7 it should be verified that the subscription -in both the primary RepServer and replicate RepServer- has reached the status indicated above before proceeding with the next step. This can be checked with **check subscription** (at both the primary and replicate RepServer), and with the RSSD procedures **rs_helpsub** (for repdef subscriptions; in the replicate RSSD only), **rs_helppubsub** (for publication subscriptions; in both the primary RSSD and replicate RSSD) or **rs_helpdbsub** (for database subscriptions; in the replicate RSSD only).
  Use when: Bulk materialization can always be used, but is most suitable for large amounts of subscription data, or when the other materialization methods are not suitable.
  Note that bulk materialization is sometimes recommended for subscriptions to function repdefs; however, the 'no materialization' method (➢p.56) is much simpler and often sufficient.

- Dump/load materialization - a bulk materialization method for database subscriptions and for a warm standby (although no subscription is involved here). The replicate database is initialized with a database dump -and optionally, log dumps- from the primary database.
  Use when: This method can be used for materializing database subscriptions (**define subscription**...**use dump marker**) and for initializing a warm standby (**create connection**...**as standby for**...**use dump marker**). For more information about coordinating dumps and the dump marker, see page 68.

- Simulated (non)atomic bulk materialization - more complex variations of bulk materialization are also possible, which require extra steps in addition to those above. See the *Replication Server Administration Guide* (➢p.13) for full details.
  Use when: These methods can be used when updates to the primary data cannot be suspended while creating the subscription.

Note that terms such as 'atomic' and 'bulk' are not RepServer keywords and do not actually appear in any RepServer commands or RSSD procedures. Also, note that the subscription-related 'bulk' is not the same as ASE's 'bulk copy program' **bcp** (although **bcp** could be used to perform bulk materialization). Only the clause **without materialization** (in **create subscription**) matches the terminology in this section.

18.2 Subscriptions: users and permissions

When creating a subscription (with either **create subscription** or **define subscription**) or dropping a subscription, the replicate RepServer uses the username and password of the RepServer session where the **create/define subscription** command is executed, to connect to the primary RepServer to perform certain actions; when using **create subscription** (except with **without materialization**) the replicate RepServer also connects to the primary dataserver to retrieve the materialization data, using the same username and password. Consequently, the username and password must be identical in the primary and replicate RepServer as well as the primary dataserver.
For this reason, it is recommended not to use the RepServer **sa** user for creating subscriptions, since this would imply that the password of the **sa** dataserver login in a participating ASE server cannot freely be changed anymore. Instead, it is recommended to create a dedicated RepServer user (with a name like **repadmin**, **ra** or **subscr_user**, for example), and maintain this username and its password in all RepServers and dataservers across the replication domain.

A subscription username must have sufficient RepServer privileges in the primary RepServer (**create object**, **primary subscribe**, or **sa**) as well as SQL access privileges in the primary dataserver (**select** on the primary table).

To complete the picture, during (de)materialization the replicate RepServer logs into the replicate dataserver as the corresponding maintenance user for inserting/deleting subscription data into/from the replicate table. This requires the maintenance user to have SQL **insert** and **delete** permissions on the replicate table.

18.3 Queues for subscription (de)materialization

When automatic materialization is performed (except for **without materialization**), the replicate RepServer builds a materialization queue, containing the subscription data from the primary table to be inserted into the replicate table.
When dropping a subscription using **with purge**, the replicate RepServer builds a dematerialization queue, containing the rows that will be deleted from the replicate table (only rows matching the conditions of the dropped subscription will be removed, and only if they also do not match other subscriptions for this replicate table).
(De)materialization queues are created and dropped automatically by RepServer. These queues can be recognized by a large, negative queue number. For example, queue **109:-2147483528** indicates a (de)materialization queue for database 109. The names of the repdef and subscription are displayed as '*repdef_name.subscr_name*' behind the queue number by **admin who** as well as in the replicate RepServer's errorlog. Whether a queue is for materialization or dematerialization can be determined from the messages in the RepServer errorlog surrounding the 'SQM starting/stopping' messages for these queues.

When the amount of data to be (de)materialized is large, the (de)materialization queue will be correspondingly large as well. This means the stable devices must be large enough to contain the entire queue.
When there is insufficient space on the stable devices, consider using incremental atomic (**create subscription**...**incrementally**) or non-atomic materialization (**create subscription**...**without holdlock**): since these methods fill the (de)materialization queue with many small transactions instead of a single large one, queue space for applied transactions can already be deallocated before the entire materialization queue is completely built. Alternatively, bulk/manual materialization (**define/activate/validate subscription**) can be used, which does not involve a materialization queue at all.
To save stable queue space in case of dematerialization, consider using **incrementally with purge**, or using **without purge** and deleting the replicate data manually.
Lastly, when a lot of data is (de)materialized, the process of creating or dropping the subscription may obviously require a considerable amount of time, disk I/O and network load.

18.4 Automatic materialization: subscription commands

All automatic materialization methods (atomic, incremental atomic, non-atomic and no materialization; ➢p.56) are handled by **create subscription**.
All commands below are executed at the replicate RepServer.

create subscription *sub_name*
{ **for** *table_repdef_name* |
for *function_repdef_name* |
for publication *pub_name* **with primary at** *dataserver.database* |
for database replication definition *db_repdef_name*
with primary at *dataserver.database* }
with replicate at *dataserver.database*
[**where** *condition* [**and** *condition*] [**and** *...more conditions...*]
[**without holdlock** | **incrementally** | **without materialization**]
[**subscribe to truncate table**] [**for new articles**]
condition: { *column_name* | *@parameter_name* } { **<** | **>** | **>=** | **<=** | **=** | **&** } *value*

Creates and activates the subscription for the specified repdef or publication, materializes the subscription data, and validates the subscription. A subscription to a publication can only be created when the publication status is 'Valid' (➢p.54).
The subscription name can be chosen freely, but must be unique for a repdef or publication only in each replicate database. The same subscription name can therefore be used multiple times (although this is not recommended). It is good practice to include a type-identifying tag such as **'_sub'** in a subscription name.

Examples: **create subscription Accounts_sub for Accounts**
with replicate at PROD.report_db
where AccountRegion = 'Europe' -- a column in the repdef 'Accounts'
incrementally

create subscription SalesData_sub
for publication SalesData_pub with primary at PROD.prod_db
with replicate at PROD.report_db for new articles

Notes:

- The replicate *dataserver.database* can be either a normal database connection or a logical connection (i.e. a warm standby pair). The latter can also be used when subscribing to a database repdef.

- A materialization method (➢p.56) must be selected for **create subscription**:
  - When subscribing to a table repdef, the default materialization method (without specifying any options) is atomic materialization; with **incrementally**, incremental atomic materialization is used; **without holdlock** specifies non-atomic materialization, and **without materialization** performs no materialization at all. When subscribing to a publication, the materialization method is used for all table repdefs in the publication.
  - When subscribing to a function repdef directly, **without materialization** must be specified (alternatively, bulk materialization can also be used, i.e. **define subscription**). When subscribing to a publication containing function repdefs, these will implicitly use **without materialization** irrespective of any specified materialization options.
  - When subscribing to a database repdef, **without materialization** must be specified (alternatively, bulk materialization can also be used, i.e. **define subscription**). When omitting this clause, the (rather general) error 2056 will be raised.

  To verify whether subscription creation is ready, check that the subscription status is 'Valid'. This can be checked with **check subscription** (in both the primary and replicate RepServer) or with the RSSD procedures **rs_helpsub** (in the replicate RSSD only), **rs_helppubsub** (in both the primary and replicate RSSD) or **rs_helpdbsub** (in the replicate RSSD only). Alternatively, the RepServer errorlog also indicates whether subscription creation has completed.

- A **where**-clause consists of one or more conditions. Each condition limits the values of columns or parameters that will be replicated through this subscription. The *column_name* or *@parameter_name* in a condition must have been declared in the **searchable columns** or **searchable parameters** clauses in the corresponding repdef. *value* is a constant, and cannot include a column name or an expression. *value* cannot exceed 255 bytes.
  A **where**-clause is not allowed for subscriptions to publications; instead, a **where**-clause can be used for a publication's articles. A **where**-clause is also not allowed for database subscriptions.
  Unlike articles, subscriptions cannot have a logical 'OR' construct in their **where**-clause. If such 'OR' functionality is needed, create a publication article

for the repdef and put the **where**-clause in the article instead of in the subscription. Alternatively, multiple subscriptions can be created for the same repdef, each with its own **where**-clause; functionally, this forms a logical 'OR' between these **where**-clauses. Lastly, an 'OR' condition may sometimes also be simulated with bitmap subscriptions (using the **&** operator; ➢p.63).

- For a publication subscription, **for new articles** creates subscriptions for articles that have been added to the publication since the subscription was created, and for articles whose subscription was explicitly dropped with **drop subscription**...**for article**. Hence, using **for new articles** is known as 'refreshing a publication'. To determine whether articles without a current subscription exist, run **check subscription**...**for publication**; to identify those actual articles, combine this output with the output from the RSSD procedure **rs_helppub**.
- **subscribe to truncate table** enables replication of the ASE **truncate table** statement to the replicate database (➢p. 63).

check subscription *sub_name*
{ **for** *table_repdef_name* |
for *function_repdef_name* |
for publication *pub_name* **with primary at** *dataserver.database* |
for database replication definition *db_repdef_name*
with primary at *dataserver.database* }
with replicate at *dataserver.database*
Displays the status of the subscription in the current RepServer. For a publication subscription, the status of each article is displayed as well. When subscribing across a route, run this command in both the primary and the replicate RepServer.
Example: **check subscription Accounts_sub for Accounts**
with replicate at PROD.report_db

drop subscription *sub_name*
{ **for** *table_repdef_name* |
for *function_repdef_name* |
for article *article_name* **in** pub_name **with primary at** *dataserver.database* |
for publication *pub_name* **with primary at** *dataserver.database* |
for database replication definition *db_repdef_name*
with primary at *dataserver.database* }
with replicate at *dataserver.database*
[**without purge** [**with suspension** [**at active replicate only**]] |
[**incrementally**] **with purge**]
Drops a subscription to a table repdef or function repdef -either directly or through an article-, a database repdef, a publication or a single article.
For a subscription to a table repdef or a publication, a dematerialization method (**with/without purge**) must be specified:

- **with purge** deletes all rows from the replicate table matching the subscription **where**-clause (provided they don't match other subscriptions for the replicate table), in a single transaction.
- **incrementally with purge** is functionally identical to **with purge** but uses multiple transactions with a small number of deleted rows (typically, some multiple of 10 rows).
- **without purge** does not remove any data from the replicate table at all; if needed, the DBA can perform dematerialization manually.
  There are two additional variations:
  - **without purge with suspension** - after the subscription is dropped, suspends the DSI, to allow the DBA to manually delete subscription data from the replicate table while no replicate transactions are applied. If the replicate table is located in a warm standby pair, suspends the DSIs for both the active and the standby database (allowing the DBA to manually delete rows from the replicate table in both databases).
  - **without purge with suspension at active replicate only** - as above, but suspends only the DSI for the active database (when the DBA deletes rows from the replicate table in the active database, these deletions are then replicated to the standby database).

For a subscription to a function repdef, **without purge** is the only allowed option, and it may therefore be omitted completely. When a publication includes a function repdef, the corresponding article subscription is always dropped **without purge**, irrespective of any options specified.
For a subscription to a database repdef, **without purge** or **without purge with suspension** (see above) are the only allowed options; if no option is specified, **without purge** is the default.

Examples: **drop subscription Accounts_sub for Accounts**
with replicate at PROD.report_db
without purge

18.5 Bulk/manual materialization: subscription commands

When using bulk/manual materialization (➢p.57), the command sequence of **define/activate/validate subscription** must be used.
All commands below are executed at the replicate RepServer.

define subscription *sub_name*
{ **for** *table_repdef_name* |
for *function_repdef_name* |
for publication *pub_name* **with primary at** *dataserver.database* |
for database replication definition *db_repdef_name*
with primary at *dataserver.database* }
with replicate at *dataserver.database*
[**where** *condition* [**and** *condition*] [**and** *...more conditions...*]
[**subscribe to truncate table**] [**for new articles**]
condition: { *column_name* | *@parameter_name* } { **<** | **>** | **>=** | **<=** | **=** | **&** } *value*
[**use dump marker**]
Creates a subscription, but does not activate or materialize it. When completed, the subscription status is set to 'Defined' - this can be verified with **check subscription** or **rs_help[pub]sub**.
The clauses **where**, **subscribe to truncate table** and **for new articles** are the same as for **create subscription** (➢p.59).
define subscription is part of the bulk materialization sequence (➢p.57); **activate/validate subscription** must be executed next, except with **use dump marker** (see below).
use dump marker can only be used for dump/load materialization when subscribing to a database repdef; when a database dump or log dump is then made from the primary database and loaded into the replicate database, the database subscription is automatically activated and validated (so **activate/validate subscription** can be skipped).
Examples: **define subscription VeryBigTable_sub for VeryBigTable_rdf**
with replicate at PROD.report_db

define subscription MyDB_sub
for database replication definition MyDB_rdf
with primary at PROD.prod_db
with replicate at REPORTING.mgt_report_db
use dump marker

activate subscription *sub_name*
{ **for** *table_repdef_name* |
for *function_repdef_name* |
for publication *pub_name* **with primary at** *dataserver.database* |
for database replication definition *db_repdef_name*
with primary at *dataserver.database* }
with replicate at *dataserver.database*
[**with suspension** [**at active replicate only**]]
For a subscription created with **define subscription**, activates the subscription; this means that distribution of replicated primary transactions to the replicate database is started. When completed, the subscription status is set to 'Active' - this can be verified with **check subscription** or **rs_help[pub]sub**.
activate subscription is part of the bulk materialization sequence (➢p.57); **validate subscription** must be executed next.
with suspension leaves the DSI suspended to allow the DBA to manually insert subscription data into the replicate table while no replicate DML is executed. In case the replicate table is located in a warm standby, suspends the DSIs for both the active and the standby database (allowing the DBA to manually delete rows from the replicate table in both databases). **with suspension at active replicate only** is identical, but suspends only the DSI for the active database (when the DBA deletes rows from the replicate table in the active database, these deletions are then replicated to the standby database).
Example: **activate subscription VeryBigTable_sub for VeryBigTable_rdf**
with replicate at PROD.report_db

validate subscription *sub_name*
{ **for** *table_repdef_name* |
for *function_repdef_name* |
for publication *pub_name* **with primary at** *dataserver.database* |
for database replication definition *db_repdef_name*
with primary at *dataserver.database* }
with replicate at *dataserver.database*
For a subscription created with **define subscription**, sets the subscription status to 'Valid' - this can be verified with **check subscription** or **rs_help[pub]sub**.
validate subscription is part of the bulk materialization sequence **define/activate/ validate subscription** (➢p.57).
Example: **validate subscription VeryBigTable_sub for VeryBigTable_rdf with replicate at PROD.report_db**

check subscription *sub_name ...*
Displays the status of the subscription in the current RepServer; see page 60 for full syntax and details.

drop subscription *sub_name ...*
Drops a subscription to a table repdef or function repdef -either directly or through an article-, a database repdef, a publication or a single article. See page 60 for full syntax and details.

18.6 RSSD tables - subscriptions

Subscription information is stored in the RSSD table **rs_subscriptions**; this table contains all subscriptions created in the current RepServer, as well as all subscriptions created in other RepServers for repdefs in the current RepServer; subscription **where**-clauses are stored in the RSSD table **rs_rules**.

18.7 Getting information about subscriptions

check subscription *sub_name ...*
Displays the status of the subscription in the current RepServer; see page 60 for full syntax and details.

rs_helpsub [*sub_name* [**,** *repdef_name* [**,** *replicate_dataserver***,** *replicate_database*]
(RSSD procedure) Without any parameters, displays a list of all subscriptions to table repdefs and function repdefs in the current, replicate RSSD. To display subscriptions to publications and database repdefs, use **rs_helppubsub** and **rs_helpdbsub**, respectively.
The parameters behave as a filter and can be specified independently. *sub_name* may contain wildcard characters to match subscription names. When the parameters match a single subscription, details are displayed, incl. the **where**-clause.
For subscriptions across a route, **'Unknown'** may be displayed by **rs_helpsub**. This does not indicate an error, but means the value cannot be determined because it is stored in a different RSSD than where **rs_helpsub** is executed.
Example: **rs_helpsub 'sub%cust%'**

rs_helppubsub [*sub_name* [**,** *pub_name* [**,** *primary_dataserver* [**,** *primary_database* [**,** *replicate_dataserver* [**,** *replicate_database*]]]]]]
(RSSD procedure) Without any parameters, displays a list of all publication subscriptions in this RSSD. The parameters behave as a filter and can be specified independently.
For subscriptions across a route, **'Unknown'** may be displayed by **rs_helppubsub**. This does not indicate an error, but means that the value cannot be determined because it is stored in a different RSSD than where **rs_helppubsub** is executed.
Use **rs_helppub** to display all subscriptions for a particular publication or article. Use **check subscription** to display the current status of a particular subscription.
Unlike **rs_helpsub**, no wildcards can be specified in *sub_name*.

rs_helpdbsub [*sub_name* [**,** *replicate_dataserver* [**,** *replicate_database*]]]
(RSSD procedure) Without any parameters, displays all subscriptions to database repdefs in the current, replicate RSSD. The parameters behave as a filter and may be specified independently. All parameters may contain wildcard characters; default= **'%'**.
For subscriptions across a route, **'Unknown'** may be displayed by **rs_helpdbsub**. This does not indicate an error, but means the value cannot be determined because it is stored in a different RSSD than where **rs_helpdbsub** is executed.

rs_helpprepdb [*replicate_dataserver, replicate_database*]
(RSSD procedure) Without any parameters, displays a list of all replicate databases with subscriptions to primary data in the current RepServer (either table/function/database repdefs or publications). When no route is involved, this is the list of all replicate databases in this RepServer. With a dataserver/database name, displays that database only when such subscriptions exist. To display the actual repdefs, publications or subscriptions, use **rs_helprep**/**rs_helpsub**, **rs_helppub**/ **rs_helppubsub** or **rs_helpdbrep**/**rs_helpdbsub**.

18.8 Subscribing to ASE 'truncate table'

The ASE T-SQL statement **truncate table** removes all rows from a table in a fast and efficient way. In ASE 15.0, **truncate table**...**partition**... truncates a specific partition. Because these row deletions are not written to the transaction log, they cannot be replicated. However, the **truncate table** statement itself can be replicated instead.
To subscribe to **truncate table** statements on the primary table, specify the clause **subscribe to truncate table** in **create/define subscription** (➢p.59/61). By default (i.e. without this clause) **truncate table** replication is disabled. To change the status of **truncate table** replication for existing subscriptions, use **sysadmin apply_truncate_table** (see below).
Example: **create subscription Accounts_sub for Accounts**
with replicate at PROD.report_db
subscribe to truncate table

Notes:

- all subscriptions for a particular replicate table must have identical settings for subscribing to **truncate table**.
- In a warm standby, **truncate table** replication is enabled by default; this can later changed with **alter logical connection** (see below).
- For a subscription to a database repdef, **truncate table** replication is disabled by default (but note that it was incorrectly enabled by default in early versions of 12.6). It can be enabled only by including **subscribe to truncate table** in **create/define subscription**. To change the setting for **truncate table** replication, drop & recreate the database subscription.
- The current status of **truncate table** replication for a subscription's replicate table or replicate database can be displayed -in the replicate RSSD only- with the RSSD procedures **rs_helpsub**, **rs_helppubsub** or **rs_helpdbsub** (➢p.62). The actual status information is stored in the RSSD table **rs_subscriptions** in the replicate RSSD; when **rs_subscriptions.status & 1073741824 > 0**, **truncate table** replication is enabled, and disabled otherwise.

sysadmin apply_truncate_table, *replicate_dataserver***,** *replicate_database***,**
{ *replicate_table_owner_name* | **''** }**,** *replicate_table_name***,** { **'on'** | **'off'** }
Executed at the replicate RepServer, enables (**'on'**) or disables (**'off'**) replication of the ASE **truncate table** statement for all existing subscriptions for the specified replicate table in the replicate database. The replicate table owner's name must be specified only if this was also done in the repdef; otherwise, specify **''** (= two single quotes). **sysadmin apply_truncate_table** takes effect immediately.
Example: **sysadmin apply_truncate_table, PROD, report_db, DailySales_tab, 'on'**

alter logical connection to *logical_dataserver.logical_database*
set send_truncate_table [**to**] { **'on'** | **'off'** }
In a warm standby, enables (**'on'**, =default) or disables (**'off'**) replication of the ASE **truncate table** statement from the active database to the standby database. The change takes effect once the connection to the standby database is resumed (it is good practice to suspend the connection first). To determine the current setting for a logical connection, use the RSSD procedure **rs_helpcfg_db**, which is included in the electronic supplement to this book (➢p.8); in 15.0.1, **admin config** can also be used (➢p.90).

18.9 Subscribing to bitmaps

RepServer supports the special datatype **rs_address**, which can be used for subscribing to bitmaps (i.e. specific bits in a column or parameter). This can be useful when individual bits have a functionally relevant meaning, for example in status fields where a group of on/off indicators is packed together in one 4-byte integer.

Warning: before using bitmap subscriptions, please pay attention to the following. With bitmap subscriptions, a primary update will not be replicated if only **rs_address** columns are updated (unless a change in the bitmap would cause a row to migrate out of its current subscription or into a different subscription); this means that the bitmap values in replicate data rows could potentially get out of sync with the bitmap values in the primary rows. Therefore, you should verify that the actual update statements on your primary data are suitable for bitmap subscriptions.

To subscribe to specific bits, use the **&** operator and a bitmask value in the **where**-clause of **create/define subscription** or **create article**. This will perform a logical 'AND' on the actual value of the column/parameter and the bitmask; when the result is non-zero, the row qualifies for the subscription.
In the example below, a bitmap indicates auxiliary employee skills. Let's assume bit 0 indicates a 'First Aid' qualification, bit 1 indicates Dutch language ability and bit 2 indicates VMS experience (indeed, not a well-normalized relational data model...):

```
create replication definition EmployeeAuxSkills with primary at PROD.staff_db
(EmpNo int, EmpName varchar(50), Skills rs_address) primary key (EmpNo)
searchable columns (Skills)

create subscription FirstAid_sub for EmployeeAuxSkills
with replicate at ADMIN.office_mgmt_db
where Skills & 1      -- folks with a First Aid qualification...  (bit 0: 2^0 = binary 001)
   and Skills & 2     -- ... who also speak Dutch                (bit 1: 2^1 = binary 010)

create subscription VMS_sub for EmployeeAuxSkills
with replicate at ADMIN.diehards_db
where Skills & 6      -- folks who speak Dutch or know VMS
                      -- (bits 1+2: 2^1 + 2^2 = binary 110)
```

Note the difference between the two **where**-clauses: the first subscription requires both bits 0 and 1 to be set; the second subscription requires either bit 1 or 2, or both (this way, bitmap subscriptions can sometimes be used to simulate a logical 'OR' condition in the **where**-clause).
The bitmask can in principle also be specified as an 8-digit hexadecimal value: on Linux for example, **Skills & 0x00000006** is equivalent to **Skills & 6** above. However, this may not work cross-platform or on other platforms, since platform-specific byte ordering may produce unexpected results when using such hexadecimal values; with integer values, this problem does not apply.
rs_address represents a 4-byte (32-bit) datatype. Columns declared as **rs_address** in the repdef should normally be 4-byte integers in the primary table. **rs_address** columns cannot be part of the **primary key** clause in a repdef.
Although undocumented (and probably unsupported by Sybase), some other column datatypes -such as ASE's **smallint**, **tinyint** and **binary** (if not longer than 4 bytes)- can also be used for **rs_address** bitmaps; however, when using this, please note that you are fully responsible yourself for issues such as alignment and byte swapping!

18.10 Common subscription creation problems

When creating a subscription, the most common problems are:

- Permission problems: during materialization, the maintenance user does not have sufficient permissions for accessing tables in the replicate or primary database. Such permission problems invariably cause the DSI to be shut down; the RepServer errorlog will contain error messages with respect to this problem. When such permission problems occur, they can usually be solved by assigning the required permissions and resuming the DSI.
- Disk partitions get full: when a primary table is large, atomic materialization may cause the disk partitions to fill up (or at least, take a long time to complete). If this happens, one approach is to add as many disk partitions as needed, and be patient. However, it may be better to abort subscription creation (see below) and use a different method instead, like 'incremental atomic' materialization (➢p.56).
- Replicate transaction log gets full: when a primary table is large, atomic materialization may also cause the transaction log of the replicate database to fill up, since the entire materialization is performed in a single transaction. If this happens, either enlarge the replicate transaction log, or retry with 'incremental atomic' materialization (➢p.56), while frequently dumping or truncating the replicate transaction log.
- Users/applications are blocked in the primary database: when using atomic materialization, users or applications trying to modify the primary table will be blocked for the duration of the materialization step due to the SQL **select**-with-**holdlock** executed against the primary table. If this is unacceptable, it may be better to abort subscription creation (see below) and use a different method, for example 'non-atomic' materialization (➢p.56).

- Connectivity problems: depending on the materialization method, the replicate RepServer may need to connect to the primary RepServer as well as the primary dataserver. If this fails, check whether these servers are correctly declared in the **interfaces** file used by the replicate RepServer, and whether the login and password used to connect, are correct (for the latter, also see section 18.2).

Aborting subscription creation
To abort subscription creation, run **drop subscription**...**without purge**. When incremental materialization was used, some materialization data may already have been inserted into the replicate table; this data should either be deleted manually, or auto-correction should be enabled (➢p.38) when retrying **create subscription**. When the DSI was suspended due to subscription problems, resume the DSI.

When **create subscription** has been aborted, its materialization queue may sometimes be left behind. If it is not dropped automatically, the queue can be dropped manually with **sysadmin drop_queue** (➢p.103). A materialization queue can be recognized by its large, negative queue number, like **109:-2147483528**. The names of the repdef and subscription are displayed as '*repdef_name*.*subscr_name*' behind the queue number by **admin who** as well as in the replicate RepServer's errorlog.

After aborting subscription creation, error message 28049 may appear in the errorlog: '**Cannot find subscription** *hex_subid* **in system tables**'. This message is harmless and can be ignored; it will disappear automatically when old queue segments are deallocated as the queue grows.

19 Warm Standby

19.1 Summary

A warm standby is a RepServer feature where some or all DML and DDL statements and executions of certain ASE system stored procedures in a primary database (known as the active database) are replicated to a replicate database (known as the standby database) . This way, the data and/or schema in the standby database are continuously kept identical with the active database. A warm standby does not use subscriptions, and does not require repdefs (although these can be created for performance reasons; ➢p.18).
A warm standby can be used as a kind of failover solution, allowing applications to continue on the standby database when the active database fails or requires downtime (note that applications must reconnect to the standby database themselves). In addition, the roles of the active database and standby database can be switched, reversing the direction of data replication.
The active-standby database pair can also act as a single ('logical') connection for the purpose of creating repdefs or subscriptions for 'normal' replication to/from other databases outside the warm standby pair. When a switchover between the active and standby database is performed, such repdefs or subscriptions are not affected.
A warm standby supports only ASE-to-ASE replication. Also, it cannot use a route between the active and standby databases. Most of the functionality of a warm standby can also be achieved with database repdefs and -subscriptions (➢p.43). Database repdefs also provide some additional features such as support for non-ASE databases, multiple replicate databases and the use of routes. For a brief comparison between the features of database repdefs and a warm standby, ➢p.47.
The steps to set up a warm standby are listed on page 67.

19.2 Warm standby commands

create logical connection to *logical_dataserver*.*logical_database*
Creates a logical connection for a warm standby. This is the first step of setting up a warm standby. When the setup is completed, this logical connection will have been mapped (with **create connection**) to two actual dataserver/database connections: one for the active database, and one for the standby database. When the connection for the active database does not yet exist, *logical_dataserver* and *logical_database* can be fictitious names (as in the first example below); otherwise, the logical connection must have the same name as the actual connection for the active database.
When setting up a warm standby with **rs_init** (➢p.98) or the RMP plug-in (➢p.115), the logical connection must be created first, since this cannot be done with these tools (unlike the RSP plug-in (➢p.116), which can create the logical connection).
Examples: **create logical connection to DUMMY_SERVER.DUMMY_DB**
create logical connection to PROD.sales_db

alter logical connection to *logical_dataserver.logical_database*
set distribution [**to**] { **on** | **off** }
Permanently enables (**on**; = default) or disables (**off**) the distributor thread for a warm standby. In a warm standby for which no subscriptions to other databases exist, the distributor may be shut down permanently to improve performance. This works because without such subscriptions, in a warm standby the DSI takes its input directly from the inbound queue; the outbound queue is not used. Note that no quotes must be specified around **on** or **off**.
To suspend the distributor thread temporarily, use **suspend distributor** (➢p.29).

alter logical connection to *logical_dataserver.logical_database*
set *logical_connection_config_parameter* [**to**] **'***value***'**
Modifies a configuration parameter for the specified logical connection. The change takes effect once the connection for the DSI for the standby database is resumed (it is good practice to suspend the connection before changing a parameter). Possible values for *logical_connection_config_parameter*, are listed on page 69.

configure logical connection ...
Identical to **alter logical connection**.

drop logical connection to *logical_dataserver.logical_database*
Drops the logical connection for a warm standby. The active and standby connections must have been dropped first (with **drop connection**).

sysadmin dropldb, *logical_dataserver*, *logical_database*
Removes the specified logical connection from the ID server. This is a troubleshooting command that should only be used when **drop logical connection** fails.

create connection to *dataserver.database*
  set error class [**to**] *error_class_name*
  set function string class [**to**] *function_class_name*
  [**set username** [**to**] *maintuser_name* **set password** [**to**] *maintuser_password*]
  [**set** *database_config_parameter* [**to**] **'***value***'** [...*more* **set** *clauses*...]]   ➢p.32
  [**set** *security_config_parameter* [**to**] **'***value***'** [...*more* **set** *clauses*...]]   ➢p.94
  [**with** { **log transfer on, dsi_suspended** }]
  [**as active for** *logical_dataserver.logical_database* |
   as standby for *logical_dataserver.logical_database* [**use dump marker**]]
Creates a connection to an active or standby database for the specified logical connection, with **as active for**... or **as standby for**... , respectively. When setting up a warm standby manually with this command, **with log transfer on** must be specified when creating the connections to the active and the standby database.
use dump marker can only be used when creating the connection for the standby database in a warm standby. First run **create connection**...**as standby for**...**use dump marker**, then make a database dump or log dump of the active database (<u>not</u> the other way around!), and load it into the standby database. Then, bring the standby database online and resume the connection to the standby.
See page 29 for further details about **create connection**.
Example: **create connection to PROD.prod_db**
set error class to rs_sqlserver_error_class
set function string class to rs_sqlserver_function_class
set username to prod_db_maintuser set password to BigSecret
with log transfer on as active for DUMMY_SERVER.DUMMY_DB

wait for create standby for *logical_dataserver.logical_database*
A blocking command, allowing a client session in RepServer to wait for the standby database creation process (**create connection**...**as standby for**) to complete. Here, 'complete' means that the connection to the standby database has been created; **wait for create standby** does not wait until the standby is initialized (for example, with a database dump from the active database).

switch active for *logical_dataserver.logical_database* **to** *dataserver.database*
[**with suspension**]
Interchanges the active and standby databases in a warm standby. *dataserver.database* must be the current standby database (which will be turned into the active database). **with suspension** leaves the connection to the new active database suspended after the switch.
See 19.4 (➢p.68) for full details on what happens internally during a switch, and the required follow-up actions by the DBA.
Example: **switch active for DUMMY_SERVER.DUMMY_DB to SPARE.spare_db**
Notes:

- The **switch active** command returns immediately. Use **admin logical_status** or **wait for switch** to determine when the switch has completed.

- After **switch active** has completed, the RepAgent for the new active database must be started manually (with **sp_start_rep_agent**).
- If it is still running, the RepAgent for the new standby (old active) database must be stopped manually (with **sp_stop_rep_agent**); otherwise, RepServer will fail to remove the secondary truncation point and the DSI will shut down.
- Client applications will not switch to the new active database automatically: this must be arranged outside RepServer. See 19.5 (➢p.69) for a common solution.

abort switch for *logical_dataserver.logical_database*
Aborts the **switch active** command (if the switchover has not yet progressed too far).

wait for switch for *logical_dataserver.logical_database*
A blocking command, allowing a client session in RepServer to wait for the **switch active** command to complete.

19.3 Tips for setting up a warm standby

The simplest way to create a warm standby is by using **rs_init** (➢p.98) or with the RSP plug-in for Sybase Central (➢p.116). A warm standby can also be set up manually, but this requires quite a series of steps (interested readers should inspect the **rs_init** log file for full details of these steps).
To set up a warm standby, the following steps must be performed:

1. Create a logical connection, either manually with **create logical connection** (➢p.65), or with the RSP plug-in for Sybase Central (➢p.116)
2. Mark the active database for replication, usually with **sp_reptostandby** (➢p.18). Optionally, the standby may also be marked for replication; this may also be done later, or not at all (only if the active and standby will never be switched).
3. Create the connection for the active database, either with **rs_init**, with the RSP plug-in for Sybase Central, or manually with **create connection**...**as active for** (➢p.29)
4. Create the connection for the standby database, either with **rs_init**, with the RSP plug-in for Sybase Central, or manually with **create connection**...**as standby for** (➢p.29). When re-initializing the standby, first drop the existing connection (if any) with **drop connection**.
5. If the standby is initialized with the **dump marker** option in the previous step, make a database dump or log dump of the active database (this must be done after the previous step!).
6. Load the database dump or log dump from the active into the standby, bring the standby online with **online database** (in ASE), and resume the DSI.

When setting up a warm standby, here are a few things to keep in mind:

- It is recommended to keep the name of the active and standby databases, as well as the name of the maintenance user for both databases, identical: if not, applications will probably fail when the active and standby are switched.
- It is recommended to keep the size and device layout of the active and standby databases identical when the standby is initialized with a database dump from the active database. This works only if the standby is at least as large as the active database. The same reasoning applies when the active and standby are switched and the new standby is later re-initialized.
- **rs_init** expects the maintenance user login for the standby database (as specified in the **rs_init** dialog) to exist in the replicate dataserver. If it does not exist, **rs_init** won't create the standby connection, but report an error. The DBA should ensure this dataserver login exists.
- In addition to the previous bullet, the maintenance user for the standby database must also exist as a database user in the standby database (i.e. be added with **sp_adduser**). If it is an alias to **dbo** (as is often done), **rs_init** may report an error when creating the standby connection; see page 98 for a workaround.
- The maintenance user for the standby database requires **replication_role** and at least object owner permission on all replicate objects. For DDL replication, at least **dbo** permission is needed.
- Error 15230 may occur during creating the active or standby connection: **'Create failed because Log transfer for database** *your_server.your_db* **is off.'** When this happens, **with log transfer on** was not specified in the **create con-**

nection command. In the **rs_init** dialogue, answer '**yes**' to the question '**Will the database be replicated:**'.

- The easiest way to initialize the standby is by loading a dump from the active database. When creating the standby connection (either with **rs_init**, the RSP plug-in, or with **create connection**), specify the option **use dump marker**. Wait until this step has completed, and then make a database dump or log dump of the active database (if the dump is made first, the standby will be waiting forever for the dump marker; if this happens, simply drop the standby connection and try again). After loading the dump into the standby database, bring the standby online with **online database** (in ASE), and resume the DSI to the standby.
- When initializing the standby with a single database dump and the **use dump marker** clause, there is no need to load subsequent transaction log dumps from the active database into the standby. When updates to the active database continued during the dump/load process, all updates that occurred before the dump will be ignored by the standby. Updates made after the dump completed will be applied to the standby through replication.
  Alternatively, the standby can be initialized with a database dump and subsequent log dumps. This scenario can be used if a making, transferring and loading a full database dump would take too long for the available maintenance window. In this scenario, the last log dump would typically (but not necessarily) contain the dump marker (by performing the log dump after **create connection**...**use dump marker**).
- To re-initialize the standby database (for example, after switching the active database), drop the connection to the standby database (if it still exists) with **drop connection**. Then, recreate the connection to the standby with either **rs_init** or **create connection** (see previous bullet).
- Instead of loading a dump from the active database into the standby (see previous bullets), the standby can also be initialized with **bcp**. In addition, RS 12.6 and ASE 12.5.1 also support the ASE statement **quiesce database**...**to** *manifest_file* to copy the active database on device level; the copy is then moved into the replicate ASE server with the ASE **mount** statement. See the *Replication Server Administration Guide* (➢p.13) for details.
- When not initializing the standby with a dump of the active database, ensure all settings for **sp_setreptable**, **sp_setrepproc** and **sp_reptostandby** are identical for the active and the standby. If not, some primary data may not be replicated properly after the active and standby have been switched.
- In a warm standby, it is usually important to keep the contents of **syslogins** and **sysusers** (etc.) identical in the active and standby servers. See 14.9 (➢p.47).

19.4 Warm standby - switching active and standby

When **switch active** is executed for a warm standby, the DBA should ensure that all client applications disconnect from the active database, and cannot reconnect while the switch is in progress.
The following steps are executed internally for **switch active**:

1. Log transfer is suspended for the active (soon-to-be-standby) database.
2. All committed transactions from the active database are read from the transaction log and applied to the standby (this is known as 'draining the queues').
3. Once all transactions are applied, the connection to the standby database is suspended. Also, the secondary truncation point is enabled in the transaction log of the standby database.
4. The 'enable marker' is written into the transaction log of the current standby (but soon-to-be-active) database. Any transactions committed in the standby database before this 'enable marker' is written will not be replicated to the soon-to-be-standby database (i.e. what was the active database before the switch). Therefore, applications that modify data should not connect to the new active database until **admin logical_status** (or **wait for switch**) indicates that the switch is complete.
5. The roles of the active and standby databases are reversed, and the RSSD is updated accordingly.
6. Log transfer is enabled for the new active (old standby) database.

The following steps must now be executed by the DBA:

7. Client applications must reconnect to the new active database. See below for a common approach.

8. The ASE RepAgent for the current active database (the old standby) must be started manually with **sp_start_rep_agent**; this does not happen automatically as part of the switch.
9. Once the ASE RepAgent is started, replication of transactions from the new active to the new standby starts.
   The connection to the new standby database remains suspended, so replicated transactions will accumulate in the outbound queue for the old active (new standby) database. The DBA must resume this connection later (see below).
10. Decide what to do with the old active (new standby) database. A switch is typically performed because there was something wrong with the active database, so you may need to re-initialise the new standby database (see the description of **create connection**...**use dump marker** on page 66).
11. Make sure the ASE RepAgent for the old active database (new standby) is shut down (use **sp_stop_rep_agent** if necessary), and verify the secondary truncation point is removed.
12. Once the new standby database is prepared and ready, resume the connection to it, if it was still suspended.

19.5 Switching client applications to the new active database

After **switch active** in a warm standby, client applications will not switch to the new active database automatically: this must be arranged outside RepServer.
A commonly used method is to solve this on network level by making applications connect to a dataserver on a fictitious hostname, which resolves to the actual host for the ASE server containing the currently active database. When executing **switch active**, the DNS resolution for the fictitious hostname is changed to the ASE server for the new active database. Applications should then be forced to reconnect to the ASE server, for example by shutting down the ASE server for the old active database.
Note that this solution assumes the following (indeed common) setup:

- The active and standby databases reside on dataservers that run on different hosts.
- The database names of the active and standby database are identical.

19.6 Configuration parameters for logical connections

The configuration parameters below apply to logical database connections for a warm standby. They can be modified (one parameter at a time) with **alter logical connection**, overriding the RepServer-wide default for the specified logical connection. Only for **rep_as_standby**, a different RepServer-wide default can be set with **configure replication server**.
Example: **alter logical connection to WARM_DS.WARM_DB**
set send_truncate_table to 'off'

Notes:

- All parameter values, including integers, must be specified as quoted strings.
- In pre-15.0.1, there is no system-supplied procedure to display non-default configuration parameter settings for a logical connection. Instead, use the RSSD procedure **rs_helpcfg_db** (included in the electronic supplement to this book; ➢p.8). In 15.0.1, **admin config** can also be used (➢p.90).
  For details about parameter storage in the RSSD table **rs_config**, see page 91.

List of configuration parameters for logical connections:

- **send_truncate_table** - enables (**'on'**; =default for ASE 11.5+) or disables (**'off'**) replication of the ASE T-SQL **truncate table** statement from the active database to the standby. For more information, see page 63.
- **replicate_minimal_columns** - has effect only for repdefs without a **send standby** clause: if **'on'** (=default), minimal columns are replicated to the standby database; if **'off'**, replicates all columns. For repdefs with a **send standby** clause, the **replicate minimal/all columns** setting in the repdefs override **replicate_minimal_columns** for the logical connection.
- **send_standby_repdef_cols** - if **'on'** or **'off'**, overrides the **send standby** clause in repdefs in the active database: if **'on'**, only the repdef columns are replicated to the standby; if **'off'**, all table columns are replicated. If **'check_repdef'** (=default), the **send standby** clause is not overridden.
- **save_interval** - either the number of minutes during which messages in the DSI queue are saved after being applied successfully to the standby database, or **'strict'**. Increasing this setting improves recoverability (through **sysadmin re-**

store_dsi_saved_segments), but requires additional disk space.
Default = **'strict'** for standby databases, meaning disk space is deallocated as soon as the transactions have been applied. The current setting is displayed by **admin who, sqm** (in the column **Save_Int:Seg**).

- **materialization_save_interval** - similar to **save_interval**, but for materialization queues (when a subscription is created in a warm standby). Default = **'strict'** for standby databases (see previous bullet).
- **(pre-12.1) md_source_memory_pool** - in 12.1, this parameter has been superseded by **md_sqm_write_request_limit**.
- **rep_as_standby** - this applies to a primary database connection or a logical connection. When **'on'**, table subscriptions can be created for table repdefs in a primary database that has been marked with **sp_reptostandby**, without the need to mark these primary tables with **sp_setreptable**. This requires the ASE RepAgent to have the option **'send warm standby xacts'** enabled. When set to **'off'** (=default), a primary table must have been marked explicitly with **sp_setreptable**.
- **(15.0) dist_stop_unsupported_cmd** - determines how to handle replicated commands for new features that are not supported by older RepServer versions. Overrides the repserver-wide setting. See p.34 for details.

19.7 Warm standby - notes and remarks

- If a stored procedure in the active database is marked for replication with **sp_setrepproc**, and this procedure executes DML in that database, only the procedure execution is replicated to the standby database, not the DML it executed. See section 14.12 (p.49) for a more detailed description of this phenomenon.
  (note: if an identical stored procedure exists in the standby (for example, as a result of DDL replication), the effect of the procedure execution in the active database will be identical in the standby database)

- There is no supported way to create custom function strings for a connection to a standby database: even though the RSSD table **rs_databases.funcclassid** may indicate **rs_sqlserver_function_class**, the standby connection actually uses **rs_default_function_class**, which cannot be customized.
  The function string class for the standby connection can only be changed with the following command, which is undocumented and unsupported.
  ***Warning:* use this command entirely at your own risk!**

  alter connection to *dataserver.database* -- specify the standby DB here
  set standby_func_class to *function_class_name*

  To activate this change, the connection to the standby database must be suspended and resumed.
  For the active database, the function string class in the RSSD table **rs_databases.funcclassid** is used, but only when the active database has repdefs/subscriptions which are replicated to/from outside the warm standby pair.

- When creating the standby database, the following configuration parameters are copied to the standby connection if they are set to a non-default value for the active connection. Note that these parameters are modified with **alter connection** (not **alter logical connection**!); details are described in section 13.3.

batch	**batch_begin**	**dsi_cmd_separator**
command_retry	**dsi_charset_convert**	**dsi_cmd_batch_size**
db_packet_size	**dsi_large_xact_size**	**dsi_keep_triggers**
dsi_fadeout_time	**dsi_max_cmds_to_log**	**dsi_max_text_to_log**
dsi_num_threads	**dsi_num_large_xact_threads**	**dsi_sql_data_style**
dsi_replication	**dsi_serialization_method**	**dsi_sqt_max_cache_size**
dump_load	**dsi_xact_in_group**	**dsi_xact_group_size**
parallel_dsi		

- A warm standby cannot use autocorrection (this can only be used for table repdefs with a subscription; ➢p.38)

19.8 RSSD tables - warm standby

A logical connection is stored in the RSSD table **rs_databases**, with columns **ltype** = **ptype** = **'L'**. The database ID for a logical connection is stored in **rs_databases.ldbid** for the active and standby databases.

19.9 Getting information about a warm standby

admin logical_status [, *logical_dataserver*, *logical_database*]
Displays status information for all logical connections. With parameters, only for that logical connection. Among other things, the active and standby database for each logical connection are displayed.

20 Functions, Function strings & Function string classes

The functionality of functions and function strings is perhaps one of the most versatile aspects of RepServer, providing almost unlimited flexibility; however, it is also one of the most complex features. Before discussing the actual commands, a summary of the main concepts is described below.

20.1 Summary of function/function string concepts

Seen from a very high level, RepServer just seems to translate primary SQL statements into identical replicate SQL statements. While that is often indeed what happens, the actual mechanism is much more advanced:

- At the primary side, RepServer converts a replicated data modification or a replicated stored procedure execution in a primary database, to a series of RepServer functions. Each function represents a basic database operation, and can be thought of as a 'package' containing the actual data elements from the primary data modification, such as the inserted column values or the stored procedure's parameter values, in a platform-independent format.
  For example, an update of a primary row is by default translated to a replicate transaction consisting of the functions **rs_begin**, **rs_update** and **rs_commit**. (note: these 'functions' are unrelated to the 'built-in functions' in SQL)
- The RepServer functions, grouped in transactions, are forwarded through the replication system to the appropriate replicate databases, according to existing subscriptions, warm standbys, etc.
- At the replicate side (in the DSI), functions are translated to SQL statements for execution in a replicate data base. This translation is based on templates called function strings; each function has such templates associated with it.
  The default, system-supplied function strings have the effect of replicating a primary SQL DML statement as a very similar replicate SQL statement. For example, the above function sequence **rs_begin** - **rs_update** - **rs_commit** is by default translated to the replicate SQL statements **begin transaction**, **update** (with the updated column values from the primary row and the name of the replicate table) and **commit transaction**, respectively. Indeed, this is precisely what is usually expected (though completely different translations are also possible).
- Function strings are related to a particular function, but they can also be seen from the perspective of a function string class. A function can have different instances of a corresponding function string, with each instance belonging to a different function string class. By associating different function string classes with different replicate database connections, different SQL statements can be generated in each replicate database for the same primary data modification.
  One application of this concept is heterogeneous replication. When replicating data between different types of databases, a function string class can be used by the DSI to generate the correct SQL syntax for each database type, and perform any required datatype conversions (➢p.27).
  For ASE databases, the Sybase-supplied function string class **rs_sqlserver_function_class** is used. Sybase-supplied function string classes are also available for other databases, including Oracle (**rs_oracle_function_class**), Microsoft SQL Server (**rs_msss_function_class**), and others (➢p.72).
- New function string classes can be created, based on an existing class. Such a derived class inherits all function strings from its parent class (➢p.73); this can be overridden for individual function strings.
- The translation from a function to an actual replicate SQL statement can be completely customized by modifying the corresponding function string to generate different SQL statements than the system-supplied defaults. For example, this feature can be used to implement special data conversions, or conflict resolution in a bi-directional replication system (for an example, ➢p.82).
  Customized function strings offer almost unlimited flexibility to generate replicate SQL statements that are completely different from the primary DML statements. For example, a primary row insertion could be replicated as a

stored procedure call by changing the function string for the **rs_insert** function to **'exec** *your_procedure_name...***'**. Similarly, a row deletion could be replicated as two inserts in two different replicate tables by changing the function string for **rs_delete** to the desired replicate **insert** statements.

- Some functions, like **rs_insert**, are specific for both a replication definition and a function string class. Other functions, like **rs_begin**, only belong to a specific function string class. Most functions have only one function string per function string class. Some functions, like **rs_select** and **rs_writetext**, can have multiple function strings. Details are described on pages 76-79.
- In a warm standby, customized function strings cannot be used (at least, not in a supported way; ➢p.70). For database repdefs/subscriptions, customized function strings are supported (➢p.45).
- All commands in the following sections are executed in the primary RepServer for the function string class involved. This is not necessarily the same RepServer as the one where the primary data resides.

20.2 Function string classes

Terminology note: some commands mention a 'function class'; this is just a synonym for 'function string class'.
The following system-supplied function string classes are available by default:

Function string class name	Used for database type:
rs_sqlserver_function_class	Sybase ASE (system-supplied base class)
rs_default_function_class	(system-supplied base class) A generic parent class for the following classes (except **rs_db2_function_class**):
rs_asa_function_class	Sybase ASA/SQL Anywhere
rs_msss_function_class	Microsoft SQL Server
rs_udb_function_class	DB2 on Unix or Windows
rs_oracle_function_class	Oracle
rs_informix_function_class	Informix
rs_ims_function_class	IMS
rs_vsam_function_class	VSAM files
rs_db2_function_class	DB2 on OS/390 (system-supplied base class)

create function string class *function_class_name*
[**set parent to** *parent_function_class_name*]
Creates a new function string class; its name cannot start with **'rs_'**.
Without **set parent**, the new class will be an empty 'base class', not containing any function strings; these must either be created explicitly with **create function string**, or a parent class must be specified, from which the function strings are inherited. If no function string exists for a function arriving at the DSI, the DSI will be suspended.
With **set parent**, the new class will be a 'derived class' of the specified parent function string class, inheriting its function strings. Not all system-supplied classes can be used as a parent class (➢p.73).
Example: **create function string class MyFunkyClass**
set parent to rs_default_function_class

alter function string class *function_class_name*
set parent to { *parent_function_class_name* | **null** }
Modifies the inheritance structure of a function string class. With *parent_function_class_name*, makes *function_class_name* a derived class from that parent function string class; with **null**, makes *function_class_name* a base class (without a parent class from which function strings are inherited). See page 73 for details about function string inheritance.

drop function string class *function_class_name*
Drops a DBA-created function string class, including all customized function strings created for the class. System-defined function string classes (starting with **'rs_'**) cannot be dropped.

move primary of function string class *function_class_name* **to** *current_repserver*
Changes the primary RepServer for the specified function string class to the current RepServer. This command must be executed in the RepServer that will be the new primary RepServer for the class (i.e. in RepServer *current_repserver*). There must be routes (in both directions) between the current RepServer and the old primary RepServer for this class.

rs_helpclass [*function_class_name*]
(RSSD procedure) Without any parameter, displays a list of all function string classes (as well as the error classes) in the current RSSD, including their primary RepServer. With parameter, displays only the specified class. To display information about class-specific function strings in the class, use **rs_helpclassfstring** (➢p.76).

admin show_function_classes
Displays a list of all function string classes in this RepServer, including their parent classes (if any), and their level of inheritance. Does not display the primary RepServer for each class.

alter connection to *dataserver.database*
set function string class [**to**] *function_class_name*
Changes the function string class for the specified database connection. When a function is translated to an actual SQL statement for this database, function strings from this class will be used as templates.
The change takes effect once the connection is resumed (it is good practice to suspend the connection before changing a parameter). When a connection is created, a function string class is defined with **create connection**, but this can later be changed with **alter connection**.
In most cases, function string classes are used for replicate databases. The function string class for a primary database is relevant only during subscription (de)materialization, when function strings for **rs_select** and **rs_select_with_lock** are used (➢p.74).
Example: **alter connection to PROD.prod_db**
set function string class to MyFunkyClass

To determine the function string class currently configured for a connection, run this query in the RSSD:

select dsname, dbname, classname 'Function string class'
from rs_databases d, rs_classes c
where d.funcclassid = c.classid

20.3 Function string inheritance

Hierarchical relationships can exist between individual function string classes, facilitating a feature known as 'function string inheritance'. From this perspective, the following types of function string classes can be distinguished:

- 'parent class' - a function string class from which another class is derived;
- 'derived class' - a function string class which has a parent class;
- 'base class' - a function string class which has no parent class.

A derived class inherits all function strings from its parent class; hence the name 'function string inheritance':

- When altering a function string in a parent class, this modification is immediately inherited by all derived classes for this parent class where this function string was not overridden (see next bullet).
- When creating a function string in a derived class, this overrides the inherited function string from the parent class (but does not affect the function string in the parent class itself).

When creating or modifying a function string, this takes effect immediately on the local RepServer; when there is an outgoing route, the modification takes effect in the destination RepServer once it has arrived in the destination RSSD.

Function string inheritance can have multiple levels: a parent class can also be a derived class at the same time. Parent classes can be established or changed with **create function string class** or **alter function string class**.
When creating a base class (i.e. a function string class without a parent class), all function strings must be explicitly created for the base class (with **create function string**); otherwise, any attempt to access a database with this function string class will cause errors in the DSI.
Notes:

- **rs_sqlserver_function_class** (the default class used for ASE connections) cannot be used as a parent class; use **rs_default_function_class** or another function class instead.
- Function strings cannot be created or modified for **rs_default_function_class** or **rs_db2_function_class**; instead, create a derived class and create customized function strings in that class.
- Function string inheritance is dynamic (unlike the static class initialization for

error classes with the RSSD procedure **rs_init_erroractions**: the latter is a one-time operation that is not maintained further).

20.4 Function string commands

{ **create function string** *repdef_name*.*function_name*[;*function_string_name*] |
create function string *function_name* }
for *function_class_name*
[**with overwrite**]
[**scan** '*input_whereclause_template*']
[**output**
{ **language** '*output_sql_template*' |
rpc 'execute *procedure_name* [**@***param*=] { *constant* | **?***variable***!***modifier***?** } [,...]' |
writetext [**use primary log** | **with log** | **no log**] |
none }]

Creates or modifies a function string for the specified function and function string class. This takes effect immediately in the primary RepServer for the function string class; for a replicate RepServer, it takes effect once the modification arrives at the replicate RSSD. **create function string**...**with overwrite** is identical to **alter function string**.

Examples: **create function string Accounts_rdf.rs_delete**
for rs_sqlserver_function_class
with overwrite output language
'delete Accounts where AccountNo = ?AccountNo!old? ;
insert LogTable values (getdate(), ?rs_origin_user!sys?,
"Deleted Account# ?AccountNo!old?") '

create function string rs_begin
for MyFunctionClass
output language
'rollback ; set chained off ; set transaction isolation level 1 ;
set arithignore off ; begin transaction ;'

Syntax notes:

- *repdef_name* must be specified for the table repdef-specific functions **rs_insert**, **rs_delete**, **rs_update**, **rs_truncate**, **rs_select**, **rs_select_with_lock**, **rs_get_textptr**, **rs_textptr_init**, **rs_writetext** and **rs_datarow_for_writetext** (➢p.76); for other functions, specifying *repdef_name* is not allowed.
- *function_string_name* can only be specified for functions that may have multiple function strings (i.e. **rs_select**, **rs_select_with_lock**, **rs_textptr_init**, **rs_get_textptr**, **rs_writetext** and **rs_datarow_for_writetext**; ➢p.76). If specified, the name must be unique for this function, repdef and function string class. If not specified, *function_string_name* defaults to *function_name*.
- '*input_whereclause_template*' and '*output_sql_template*' are templates for generating SQL statements. These templates consist of literal text and symbolic variables representing the replicated data values. The total size of the generated SQL statements cannot be more than 64Kb. Details about these templates are described on page 79. Note that single quotes must be used as delimiters. For the semantics of the semicolon in the templates, see page 79.
- **output language** '*output_sql_template*' specifies how to generate the SQL statements to be executed in the replicate database (except for **rs_select**/ **rs_select_with_lock** during subscription materialization: these apply to the primary database).
- **output rpc** specifies a local stored procedure or a remote procedure call should be executed (most of this can also be achieved with **output language**).
- **output writetext** specifies that CT-Lib calls be used for updating replicate **text/image** data; **with log** and **no log** specify the corresponding transaction logging behaviour. **use primary log** will log these operations only if the primary DML did as well.
- **output none** applies only the **rs_writetext** function; it performs no action. For other functions, to generate a replicate SQL statement that performs no action, specify **output language ' '** (= a single space).
- **scan** '*input_whereclause_template*' can be specified only for the functions **rs_select** and **rs_select_with_lock**. It is only necessary to define this clause when multiple subscriptions with different **where**-clauses exist for the repdef, and which require non-standard (de)materialization queries.
  rs_select and **rs_select_with_lock** specify how to generate SQL statements for automatic materialization (executed in the primary database) and for dema-

terialization **with purge** (executed in the replicate database; for **rs_select** only). Note that a customized function string must be in the function string class used by these databases.
During (de)materialization, *input_whereclause_template* is matched to each subscription's **where**-clause; the corresponding *output_sql_template* generates the SQL statements to query the primary table (for materialization) or the replicate table (for dematerialization). A blank, empty input template (=default) matches all **where**-clauses that don't match any other template. For more information, see the *Replication Server Administration Guide* (➢p.13).

- Function strings cannot be created or modified for **rs_default_function_class** or **rs_db2_function_class**; instead, create a derived class and create customized function strings for that class.
- When errors 15287 (**'No site is currently owning function 'rs_*xxx*'. Please designate a primary site [...]'**) or 15162 (**'This function string 'rs_*xxx*' can only be created at the primary of the class'**) are raised, the following must first be run at the primary RepServer (this needs to be done only once):
  create function string class *function_class_name*

{ **alter function string** *repdef_name.function_name*[;*function_string_name*] |
alter function string *function_name* }
for *function_class_name*
[**scan** '*input_whereclause_template*']
[**output**
{ **language** '*output_sql_template*' |
rpc 'execute *procedure_name* [**@***param***=**] { *constant* | **?***variable***!***modifier***?** } [,...]**'** |
writetext [**use primary log** | **with log** | **no log**] |
none }]
Replaces an existing function string by dropping and recreating it in a single operation; this is identical to **create function string**...**with overwrite**. The change takes effect immediately once the modification arrives at the RSSD. See **create function string** (➢p.74) for details about the various clauses of this command.
To restore the default function string for a function, omit the **scan** and **output** clauses completely. Note that this is different from **output language ' '**, which is an empty function string generating a SQL statement (a space) that performs no action at all.
Examples: **alter function string Accounts_rdf.rs_delete**
for rs_sqlserver_function_class
output language 'exec sp_delete_Account ?AccountNo!old?'

-- restore the default function string:
alter function string Accounts_rdf.rs_delete
for rs_sqlserver_function_class

{ **drop function string** *repdef_name.function_name*[;*function_string_name*] |
drop function string *repdef_name.function_name*[;**all**] |
drop function string *function_name* }
for *function_class_name*
Drops a function string for the specified function and function string class. For functions that can have multiple function strings, **';all'** drops all function strings for the function. When dropping a repdef, all its repdef-specific functions and corresponding function strings are dropped automatically as well.
Note: be careful about dropping function strings: when a function arrives at the DSI for which no function string is available, an error is reported and the DSI is shut down. To revert a customized function string back to its default, either use **alter function string** without **scan** or **output** (see above), or use **rs_default_fs** (➢p.81). When a function string has been dropped already, use **create function string** (without **scan** or **output**) to recreate the default function string.

20.5 RSSD tables - functions, function strings & -classes

Functions are stored in the RSSD table **rs_functions**. Function strings are stored in the RSSD table **rs_funcstrings**; the actual text of the input/output templates of the function strings is stored in the RSSD table **rs_systext**. Function string classes are stored in the RSSD table **rs_classes**, with **rs_classes.classtype** = **'F'**.
For class-specific functions (➢p.77), **rs_functions.objid** = **0x0**; for repdef_specific functions (➢p.54), **rs_functions.objid** is equal to the **rs_object.objid** for the repdef.
When a RepServer has an outgoing route, these tables (among others) are replicated to the destination RSSD.

20.6 Getting information about function strings

rs_helpfstring *repdef_name* [, *function_name*]
(RSSD procedure) For all function string classes, displays function strings for repdef-specific functions (➢sections 20.8,20.9) for the specified repdef; if *function_name* is specified, only for the specified function. *function_name* is matched against a leading substring. Note that inherited function strings are not displayed for derived classes.

rs_helpclassfstring *function_class_name* [, *function_name*]
(RSSD procedure) Displays function strings for class-specific functions (➢p.77) for the specified class; with *function_name*, only for the specified function. Each parameter is matched against leading substrings.
To display function strings for a function in all classes, **NULL** can be specified for *function_class_name*, but the output of **rs_helpclassfstring** unfortunately does not include the class name. Instead, use one of the RSSD queries from the electronic supplement to this book (➢p.8).

Note that repdef-specific function strings are not displayed by **rs_helpclassfstring**. When a class has no class-specific function strings, **rs_helpclassfstring** produces no output at all, even when the class exists. Also note that inherited function strings are not displayed for derived classes.
The electronic supplement to this book (➢p.8) contains RSSD queries to display the repdef-specific function strings in a class, and to display all customized function strings for repdef-specific functions.

rs_helpfunc [*repdef_name* [, *function_name*]]
(RSSD procedure) Without any parameters, displays all functions defined in this RSSD, ordered by type (repdef-specific functions for table- and function repdefs, and class-specific functions). With parameters, only displays functions for the specified repdef and/or function.

20.7 Function categories

RepServer functions can be divided in the following categories:

- Table repdef-specific functions, like **rs_insert**, to access or modify replicate (or primary) data. Instances of these functions (and their function strings) are specific for a table repdef. These functions are described in the table on page 76.
- Function repdef-specific functions, also known as 'user-defined functions', created automatically by RepServer for function repdefs; the function name is identical to the name of the function repdef. Each function (and its function strings) is specific for a particular function repdef; see page 77.
- Class-specific functions, like **rs_begin**, mainly for transaction control. These functions are not related to a repdef; their function strings are only specific for a function string class. These functions are described in the table on page 77.

For details about all functions, see the *Replication Server Reference Manual* (➢p.13).

20.8 Table repdef-specific functions (data access)

The functions for table repdefs are listed below:

Repdef-specific functions	Max# func. strings per class, repdef	Function description
rs_insert	1	Inserts a row into a replicate table.
rs_delete	1	Deletes a row from a replicate table.
rs_update	1	Updates a row in a replicate table, except for **text/image** data (for this, use the functions in the table below).
rs_truncate	1	Truncates a replicate table or (in ASE 15.0 + RS 15.0) an individual table partition (➢p.79), when **truncate table** replication is subscribed to.
rs_select	≥ 1	Selects rows from a primary table for materialization of **create subscription** ...**without holdlock**; selects rows from a replicate table for dematerialization of **drop subscription**...**with purge**. See the description of the **scan** clause on page 74.

rs_select_with_lock	≥ 1	Same as **rs_select**, but uses **holdlock**. **rs_select_with_lock** is used for materialization only.

Repdef-specific functions for text/image columns	Max# func. strings	Function description
rs_datarow_for_writetext	≥ 1	Retrieves the primary key columns and searchable columns for a data row whose **text/image** column is updated; does not return the **text/image** data itself.
rs_get_textptr	≥ 1	Retrieves the text pointer for a **text/image** column.
rs_textptr_init	≥ 1	Allocates a text pointer for a **text** or **image** column.
rs_writetext	≥ 1	Modifies replicate **text/image** data.

For the functions in the above table, as well as for their function strings, multiple instances can exist in a function string class, where each instance is specific for a table repdef (the official RepServer documentation uses the term 'replication definition scope'). For these functions, **create/alter/delete function string** must be run at the RepServer where the repdef was created. Also, the repdef name must always be specified like this:

create function string *table_repdef_name*.*function_name*
for *function_class_name ...*

The functions **rs_datarow_for_writetext**, **rs_get_textptr**, **rs_textptr_init** and **rs_writetext** are automatically created for each **text** or **image** column in a table repdef, with *function_string_name* equal to the name of the corresponding **text/image** column. Consequently, with multiple **text/image** columns in the repdef, there will be multiple function strings for these functions for that repdef.
For **rs_datarow_for_writetext**, **rs_get_textptr**, **rs_textptr_init** and **rs_writetext**, an additional function string name can optionally be specified like this:

create function string *table_repdef_name*.*function_name*;*column_name*
for *function_class_name ...*

For **rs_select** and **rs_select_with_lock**, *function_string_name* may also be specified explicitly when multiple function strings exist (see the description of the **scan** clause on page 74). In this case, the function string name can be chosen freely, but must be unique for that function.
The functions **rs_insert**, **rs_delete**, **rs_update**, **rs_truncate**, **rs_select** and **rs_select_with_lock** are created (and dropped) automatically for a table repdef.

To display the actual function strings for these repdef-specific functions, use **rs_helpfstring** (➢p.76).

20.9 Function repdef-specific functions ('user-defined')

User-defined functions are functions whose names do not start with **'rs_'**. A user-defined function is created (and dropped) automatically when creating (or dropping) a function repdef. The user-defined function will have the same name as the function repdef. There can be only one function for a function repdef in a function string class; other repdef-specific functions (like **rs_select** etc.) are not possible.
A user-defined function, as well as its function strings, are specific for the corresponding function repdef (the official RepServer documentation uses the term 'replication definition scope').
For user-defined functions, **create/alter/delete function string** must be run at the RepServer where the function repdef was created. Also, the repdef name must always be specified like this:

create function string *repdef_name*.*function_name*
for *function_class_name ...*

To display the actual function strings for user-defined functions, use **rs_helpfstring** (➢p.76).
Note: User-defined functions can also be created, modified and dropped with the obsolete commands on page 83, but this is not recommended. In fact, that is where the name 'user-defined' function originates from, although today's user-defined functions are really created implicitly by **create function replication definition**.

20.10 Class-specific functions (transaction control)

The functions described below mainly represent transaction control functionality. These functions are not related to a particular repdef; their function strings are specific only to the function string class for which they are created (the official RepServer documentation uses the term 'function string class scope').

Class-specific functions	Function description
rs_begin	Starts an explicit transaction in a replicate database
rs_commit	Commits a transaction in a replicate database.
rs_rollback	Rolls back a replicated transaction. Used only internally by parallel DSI.
(15.0) rs_batch_start, **rs_batch_end**	SQL commands to marking start/end of a command batch in replicate non-ASE dataservers (➢p.34)
rs_usedb	Changes the default database in a dataserver.
rs_check_repl	Checks if a primary table is marked for replication.
rs_get_lastcommit	Retrieves data from the **rs_lastcommit** table.
rs_marker *@rs_api*	Passes the *@rs_api* parameter to RepServer via the stored procedure **rs_marker**. ***Warning:*** if used to simulate atomic materialization (see the *Replication Server Administration Guide*; ➢p.13) be careful not to make syntax errors in the *@rs_api* argument!
rs_get_charset	Returns the character set used by a dataserver.
rs_get_sortorder	Returns the sort order used by a dataserver.
rs_raw_object_serialization	Used for replicating Java columns as serialized data.
rs_repl_off	Executes **set replication off** in the replicate ASE database.
(15.0) rs_repl_on	Executes **set replication on** in the replicate ASE database.
rs_setproxy	Assumes the identity of a different dataserver login, using **set proxy/set session authorization**.
rs_triggers_reset	Executes **set triggers off** to disable all triggers in the replicate ASE database (for the DSI session only).
(ASE 15.0, RS 15.0) **rs_set_dml_on_computed**	Replicates materialized computed columns when these are included in the repdef, using **set dml_on_computed on**
(ASE 12.5.4, RS 12.6 esd#5) **rs_set_ciphertext**	Replicates encrypted ASE columns without decrypting them, using **set ciphertext on**.
(ASE 15.0.2, RS 15.1) **rs_set_timestamp_insert**	Replicates actual primary values of ASE timestamp columns, using **set timestamp_insert on**
rs_initialize_threads *@rs_id*	Sets the sequence of all entries in the RSSD table **rs_threads** to 0 (applies to parallel DSI only).
rs_get_thread_seq *@rs_id*	Returns the sequence number for entry *@rs_id* in the RSSD table **rs_threads**.
rs_get_thread_seq_ **noholdlock** *@rs_id*	Same as **rs_get_thread_seq**, but without using **holdlock**.
rs_update_threads *@rs_id*, *@rs_seq*	Updates the sequence number for entry *@rs_id* in the RSSD table **rs_threads** to *@rs_seq*.
(pre-15.0) **rs_set_isolation_level3**	Sets ANSI transaction isolation level 3 in the replicate database for each parallel DSI EXEC session.
(15.0) **rs_set_isolation_level**	Sets the ANSI transaction isolation level (0, 1, 2 or 3) in the replicate database for a DSI EXEC session.
rs_dsi_check_thread_lock	Checks if the DSI EXEC session is blocking other sessions while waiting to commit its replicate transaction; if so, its transaction is rolled back. This function string is related to the config. parameter **dsi_commit_check_locks_intrvl** (➢p.97).
rs_trunc_reset	Resets the secondary truncation point in a warm standby when switching databases.
rs_trunc_set	Sets the secondary truncation point in a warm standby when switching databases.
rs_dumpdb	Initiates a coordinated database dump (➢p.117). Note that there is no system-supplied default function string for this function, so a custom function string must be created.
rs_dumptran	Like **rs_dumpdb**, but for transaction log dumps.
rs_ticket_report	Executes the replicate stored procedure **rs_ticket_report** (➢p.132)

Function strings for the class-specific functions in the above table are usually not customised. Should this be required anyway, run **create/alter/delete function string** at the primary RepServer for the class. Syntax must be like the following (i.e. no repdef name must be specified):

> **create function string** *function_name*
> **for** function_class_name …

To display the actual function strings for these class-specific functions, use **rs_helpclassfstring** (➢p.76).

20.11 SQL input/output templates for function strings

The input/output language templates in the **scan/output** clauses of **create/alter function string** are used for generating the SQL statements to be executed in the replicate (or primary) database. These templates may contain the following elements:

- Literal text ('**insert MyTable values**' and the characters '**(**' , '**,**' and '**)**' in the first example below).
- Repdef variables, representing columns and parameters from the repdef ('**MyCol**' in the first example below).
- System variables, representing information about the replicated transaction itself, as described in the table on page 80 ('**rs_origin_begin_time**' in the first example below).
- Variable modifiers, with the syntax **?***variable***!***modifier***?** representing actual values in the system variables, as described in the table below ('**new**' and '**sys_raw**' in the first example below).

Examples (for a table repdef and function repdef, respectively):
create function string MyRepDef.rs_insert for MyFuncClass output language 'insert MyTable values (?MyCol!new?, ?rs_origin_begin_time!sys_raw?)'

create function string YourRepDef.your_proc for MyFuncClass output language 'exec your_replicate_proc ?your_p1!param?, ?your_p2!param_raw? insert LogTable values ("Called proc: ?your_p1!param?, ?your_p2!param_raw? ") '

Notes:

- Single quotes <u>must</u> be used as delimiters for a function string language template.
- The syntax characters **'**, **?** and **!** in the templates will not occur in the generated SQL statements. To make these characters appear in the final SQL statement, repeat each character: **''**, **??**, **!!** are evaluated as **'**, **?** and **!**, respectively.
- A semicolon (**;**) in a template is replaced by the character defined in the configuration parameter **dsi_cmd_separator** (default='**\n**';➢p.32), provided the configuration parameter **batch** (➢p.32) is set to **'on'** (=default). By specifying two semicolons (;;) in an input/output template, this replacement will not occur and a single semicolon will be part of the generated SQL statements.
- When creating or altering a function string, you should make sure the generated SQL statement is syntactically correct since RepServer does not verify this: if the replicate SQL statement contains errors, the dataserver returns an error and the DSI will shut down. If this happens, first correct the function string, and then resume the DSI (when a route is used, wait until the modified function string arrives in the replicate RSSD before resuming the DSI).
- The total length of the SQL statements generated for a function string must not exceed 64 Kb.
- In ASE 15.0 + RS 15.0, the **rs_truncate** function, when used to replicate truncation of a table partition, has a position-based function string parameter **?1!param?** which corresponds to the name of the partition being truncated. When a table is truncated (instead of a partition), this parameter is empty.

The following variable modifiers can be used:

Variable modifier	Effect on preceding variable
new or **new_raw**	Represents the value of a column in an inserted row, or the new value of an updated column
old or **old_raw**	Represents the value of a column in a deleted row, or the old (i.e. pre-update) value of an updated column
param or **param_raw**	Represents the value of a stored procedure parameter

user or **user_raw**	Can be used only in input and output templates for **rs_select** or **rs_select_with_lock** function strings. Represents the constant value for the preceding column or parameter as specified in the **where**-clause for the corresponding subscription (➢p.74)
sys or **sys_raw**	Used with system-defined variables (➢p.80)
text_status	Status indicator for a **text**, **image** or **rawobject** column. Possible values are: – **0x0000** - **text/image** column pointer is **NULL**, and no primary **text/image** data was modified – **0x0002** - **text/image** column pointer is initialized due to modifications to primary **text/image** data – **0x0004** - actual **text/image** data follows – **0x0008** - no **text/image** data follows because there is nothing to be replicated **0x0010** - **text/image** column pointer is **NULL**

For the modifiers **new**, **old**, **sys**, **param** and **user**, the following formatting is applied when data values are expanded in function strings:

- Character strings and date/time values are enclosed in single quotes ('*string*');
- For character strings and date/time values, each single quote (') inside the string is changed to two single quotes ('') (to preserve its meaning as an individual character).
- For character strings, each backslash-newline pair of characters (**\n**) inside the string is changed to **\\nn** (to preserve the individual characters).
- Values of **money** datatypes are preceded by the currency symbol (usually **'$'**).
- Values of binary datatypes are preceded by **'0x'**.

For the modifiers **new_raw**, **old_raw**, **sys_raw**, **param_raw** and **user_raw**, no such formatting is applied to data values. Because values of variables are expanded to plain ASCII characters in a function string, this formatting aspect should be taken into account when writing function strings in order to avoid syntax errors in the generated SQL statements. For example, the following examples will both generate syntactically correct SQL (assuming **MyTable** has one character column)

... **output language 'insert MyTable values (?MyColumn!new?)'**
... **output language 'insert MyTable values ("?MyColumn!new_raw?")'**

20.12 System variables in input/output templates

System variables contain information about the transaction being replicated, such as the primary database where the transaction originated, and the start- and commit times of the primary transaction.
The existing system variables are listed in the table below. These variables can be used in SQL templates for all functions; however, for **rs_select** and **rs_select_with_lock**, many variables are not relevant. Note that some variables may not always have a value, for example **rs_deliver_as_name** for a table repdef. When a system variable has no value, it evaluates to SQL **NULL**.

Most system-defined variables have a datatype of **varchar(30)**, except where indicated differently between parentheses. Note that actual values of system variables are expanded to ASCII format in a function string. Also note how ***_raw** modifiers affect this formatting (➢p.80).
All system-defined variables must use the **sys** or **sys_raw** modifier.

System variable	**Contents of variable**
rs_destination_db	Replicate database name
rs_destination_ds	Replicate dataserver name
rs_destination_ldb	Replicate logical database name (in a warm standby)
rs_destination_lds	Replicate logical dataserver name (in a warm standby)
rs_destination_ptype (**char(1)**)	Indicates whether the replicate logical database indicated by the variables **rs_destination_ldb** and **rs_destination_lds** is the active (**'A'**) or the standby (**'S'**) database
rs_destination_user	User (= ASE login) to execute the replicate transaction
rs_origin_user	User who executed the primary transaction
rs_origin (int)	Database ID of the primary database
rs_origin_db	Primary database name
rs_origin_ds	Primary dataserver name
rs_l_origin	Database ID of the primary database (when the primary

(**int**)	is part of a warm standby)
rs_origin_ldb	Primary logical database name (in a warm standby)
rs_origin_lds	Primary logical dataserver name (in a warm standby)
rs_deliver_as_name (**varchar(200)**)	Replicate procedure to be invoked for a function repdef.
rs_origin_begin_time (**datetime**)	Date/time when the primary transaction was started
rs_origin_commit_time (**datetime**)	Date/time when the primary transaction was committed With parallel DSI, this is only reliable for **rs_commit**
rs_origin_xact_id (**binary(120)**)	Transaction ID of the primary transaction
rs_origin_xact_name	Transaction name of the primary transaction
rs_origin_qid (**varbinary(36)**)	Queue ID of the first statement in the primary transaction
rs_secondary_qid (**varbinary(36)**)	Queue ID of the transaction in a (de)materialization queue
rs_last_text_chunk (**int**)	If **1**, indicates this is the last chunk of **text/image** data; if **0**, more data will follow.
rs_writetext_log (**int**)	If **0**, **rs_writetext** is still logging **text/image** data in the primary database transaction log; if **1**, it's ready.
rs_dump_dbname	Database name where a database dump or transaction log dump originated
rs_dump_label	Label information for a dump: in ASE, this variable contains the date/time when the dump indicated by the variable **rs_dump_dbname** originated
rs_dump_timestamp (**varbinary(16)**)	The value of the ASE database timestamp (**@@dbts**) at the moment when the dump indicated by the variable **rs_dump_dbname** originated
(RS 15.1) rs_dump_status	For use with the **rs_dumptran** function: if **1**, the **dump transaction** command included **with standby_access**; if **0**, it did not.
rs_default_fs (**text**)	System-supplied default function string text for the function. Applies to repdef-specific functions only, and must use the **sys** modifier. See below for details.

rs_default_fs
The variable **rs_default_fs** is a special case: it represents the default, system-supplied function string for a repdef-specific function. By including **rs_default_fs** in a customized function string, the default functionality of the function can be extended with custom processing.
For example, the following function string logs every row deletion in a separate table:

create function string MyRepDef.rs_delete for MyFuncClass output language '?rs_default_fs!sys? ; insert MyLogTable values (?MyKeyCol!old?, "Row was deleted from ?rs_origin_ds!sys_raw?.?rs_origin_db!sys_raw? by ?rs_origin_user!sys_raw? at ?rs_origin_begin_time!sys_raw? ")'

Notes:

- In this example, the semicolon after **?rs_default_fs!sys?** is essential: although undocumented, it appears that any other function string text is ignored once **rs_default_fs** is included in the template. This effect seems to be limited to the first semicolon following **rs_default_fs**.
- **rs_default_fs** applies to repdef-specific functions only.
- **rs_default_fs** can only use the **sys** modifier.
- **rs_default_fs** can only be used for dataservers that can process ASE T-SQL syntax.
- Minimal column replication (➢p.49) does not combine well with customized function strings for most repdef-specific functions: since not all columns may be replicated, customized function strings cannot refer to columns that are not in the **primary key** clause of the repdef. Custom function strings can only be created for **rs_update** and **rs_delete**, and only by using **rs_default_fs**. For **rs_insert**, all columns are always replicated, so no restrictions apply.

20.13 Tricks with function strings

Creating custom function strings offers enormous possibilities: practically anything that can be done in SQL can be put in a function string. To illustrate what's possible, here are just a few examples.

Conflict resolution for conflicting updates

In a replication system where multiple primary tables are replicated to a single replicate table, conflicts between different updates may occur. As an example, imagine a central inventory table to track product inventory in a central warehouse. Each sales office has its own copy of the table; for each sale, the central replicate table should be updated to reflect the decreased inventory count.
The problem is that the replicate **update** statement specifies the new value of the column in the primary table as an absolute value instead of a relative value, i.e.:

```
update Inventory set Quantity = 105     -- old value was 110; 5 units were sold
where ProductID = 9876
```

Consequently, updates from different sales offices will overwrite each other's values causing the central inventory table not to reflect the proper inventory count. Instead, the central table's count should simply be reduced by the amount sold (in the above example, 5). This can be achieved with the following function string, where **?Quantity!old?-?Quantity!new?** represents the amount by which the column has changed:

```
alter function string Inventory.rs_update
for rs_sqlserver_function_class
output language
'update Inventory
 set Quantity = Quantity - (?Quantity!old? - ?Quantity!new?)
 where ProductID = ?ProductID!new?'
```

Actually, to make the whole thing work, there's more to it: the primary tables in the sales offices must somehow also be synchronized with the actual inventory count of the central table, for example by replicating the central table back to the sales offices databases. If you're facing this kind of design problem, it is recommended consulting the *Replication Server Design Guide* (➢p.13) for background information about replication system design issues.

The replicate database as archive: suppressing delete statements

Let's assume the replicate database is used as an archive of historical data. All insertions and updates should be replicated, but no data should be deleted from the archive, even when it is deleted from the primary database. One way of implementing this is with an empty (single-space) function string for **rs_delete**:

```
alter function string MyTable.rs_delete
for rs_sqlserver_function_class
output language ' '
```

With this function string, a primary delete is not applied to the replicate database. (Alternatively, it is also possible to suppress replication of certain primary statements by preceding them with the ASE statement **set replication off** (➢p.18) in the primary database)

Replicating ad-hoc SQL statements

Let's assume the following table is replicated:

```
create table RepSQL (cmd varchar(255))
```

... and this function string exists for **rs_insert** for this table's repdef:

```
alter function string RepSQL.rs_insert
for rs_sqlserver_function_class
output language 'rollback ; ?cmd!new_raw?'
```

Now, by inserting a SQL statement as a string into this primary table, that SQL statement will be executed in all replicate databases using this function string class:

```
-- inserted in the primary database:
insert RepSQL values ('reorg rebuild MyTable PKIndex')
```

```
-- executed in the replicate database:
reorg rebuild MyTable PKIndex
```

One possible application of this trick is to keep passwords for identically named logins synchronized across different servers. In ASE, this could be done as follows:

```
-- inserted in the primary database:
insert RepSQL values
('exec sp_password current_pwd, new_pwd, login_name')
```

To make this last example work, the maintenance user for the replicate database must have **sso_role** permission (this is required to run **sp_password**).

Notes:

- The **rollback** in the function string avoids errors for statements or procedures that cannot run in a transaction (like **sp_password**, **reorg**, and many others).
- Any output from the SQL statement (such as output of stored procedures), will end up in the replicate RepServer's errorlog.
- In this example, note that the table **RepSQL** doesn't actually need to exist in the replicate database. The rows in the primary table can be deleted regularly - but create an empty function string for **rs_delete** first (or use the ASE **truncate table** statement).

20.14 User-defined functions: obsolete commands

The commands described in this section represent functionality from old versions of RepServer, where stored procedure executions could be replicated with table (!) repdefs. These commands have become obsolete since RepServer version 11.0 when procedure replication could be implemented more easily with function repdefs (i.e. **create/alter/drop function replication definition**).
Although these commands are not needed anymore today, they are still supported, and included here for completeness. Nevertheless, their use is not recommended unless you really understand what you're doing. For more information, see the appendix about *'Asynchronous Procedures'* in the *Replication Server Administration Guide* (➢p.13). These functions do not support identifiers longer than 30 bytes.

create function *repdef_name.function_name* **(** [@*param datatype* [, ...]] **)**
Creates a user-defined function.

alter function *repdef_name.function_name*
add parameters @*param datatype* [,...]
Adds parameters to a user-defined function.

drop function *repdef_name.function_name*
Drops a user-defined function.

21 Error classes

Error actions define how RepServer handles dataserver errors encountered by the DSI. An error class is a collection of error actions which can be associated with a (replicate) database connection. By creating different error classes, different error handling actions can be defined for each replicate database. Note that an error class or an assigned error action is unrelated to a particular repdef or subscription.
rs_sqlserver_error_class is the default error class, aimed at ASE databases. For non-ASE databases, custom error classes can be created.

assign action { **ignore** | **warn** | **retry_log** | **log** | **retry_stop** | **stop_replication** }
for *error_class_name* **to** *dataserver_error_no* [, *...more dataserver errors...*]
Defines an error action for one or more error numbers for the specified error class.
Example: **assign action ignore for rs_sqlserver_error_class to 2601**

The possible error actions are the following (the corresponding value of the **rs_erroractions.action** column is indicated between parentheses):

- **ignore** (**action=1**) - the SQL statement is considered to be successfully completed (even if it actually failed); continues with the next SQL statement in the transaction.
- **warn** (**action=3**) - identical to **ignore**, but also writes a warning message to the RepServer errorlog.
- **log** (**action=4**) - rolls back the current transaction, logs it into the RSSD exceptions log (➢p.85), writes a message to the RepServer errorlog, and continues with the next transaction.
- **retry_log** (**action=5**) - rolls back the current transaction and retries it. If it still fails after the number of retries configured with **command_retry** (➢p.85; default=3), logs the transaction into the RSSD exceptions log (➢p.85), writes a message to the RepServer errorlog, and continues with the next transaction.
- **retry_stop** (**action=6**) - same as **retry_log**, but suspends the DSI if the transaction keeps failing; does not log the transaction into the RSSD exceptions log.
- **stop_replication** (**action=2**) - the default action: rolls back the current transaction, suspends the DSI and writes an error message to the RepServer errorlog.

Notes:

- **assign action** immediately affects the error handling of all DSIs in the RepServer where **assign action** is executed. DSIs in replicate RepServers are affected immediately once the corresponding RSSD modifications have been replicated to the replicate RSSD.
- **assign action** must be executed at the primary RepServer for the error class.
- Once assigned, an error action cannot be dropped. To change the action, re-assign it with **assign action**. Re-assigning the action **stop_replication** effectively drops an action by reversing it to the default.
- When assigning an action for the first time for the default ASE error class **rs_sqlserver_error_class**, you'll have to run the command **create error class rs_sqlserver_error_class** once to initialize the class (**rs_init_erroractions** is not required). When using routes, run this command at a primary RepServer.
- ***Warning:*** ignoring errors may lead to inconsistent data in the replicate database since replicate DML may not have been executed successfully, or transactions may not been applied completely (remember that replicating entire transactions is a basic principle of RepServer; ➢p.**9**).

create error class *error_class_name*
Creates a new, empty error class. After creating the error class, the RSSD procedure **rs_init_erroractions** can be used to initialize the error class.
Error class names may not start with **'rs_'**.
Example: **create error class MyErrorClass**

drop error class *error_class_name*
Drops the specified error class, including all defined error actions for this class. The error class must not be used by a database connection.
The system-defined error class **rs_sqlserver_error_class** cannot be dropped.

move primary of error class *error_class_name* **to** *current_repserver*
Changes the primary RepServer for the specified error class to the current RepServer. This command must be executed in the RepServer that will be the new primary RepServer for the class (i.e. in RepServer *current_repserver*). There must be routes (in both directions) between the current RepServer and the old primary RepServer for this class.
Example: **move primary of error class MyErrorClass to PROD_BACKUP**

rs_init_erroractions *new_error_class_name*, *template_error_class_name*
(RSSD procedure) Initializes a newly created error class by copying all assigned error actions from an existing ('template') error class. This is a one-time operation; no further relationship will be maintained between these error classes (unlike function string inheritance for function string classes, which is dynamic).
Example: **rs_init_erroractions MyErrorClass, rs_sqlserver_error_class**

rs_helpclass [*error_class_name*]
(RSSD procedure) Without parameter, displays a list of all error classes (as well as function string classes) in this RSSD. With parameter, displays only the specified class. Note that **rs_helpclass** does not show the actions assigned to error numbers in the error class. To display these actions, run this query in the RSSD (all errors that are not displayed are handled as **stop_replication**):

```
select ds_errorid, action = v.name
from rs_erroractions e, rs_classes c, rs_tvalues v
where e.errorclassid = c.classid
and e.action = v.value
and v.type = 'ERR'
and c.classname = 'error_class_name'
order by 1
```

rs_helperror *dataserver_error_number* [,**'v'**]
(RSSD procedure) For all error classes in this RSSD, displays the error action associated with the specified dataserver error number. With **'v'**, displays the corresponding ASE error message text (useful only for error numbers in ASE).

alter connection to *dataserver.database*
set error class [**to**] *error_class_name*
Changes the error class for the specified database connection, taking effect once the connection is resumed (it is good practice to suspend the connection before changing a parameter). When a connection is created, an error class is specified with **create connection**, but this can later be changed with **alter connection**.

Changing the error class is meaningful only when the connection corresponds to a replicate database; it has no effect for a primary-only database or for materialization queries on primary data.
To determine the error class configured for a connection, run this query in the RSSD:

select dsname, dbname, classname 'Error class'
from rs_databases d, rs_classes c
where d.errorclassid = c.classid

alter connection to *dataserver.database*
set command_retry [**to**] *nr_retries*
Defines the number of times a failed transaction is retried when the **retry_log** or **retry_log** action has been assigned to the corresponding error.
configure replication server sets the server-wide default value (default=3); **alter connection** overrides this for a particular connection. Modified values take effect after resuming a connection.
Examples: **alter connection to REP2.salesdb set command_retry '6'**
configure replication server set command_retry to '4'

21.1 RSSD tables - error classes

Error classes are stored in the RSSD table **rs_classes**, with **rs_classes.classtype** = **'E'**. The assigned error actions in a class are stored in the RSSD table **rs_erroractions**. When a RepServer has an outgoing route, these tables are replicated to the destination RSSD.

22 RSSD exceptions log

Transactions causing problems in the DSI may be skipped (for example with **resume connection**...**skip transaction**) and logged in the RSSD exceptions log. Transactions may also be logged directly (and not skipped) with **sysadmin log_first_tran**.
The RSSD exceptions log consists of the RSSD tables **rs_exceptshdr**, **rs_exceptscmd** and **rs_systext** (only for rows with **rs_systext.texttype** = **'C'**; **rs_systext** is also used for other purposes, like storing function strings).
The maximum number of statements and the maximum amount of **text/image** data to be logged can be configured with parameters **dsi_max_cmds_to_log** and **dsi_max_text_to_log**, respectively (➢p.33). By default, everything is logged.
In addition, the RSSD table **rs_exceptslast** contains the queue ID for the last transaction written to the RSSD exceptions log tables, for each primary database (this does not include transactions skipped by **sysadmin log_first_tran**).

rs_helpexception [*transaction_ID* [, **'v'**]]
(RSSD procedure) Displays transactions in the RSSD exceptions log. Without any parameters, displays a list of transactions, identified by a unique transaction ID. With *transaction_ID*, displays additional details for that transaction; when **'v'** is also specified, displays the full text of the transaction. With **'v'**, the output of **rs_helpexception** may look a bit puzzling, but the actual replicate SQL statements for this transaction are usually quite easily visible.
Example: **rs_helpexception 117, 'v'**

rs_delexception [*transaction_ID*]
(RSSD procedure) Without any parameter, displays a summary list of transactions in the RSSD exceptions log, identical to **rs_helpexception**. With *transaction_ID*, deletes that specific transaction from the RSSD exceptions log.
To delete many exceptions in a single query according to certain criteria, use one of the RSSD queries from the electronic supplement to this book (➢p.8).

23 Routes

23.1 Summary

A route is a one-way connection from one RepServer (the 'source') to another RepServer (the 'destination'). A route allows the destination RepServer to subscribe to repdefs/publications, and to execute request functions (➢p.41). Routes can provide load balancing and reduce downtime, but they also increase latency and overall system complexity.
A route can be direct or indirect. An indirect route runs via one or more other 'intermediate' RepServers, while a direct route does not. Also see page 89.

In 12.6, a route can only be created when the source RepServer has a classic ASE RSSD. To create a route for a source RepServer with an embedded RSSD (➢p.110),

15.0 is required.
In all RepServer versions, routes cannot be used for the connection to the active or standby database in a warm standby. However, similar functionality is available through database repdefs (➢p.43), which can be subscribed to across a route.

Each route has an associated RSI ('RepServer Interface') thread in RepServer. RSI queues (outbound only) have a positive, 8-digit number. For example, **'16777321:0 REP2B'** (as shown by **admin who**) indicates an RSI queue to destination RepServer **REP2B**.

23.2 Route commands

create route to *destination_repserver*
[**set username** [**to**] *repserver_user_name*]
[**set password** [**to**] { **'***password***'** | **null** }]
[**set** *route_config_parameter* [**to**] **'***value***'** [*...more* **set** *clauses...*]] ➢p.88
[**set** *security_config_parameter* [**to**] **'***value***'** [*...more* **set** *clauses...*]] ➢p.94
Creates a direct route from the current (=source) RepServer to the specified destination RepServer. The destination RepServer must be running, must be part of the same replication domain as the current RepServer (i.e. use the same ID server), and its servername must be defined in the **interfaces** file (Windows: **SQL.ini** file) used by the source RepServer.
The username and password (by default, *destination_repserver*_**rsi** and *destination_repserver*_**rsi_ps**) are used to log into the destination RepServer; without **set password**, or with **null** (without quotes!), a blank password is used. The username and password are inserted into the RSSD table **rs_maintusers** in the source RSSD. When using network security mechanisms (Kerberos, DCE), the username/password can be omitted. For *route_config_parameter*, see page 88. For *security_config_parameter*, see page 94.
For **create route** to succeed, log transfer must be enabled for the source RSSD, and the RepAgent must be running in the source RSSD. To test whether a route is working properly, create a table repdef for a non-existent table in the source RepServer, and verify that it arrives in the replicate RSSD.
In 15.0, when creating a route for a source RepServer with an embedded RSSD:

- RepServer automatically configures and starts the ERSSD RepAgent (**dbltm**, an OpenServer application); a RepAgent **.cfg** file is created in **$SYBASE**.
- The name of the ERSSD RepAgent must be in the **interfaces** file (Windows: **SQL.INI**); it is defined by the configuration parameter **erssd_ra** (➢p.88).
- After RepServer startup, the ERSSD RepAgent is not started until the period set by **rec_daemon_sleep_time** has passed (default=120 seconds).

Example: **create route to REP2**
set username REP2_rsi set password REP2_rsi_ps

create route to *destination_repserver* **set next site** [**to**] *intermediate_repserver*
Creates an indirect route from the current (=source) RepServer to the specified destination RepServer, via the specified intermediate RepServer.
Direct routes must already exist from the source RepServer to the intermediate RepServer and from the intermediate RepServer to the destination RepServer.
Example: **create route to REP2 set next site to REP3**

drop route to *destination_repserver* [**with nowait**]
Executed in the source RepServer, drops the route to the specified destination RepServer. Before dropping a route, all subscriptions at the destination RepServer for primary data in the source RepServer must be dropped. Also, any indirect routes using this route must have been dropped.
In 15.0, for a source RepServer with an embedded RSSD, when dropping the last outgoing route, RepServer automatically stops the ERSSD RepAgent and disables log transfer for the ERSSD.
with nowait is for troubleshooting, and to be used as a last resort only (for example when destination RepServer is unavailable). **with nowait** forcefully closes and drops the route at the source RepServer, regardless of other RepServers in the route. In the process, error messages may be written to the errorlogs of the involved RepServers.
After using **with nowait**, the command **sysadmin purge_route_at_replicate** (see below) should be executed in the destination RepServer to clean up the route. If subscriptions were still active in the destination RepServer, manual cleanup of **rs_subscriptions** in the destination RSSD may also be required.

sysadmin purge_route_at_replicate, *source_repserver*
Executed at the destination RepServer, removes all information about the route from the source RepServer from the destination RSSD. Use this command after a route was dropped (in the source RepServer) with **drop route**...**with nowait**.

alter route to *destination_repserver*
{ **set username** [**to**] *repserver_user_name* |
set password [**to**] { '*password*' | **null** } |
set *route_config_parameter* [**to**] '*value*' | ➢p.88
set *security_config_parameter* [**to**] '*value*' | ➢p.94
set security_services [**to**] **'default'** }
Modifies route-specific settings for the route to the specified destination RepServer. **set security_services to 'default'** resets all network security features for this route to their server-wide defaults (➢p.94). The other options are similar to **create route**. Unlike **create route**, **alter route** can set only one attribute at a time. Most changes to configuration parameters take effect once the route is resumed.
Examples: **alter route to REP2 set username REP2_rsi**
alter route to REP2 set password REP2_rsi_mypassword
Notes:

- By specifying **set username** (and **set password**) for an indirect route, it is changed to a direct route.
- Specifying **set username** for a direct route changes the username for connecting to the destination RepServer (as stored in the RSSD table **rs_maintuser** in the source RSSD; ➢p.108).
- **set password** changes the password for connecting to the destination RepServer (as stored in the RSSD table **rs_maintuser** in the source RSSD; ➢p.108).
- When changing the username or password for a route, the corresponding actual username and password in the destination RepServer must be changed separately by the DBA (with **alter user**).

alter route to *destination_repserver*
set next site [**to**] *intermediate_repserver*
Changes the (direct or indirect) route from the current (=source) RepServer to the specified destination RepServer to an indirect route via the specified intermediate RepServer.
Direct routes must already exist from the source RepServer to the intermediate RepServer and from the intermediate RepServer to the destination RepServer. It is recommended to quiesce the current RepServer (➢p.116), and quiesce the route (with **admin quiesce_force_rsi**; ➢p.88) before altering it.
Example: **alter route to REP2 set next site to REP4**

configure route ...
Identical to **alter route**.

resume route to *destination_repserver*
[**skip transaction with large message**]
Resumes the route to the specified RepServer, which must currently be suspended. With **skip transaction with large message**, ignores the first transaction with a message larger than 16Kb (this applies only to direct routes with a replicate site version of **1210** or earlier).

suspend route to *destination_repserver*
Suspends the route to the specified RepServer.

23.3 RSSD tables - routes

Information about outgoing and incoming routes in a RepServer are stored in the RSSD table **rs_routes**. When a route is direct, **rs_routes.through_rsid** = **rs_routes.dest_rsid**; for indirect routes, these columns have different values. Join **rs_routes** with the RSSD table **rs_sites** to find the names corresponding to these RepServer IDs.
When a route exists, the following RSSD tables in the source RSSD are replicated to the destination RepServer RSSD: **rs_databases**, **rs_objects**, **rs_columns**, **rs_routes**, **rs_classes**, **rs_funcstrings**, **rs_erroractions**, **rs_functions**, **rs_systext**, **rs_dbreps** and **rs_dbsubsets**. Consequently, when repdefs, function strings, error classes etc. are created or modified in the source RepServer, these changes are replicated to the destination RSSD. Therefore, a RepAgent should always be running in the source RSSD when a RepServer has an outgoing route.

23.4 Getting information about routes

rs_helproute [*destination_repserver*]
(RSSD procedure) Displays information about routes in the RSSD table **rs_routes**. With a parameter, displays only routes involving that RepServer; otherwise displays all known routes. When a route is indirect, the output shows **'(Next site:...)'**.
rs_helproute does not display route-specific configuration settings (see below).

admin show_connections
Displays the current status of outgoing routes -indicated as 'RSI'- (as well as database connections) from this RepServer.

admin who, rsi
Displays status info and some statistics for all outgoing routes from this RepServer.

admin quiesce_force_rsi
Determines whether the RepServer is currently quiescent, and forces the RepServer to flush its RSI queues for all outgoing routes. It is recommended to suspend incoming routes and incoming log transfer before running **admin quiesce_force_rsi**; otherwise, the RSI queues may keep receiving new, incoming messages.

23.5 Configuration parameters for routes

The following configuration parameters apply to routes. They can be modified (one parameter at a time) with **configure replication server** to set RepServer-wide defaults; when specified with **create route** or **alter route**, these server-wide defaults are overridden for the specified route.
Notes:

- All parameter values, including integers, must be specified as quoted strings.
- Except for **disk_affinity**, all parameters are stored in the RSSD table **rs_config**, and changes take effect once the route is resumed (it is good practice to suspend the route before changing a parameter). For details about parameter storage in **rs_config**, see page 91.
- In pre-15.0.1, there is no system-supplied procedure to display non-default configuration parameter settings for a route. Instead, use the RSSD procedure **rs_helpcfg_route** (included in the electronic supplement to this book; ➢p.8). In 15.0.1, **admin config** can also be used (➢p.90).

List of configuration parameters for routes:

- **disk_affinity** - when set to a disk partition name, tries to allocate disk space for this route's queues on that partition (➢p.101). When **'off'** (=default), space is allocated on the next free segment in the current (or next) partition.
- **(15.0) erssd_ra** - the name of the RSSD RepAgent for a RepServer with an embedded RSSD; default= '*ERSSD_name*_**rs**'. This name must be in the **interfaces** file (Windows: **SQL.INI**).
- **rsi_batch_size** - the number of bytes sent to the destination RepServer before requesting a truncation point (allowing to delete sent messages from the source RSI queue). In 15.0.1, possible values are from **1024** to **134217728**; default = **262144**. In pre-15.0.1, possible values are from **1024** to **262144** (=default).
- **rsi_fadeout_time** - the number of seconds of idle time before the connection to the destination RepServer is temporarily closed. The default is **-1** (meaning the connection is never closed).
- **rsi_packet_size** - the network packet size (in bytes) for the connection to the destination RepServer. Possible values are from **1024** to **8192**; default = **2048**.
- **rsi_sync_interval** - the number of seconds between sending RSI synchronization messages to the destination RepServer. This must be > **0**; default = **60**.
- **rsi_xact_with_large_msg** - only for direct routes with a route version of 12.1 or earlier, specifies what happens when a large message is encountered. Possible values are **'skip'** (the message) and **'shutdown'** (the connection; =default).
- **save_interval** - the number of minutes (default = **0**) messages in the RSI queue are saved after being applied successfully to the destination RepServer. Increasing this setting improves recoverability (through **sysadmin restore_dsi_saved_segments**), but requires additional disk space. The current setting is displayed by **admin who, sqm** (in the column **Save_Int:Seg**).
- The configuration parameters related to network security, as described on page 94, can also be defined for a specific route.

Examples: **alter route to REP2 set rsi_packet_size to '8192'**
configure replication server set rsi_sync_interval to '120'

23.6 Direct & indirect routes

Routes can be direct or indirect. An indirect route runs via one or more other 'intermediate' RepServers, which do not process transactions but only forward them. A direct route has no intermediate RepServers.
For replication functionality, direct or indirect routes are equivalent. Indirect routes can provide better performance than direct routes in certain replication topologies where the same data is replicated to multiple destination RepServers.
Direct routes can be changed to indirect routes and vice versa:

- A direct route is created with **create route**...**set username**.
- An indirect route is created with **create route**...**set next site**, provided the necessary direct routes to and from the intermediate RepServer already exist.
- A direct route is changed to an indirect route with **alter route**...**set next site**.
- An indirect route is changed to a direct route with **alter route**...**set username**.

It is possible to create an indirect route with multiple intermediate RepServers; however, note that this is likely to increase overhead, complexity and latency. To create a route from RepServer A to RepServer D via RepServers B and C (i.e. A→B→C→D), follow these steps:

1. In RepServers A, B, C, create direct routes A→B, B→C and C→D, respectively;
2. In B, create an indirect route from B→D with C as the intermediate site;
3. In A, create an indirect route from A→D with B as the intermediate site;
4. When a repdef is now created at RepServer A, it should be replicated to the RSSD of RepServer D (check with the RSSD procedure **rs_helprep**).

For steps 2 and 3, the indirect route can either be created directly with **create route**...**set next site**, or a direct route can be created first, which is then made indirect with **alter route**...**set next site**.

23.7 Site-, System- and Route versions

The version of an individual RepServer is known as its 'site version'. This is a 4-digit integer; for example, **1260** for RS 12.6.
Two RepServers with a route between them may well be running different versions of the RepServer software (for example, 12.6 and 15.0.1). Each route has a 'route version' associated with it, indicating the lowest 'site version' of the RepServers involved in the route. The route version indicates which RepServer features are supported over the route. For example, to replicate **char(1500)** columns in ASE 12.5 over a route, the route version must be **1250** or higher.

admin version
Displays the detailed version ID of the current RepServer.

admin show_site_version
Displays the site version (see above) for this RepServer.

sysadmin site_version [, *version*]
Displays or sets the site version (see above) for this RepServer. Do not use quotes around *version*.

sysadmin system_version [, *version*]
Executed in the ID server, displays or sets the system version (see above) for a replication domain, indicating that all RepServers known in this ID server have at least that site version. Valid system version numbers include **1200**, **1210**, **1250** and **1260** (as well as others, corresponding to earlier RepServer releases). For a newly installed RepServer, the system version is **1102**. Do not use quotes around *version*.

admin show_route_versions
Displays the 'route version' (a RepServer version number) for all routes to and from this RepServer.

sysadmin fast_route_upgrade, *destination_repserver*
Upgrades the route from the current RepServer to the destination RepServer. This updates the 'route version' to the lowest 'site version' of the two RepServers; both RepServers will then be able to use all RepServer features supported by the new route version.

Also, upgrading a route will re-materialize the subscriptions for the RSSD tables. Upgrading a route may fail if the source RepServer has already used RepServer features that were not available in the destination RepServer. In this case, the route must be upgraded with the RSM Server commands **route_upgrade** etc. (see below) or with the RepServer plug-in for Sybase Central.

route_upgrade *source_repserver.destination_repserver*
(RSM command) Executed in RSM Server (➢p.116), this RSM command upgrades the route from *source_repserver* to *destination_repserver* to the lowest 'site version' of either RepServer (see above).

route_upgrade_recovery *source_replication_server.remote_replication_server*
(RSM command) Executed in RSM Server (➢p.116), this RSM command recovers a failed route upgrade.

route_upgrade_status
(RSM command) Executed in RSM Server (➢p.116), this RSM command displays whether routes need to be upgraded or recovered from a failed upgrade attempt.

24 Configuration parameters

RepServer configuration parameters can be divided in RepServer-wide parameters (set by **configure replication server**), and parameters specific for connections, routes, etc. (set by **alter connection/alter route** etc.):

Config. parameters for:	**Described at:**
database connections	page 32
parallel DSI	page 96
RepServer-wide settings	page 91
network security	page 94
warm standby	page 69
routes	page 88
monitor counters	page 122
embedded RSSD	page 110

24.1 Configuration parameters - commands

configure replication server set *config_param* **to** '*value*'
Sets the configuration parameter *config_param* for this RepServer. Note that '*value*' must be specified as a quoted string, even when the actual value is an integer.
Configuration parameters set by **configure replication server** act as RepServer-wide defaults. For individual connections or routes, some of these server-wide settings (as indicated in the respective sections) can be overridden with **create/alter** [**logical**] **connection** or **create/alter route**.
When a configuration parameter is changed, the moment it takes effect depends on the type of parameter:

- For most parameters related to connections or routes, changes take effect after the connection or route is resumed (it is good practice to suspend the connection or route before changing the parameter).
- For most RepServer-wide parameters, changes take effect after a RepServer restart. The parameters for monitor counters (➢p.122) are dynamic; most **msg_*** parameters for network security (➢p.94) are also dynamic.

Example: **configure replication server set memory_limit to '100'**

(15.0.1) admin config [, '*name*']
(15.0.1) admin config, 'connection', *dataserver*, *database* [, '*name*']
(15.0.1) admin config, 'logical_connection', *logical_ds*, *logical_db* [, '*name*']
(15.0.1) admin config, 'route', *destination_repserver* [, '*name*']
Displays configuration parameters, including config-, run- and default values, datatype and allowed values, and whether a change takes effect immediately. With **'connection'**, **'logical_connection'** or **'route'**, displays all parameters applying to the specified connection, logical connection or route. Without any of these, displays all RepServer-wide parameters only. With '*name*', displays only those parameters that contain the specified substring (no wildcards can be used).

rs_configure [*config_param* [, '*value*']]
(RSSD procedure; deprecated!) Without any parameters, displays some -but not all- RepServer-wide configuration parameters; non-default parameter settings for specific connections or routes are not displayed. With *config_param*, displays only parameters

starting with this string. With '*value*', changes the parameter.
Warning: Please do not use **rs_configure** to change parameter settings, but use **configure replication server** instead (since this behaves more consistently).

24.2 RSSD tables - configuration parameters

With few exceptions, all configuration parameters are stored as rows in the RSSD table **rs_config** (**disk_affinity** is stored the RSSD table **rs_diskaffinity**; ➢p.101). The value of a configuration parameter is stored in the **charvalue** column of **rs_config**. The **objid** column indicates the scope of the configuration parameter setting:

- For rows with **rs_config.objid** = **0x0**, the parameter is a RepServer-wide default value. These rows are modified with **configure replication server**.
  Most configuration parameters are inserted into **rs_config** when the RSSD is created, along with their default values. Some RepServer-wide configuration parameters do not exist in **rs_config** by default, but only when a non-default value has been set with **configure replication server**.
- For rows with **rs_config.objid** <> **0x0**, the parameter is a non-default setting for a specific database connection, logical connection, or route, overriding the RepServer-wide default setting for that parameter. These rows are inserted or modified with **create/alter** [**logical**] **connection** and **create/alter route**.

How connection- or route-specific parameters are stored in rs_config
For a connection- or route-specific parameter, **rs_config.objid** indicates which connection or route the parameter applies to: if the parameter applies to a connection, this column contains the database ID; if it applies to a route, it contains the route ID. Unfortunately, it isn't always easy to decode **rs_config.objid**, since its value is in hexadecimal, and may also be byte-swapped in a platform-dependent way.
The RSSD procedures **rs_helpcfg_db** and **rs_helpcfg_route**, which are included in the electronic supplement to this book (➢p.8), properly decode **rs_config.objid**. These procedures can be used to display non-default configuration parameter settings for a specific connection or route (note that there is no system-supplied procedure to display this information).
In 15.0.1, **admin config** (➢p.90) also displays the connection- and route-specific parameters, but requires specifying the name of the connection or route.

Once a connection- or route-specific parameter setting exists, the corresponding row in **rs_config** is not deleted until the connection or route itself is dropped. To reset the parameter for that connection or route to the RepServer-wide default, the corresponding row must be deleted manually from **rs_config** (obviously, the parameter can also be set explicitly to the current RepServer-wide default with **alter** [**logical**] **connection** or **alter route**, but any subsequent changes to the RepServer-wide default will not apply to the connection or route in question). To delete the row for a connection- or route-specific parameter from **rs_config**, it may be required to decode the value of **rs_config.objid**; again, see the RSSD procedures **rs_helpcfg_db** or **rs_helpcfg_route** for inspiration (➢p.8).

Run values and configured values
For parameter settings changed with **configure replication server**, no separate run value and config value are maintained in the RSSD: when a parameter value is set, this is reflected immediately in **rs_config.charvalue**. In 15.0.1, **admin config** (➢p.90) displays the config and run values, which are maintained in RepServer memory.
For most connection- or route-specific parameters, changes only become active once the corresponding connection or route is resumed (so it may need to be suspended first). For most RepServer-wide parameters, changes become active only after a RepServer restart. Since there is no way of telling when a parameter in **rs_config** was last updated, it may not be possible to determine whether a parameter setting in **rs_config** has already taken effect.
If it is required to keep track of each configuration parameter change, create a trigger on **rs_config** to log each inserted, modified and deleted row into a different, user-created table. The electronic supplement to this book (➢p.8) contains an example.

To display RepServer-wide settings, use the RSSD procedure **rs_helpcfg** (in the electronic supplement to this book; ➢p.8). In 15.0.1, **admin config** can also be used (➢p.90).

24.3 RepServer-wide configuration parameters

The configuration parameters in this section can be changed with **configure replication server** (do not use the deprecated RSSD procedure **rs_configure**!). For most

RepServer-wide configuration parameters, unless mentioned otherwise, changes take effect only after a RepServer restart.
The current settings can be displayed with **admin config** (in 15.0.1) or with the RSSD procedure **rs_helpcfg** (included in the electronic supplement to this book; ➢p.8).
List of RepServer-wide configuration parameters:

- **byte_order** - a read-only parameter indicating the byte ordering used by RepServer on this platform (this is used by some RSSD stored procedures).
- **current_rssd_version** - a read-only parameter indicating the current RepServer version; for example **'1260'** for version 12.6. Only to be modified by the **rs_init** utility during an upgrade or downgrade!
- **minimum_rssd_version** - a read-only parameter indicating the lowest RepServer version that can use this RSSD. Only to be modified by the **rs_init** utility during an upgrade or downgrade!
- **prev_rssd_version** - a read-only parameter indicating the value of **current_rssd_version** before an upgrade. To be modified only by **rs_init**!
- **prev_min_rssd_version** - a read-only parameter indicating the value of **minimum_rssd_version** before an upgrade. To be modified only by **rs_init**!
- **rsm_proc_compat_version** - a read-only parameter related to RSM Server. Do not modify manually!
- **prev_rsm_proc_compat_version** - a read-only parameter related to RSM Server. Do not modify manually!
- **cm_max_connections** - the maximum number of outgoing connections for this RepServer (default = **64**).
- **cm_fadeout_time** - the number of seconds (default = **300**; minimum = **1**) of idle time before the RSSD connection is closed. When set to **-1**, it will never be closed.
- **ha_failover** - when **'on'** (default = **'off'**), ASE-to-ASE failover is enabled for connections to ASE databases; this uses the High Availability feature in ASE (**ASE_HA**). Note that this does not apply to the RSSD connection; RSSD failover is enabled by setting the line **RSSD_ha_failover=yes** (default = **no**) in the **.cfg** file.
- **id_server** - the name of the ID server for this RepServer (➢p.106). Do not change this parameter unless you know what you're doing!
- **oserver** - the name of this RepServer. Do not change this parameter unless you know what you're doing!
- **init_sqm_write_delay** - the time (in milliseconds) an SQM thread will wait before writing a not-completely-filled block of messages to disk. If no new messages have arrived after this time, the wait time is doubled; when the wait time reaches the current setting of **init_sqm_write_max_delay**, the block is written anyway (default = **1000** = 1 second). In 15.0.1, this setting takes effect immediately without a RepServer reboot.
- **init_sqm_write_max_delay** - the maximum SQM write waiting time: see **init_sqm_write_delay** (default = **10000** = 10 seconds). In 15.0.1, this setting takes effect immediately without a RepServer reboot.
- **memory_limit** - the maximum amount of memory (in Mb; default = **40** in 15.0; **20** in pre-15.0) that can be allocated by RepServer. In 15.0.1, this setting takes effect immediately without a RepServer reboot (note: the **rs_config** table still contains the parameter **memory_max**, although this is now obsolete and was replaced by **memory_limit** since version 11.5).
- **num_client_connections** - the maximum number of incoming client connections (default = **30**) for this RepServer.
- **num_concurrent_subs** - the maximum number of automatic (= atomic + non-atomic; ➢p.56) subscription (de)materializations (default = **10**) that can be executed concurrently.
  In 15.0.1, this setting takes effect immediately without a RepServer reboot.
- **num_msgqueues** - the maximum number of OpenServer message queues (default = **178**); this must be > **num_threads**.
- **num_msgs** - the maximum number of OpenServer message queue messages (default = **45568**).
- **num_mutexes** - the maximum number of OpenServer mutexes (default = **1024**); this must be > **num_threads**.

- **num_stable_queues** - the maximum number of stable queues (default = **32**).
- **num_threads** - the maximum number of OpenServer threads (default = **50**).
- **password_encryption** - when set to **1**, any passwords for maintenance users or routes that are created or modified, will be stored in the RSSD in encrypted form. Note the following:
  - Only newly changed or created passwords are affected; existing passwords remain in the RSSD in plaintext form. To also encrypt existing passwords, use **rs_init** to enable password encryption.
  - Passwords in the **.cfg** file are not encrypted by this option: this happens only when password encryption is enabled through the **rs_init** utility.
  - Despite their encrypted storage, passwords are still sent over the network in plaintext. To encrypt these as well, use the **send_enc_password** option (see below), SSL or a security mechanism (➢p.94).

  When **password_encryption** is set to **0** (=default), plaintext, unencrypted passwords are stored in the RSSD.
  To disable password encryption, set **password_encryption** to **0** and update the RSSD tables **rs_users** and **rs_maintusers** manually with plaintext passwords (set columns **password**='yourpasswd', **use_enc_password=0, enc_password =NULL**). Also, edit the **.cfg** file: for all keywords ending in '**_pw_enc**', remove '**_enc**', and enter plaintext passwords. Finally, restart RepServer.
- **send_enc_password** - when **'on'** (default = **'off'**) RepServer uses login password encryption for all its client connections (similar to the **-X** option on **isql**). Note that this does not apply to the first connection to the RSSD; to use encryption for all RSSD connections (irrespective of **send_enc_password**), set **RS_send_enc_pw** to **on** in the **.cfg** file (default = **'off'**).
- **queue_dump_buffer_size** - when running **sysadmin dump_queue**, this is the maximum number of bytes that will be dumped. Any data exceeding this size is not dumped but discarded. Possible values are **1000** to **32768** (default = **1000**). In 15.0.1, this setting takes effect immediately without a RepServer reboot.
- **rec_daemon_sleep_time** - the time (in seconds; default = **120**) the recovery daemon (dREC thread) sleeps before checking the RSSD table **rs_recovery** for recovery actions.
- **rssd_error_class** - a read-only parameter, indicating the error class used for the RSSD (default = **'rs_sqlserver_error_class'**).
- **sqm_warning_thr1** - the percentage (**1**..**100;** default = **75**) stable device partitions must be filled for a first warning to be logged to the RepServer errorlog. In 15.0.1, this setting takes effect immediately without a RepServer reboot.
- **sqm_warning_thr2** - the percentage (**1**..**100;** default = **90**) stable device partitions must be filled for a second warning to be logged to the RepServer errorlog. In 15.0.1, this setting takes effect immediately without a RepServer reboot.
- **sqm_warning_thr_ind** - the percentage (**51**..**100;** default = **70**) the stable device partitions must be filled by a single queue for a warning to be logged to the RepServer errorlog. In 15.0.1, this setting takes effect immediately without a RepServer reboot.
- **sqm_recover_segs** - the number of stable queue segments (default=**1**) allocated before the RSSD table **rs_oqid** is updated with recovery information. In 15.0.1, this setting takes effect immediately without a RepServer reboot.
- **sre_reserve** - the amount of additional memory to be allocated for new subscriptions in certain internal structures, expressed as a percentage of the currently allocated amount of memory for those structures. Possible values are **0** to **500** (default = **0**). A setting **100** indicates to double the current memory.
- **sqm_write_flush** - this setting applies only to disk partitions on a file system (it has no effect on raw partitions or on Windows). When set to **'on'** (=default) a write operation is guaranteed to be written to disk (the file is opened with the O_DSYNC flag). When **'off'**, writes may be buffered by the file system.
  In 15.1, this can also be set to **'dio'**, which will use Direct I/O (the file is opened with the O_DIRECT flag); on supported platforms (Direct I/O is not available in all O/Ss); this should always be used instead of **'on'** (i.e. O_DSYNC).
  On Unix, Direct I/O or raw devices are recommended for best performance.
- **smp_enable** - when **'on'** (default = **'off'**), allows RepServer to use multiple CPUs. The number of CPUs that may be used by RepServer must be configured on OS level.

- **sqt_max_cache_size** - the maximum size (in bytes; default = **1048576** = 1 Mb) of the SQT caches for both the distributor and the DSI. In 15.0.1, this setting takes effect immediately without a RepServer reboot. Overridden by **dsi_sqt_max_cache_size** (➢p.33) or **dist_sqt_max_cache_size** (➢p.33), if defined.
- **(pre-12.0) sqt_max_prs_size -** this parameter is obsolete since 11.0. It still exists in the RSSD but has no function anymore.
- **sqt_init_read_delay** - the time (in milliseconds) an SQT thread will sleep while waiting for an SQM thread before checking its incoming queue for new instructions. When the queue then appears empty, the sleep time is doubled (up to the current setting of **sqt_max_read_delay**). Possible values are **1000** to **86400000** (=24 hours) (default = **2000** = 2 seconds).
  In 15.0.1, this setting takes effect immediately without a RepServer reboot.
- **sqt_max_read_delay** - the maximum SQT sleep time: see **sqt_init_read_delay** (default = **10000** = 10 seconds). In 15.0.1, this setting takes effect immediately without a RepServer reboot.
- **sts_cachesize** - the number of rows cached in memory for each cached RSSD table (default = **100**). Also see **sysadmin stscache** (➢p.122).
  In 15.0.1, this setting takes effect immediately without a RepServer reboot.
- **sts_full_cache_***RSSD_table_name* - when setting such a parameter to **'on'**, that specific RSSD table will be cached completely in RepServer memory. Examples: **sts_full_cache_rs_objects**, **sts_full_cache_rs_functions**. When **'off'**, the table is not fully cached. Also see page 121.
  In 15.0.1, this setting takes effect immediately without a RepServer reboot.
- **sub_daemon_sleep_time** - when an error occurs while materializing a subscription, the time (in seconds) before materialization will be retried. Possible values are **1** to **31536000** (=365 days) (default = **120** = 2 minutes).
- **varchar_truncation** - when set to **'on'**, incoming data exceeding the column length in the repdef is silently truncated to that length. When **'off'** (=default), RepServer ignores primary rows with data exceeding the repdef column length; when data exceeds the repdef length in the DSI (as a result of character set conversion), the DSI is shut down.
- **(15.0) deferred_queue_size** - defines the size of the Open Server deferred queue (default = **1024**).
- **(15.1) sqm_seg_prealloc** - when **'on'** (=default), pre-allocates new disk segments in the background for better performance. When **'off'**, allocates a segment only when needed (=pre-15.1 behaviour).

24.4 Configuration parameters for network security

Network security protects network communication against interception and tampering by applying encryption techniques. Available configuration parameters:

- **use_ssl** - when **'on'** (default=**'off'**), uses SSL for encrypting all network traffic for all connections. This requires the license keys for the **REP_SSL** and **REP_SERVER** options to be installed in the SySam license file (➢p.13). Using SSL requires a number of setup steps, partly external to RepServer; see the *Replication Server Configuration Guide* (➢p.13) for details. Changes to this parameter take effect after a RepServer start. Note that using SSL may impact performance. Also note that SSL is independent of the security mechanisms described under **use_security_services** below.
- **security_services** - not a parameter, but a special clause of **configure replication server**: **set security_services to 'default'** resets the RepServer-wide default for all network security parameters below (except **use_security_services**) to '**not required**'.
- **use_security_services** - when **'on'** (default=**'off'**), enables a security mechanism (Kerberos or DCE) to provide a number of network security options as described below. Note that these security mechanisms are independent of SSL (described above). Using security services requires a number of setup steps, partly external to RepServer; see the chapter *Managing Replication Server Security* in the *Replication Server Administration Guide* (➢p.13) for details. Changes to this parameter take effect after a RepServer reboot.
  The following parameters require that **use_security_services** is set to **'on'**. Each parameter can be set as a server-wide default (with **configure replication server**) and for a particular connection (with **create/alter connection**) or route (**create/alter route**). Note that enabling these options may impact performance.

Available network security options:

- **msg_confidentiality** - when set to **'required'**, network packets will be encrypted; default = **'not_required'**.
- **msg_integrity** - when set to **'required'**, the source of network packets is verified; default = **'not_required'**.
- **msg_origin_check** - when set to **'required'**, network packets are checked for tampering; default = **'not_required'**.
- **msg_replay_detection** - when set to **'required'**, network packets are checked to ensure they have not been intercepted and resent; default = **'not_required'**.
- **msg_sequence_check** - when set to **'required'**, network packets are checked to arrive in the right order; default = **'not_required'**.
- **mutual_auth** - when set to **'required'**, the identity of the other servers is verified before connecting; default = **'not_required'**.
- **unified_login** - when set to **'required'**, logins are performed with a credential; when **'not_required'** (=default), logins must specify a username and password.
- **security_mechanism** - the name of the security mechanism used, as specified in the SECURITY section of **libtcl.cfg** file (located in the **$SYBASE/$SYBASE_OCS** installation tree). Default = first mechanism listed in **libtcl.cfg**.

The following parameters apply only to connections to the ID server, and can be set only as a server-wide default (with **configure replication server**). Their function is identical to the corresponding parameter above, but without **'id_'**:

id_msg_confidentiality	**id_msg_integrity**	**id_msg_origin_check**
id_msg_replay_detection	**id_unified_login**	**id_security_mechanism**
id_mutual_auth	**id_msg_sequence_check**	

admin security_property [, *mechanism_name*]
Displays the available network-based security mechanisms for this RepServer.

admin security_setting [,] [*idserver_name* | *repserver_name* | *dataserver.database*]
Displays network-based security settings for all connections, or only for a connection to the specified ID server, RepServer or database.

25 Parallel DSI

By default, replicate transactions are applied serially over a single DSI EXEC connection to the replicate database. Parallel DSI is a performance improvement where multiple replicate transactions are applied concurrently using multiple DSI EXEC connections for one replicate database. The replicate transactions are still committed in the same order as in the primary database. For a replicate connection, one DSI thread always exists (irrespective of parallel DSI), doing the scheduling for the DSI EXEC thread(s). The performance of a parallel DSI can be optimised by tuning certain aspects (by configuring the parameters described below):

- 'Large' transactions (as defined by **dsi_large_xact_size**) may already be applied at the replicate database even when they have not yet been committed in the primary.
- To guarantee that replicate transactions are committed in the same order as in the primary database, a 'serialization method' is used for each parallel DSI (as defined by **dsi_serialization_method**). Different methods are available for minimising lock contention between the parallel transactions.
- 'Transaction partitioning' rules are used (defined by **dsi_partitioning_rule**) to determine how to parallellize the transaction stream. Again, the aim is to minimise lock contention between the parallel transactions.

Notes:

- Parallel DSI may improve throughput and reduce latency. However, it is not guaranteed to actually deliver such improvements. It is recommended to evaluate the performance effects of different options for serialization and partitioning. It is recommended to use **dsi_commit_control** = **'on'.**
- Parallel DSI can be used in a warm standby, but must be configured for the connection to the standby database (i.e. not for the logical connection).
- In RS pre-12.5, parallel DSI could only be used for replicate ASE databases. With **dsi_commit_control** = **'on'**, parallel DSI can also be used for non-ASE replicate databases.
- When row-level locking is used for a replicate table, parallel DSI introduces a

potential risk that **update** or **delete** statements are replicated in the wrong order, making it look as if they were not replicated at all (a.k.a. the 'missing update'). To reduce/avoid this problem, use one of the following configurations:

- with **dsi_commit_control** = **'on'**, set **dsi_serialization_method** to **'wait_for_commit'** or **'single_transaction_per_origin'**
- with **dsi_commit_control** = **'off'**

25.1 Configuration parameters for parallel DSI

The following configuration parameters apply to the parallel DSI aspects of a connection. They can be modified (one parameter at a time) with **configure replication server** to set RepServer-wide defaults; when specified with **create/alter connection**, this overrides the server-wide defaults for the specified connection.
Example: **alter connection to PROD.prod_db set parallel_dsi to 'on'**

Notes:

- All parameter values, including integers, must be specified as quoted strings.
- In pre-15.0.1, there is no system-supplied procedure to display all non-default configuration parameter settings for a connection (some, but not all, connection-specific settings are displayed by **admin who, dsi**). Instead, use the RSSD procedure **rs_helpcfg_db** (included in the electronic supplement to this book; ➢p.8). In 15.0.1, **admin config** can also be used (➢p.90).
  For details about parameter storage in the RSSD table **rs_config**, see page 91.

List of configuration parameters for parallel DSI:

- **dsi_num_threads** - specifies the number of DSI threads to be used for parallel DSI. Default = **1**, meaning parallel DSI is not used. Maximum value = **255**.
- **parallel_dsi** - a quick way to configure parallel DSI. When **'on'**, these values are set for the DSI: **dsi_num_threads=5**, **dsi_num_large_xact_threads=2** **dsi_serialization_method='wait_for_commit'**, **dsi_sqt_max_cache_size= 1000000** (bytes); nevertheless, these parameters can still be overridden individually (with **alter connection**). When **'off'** (=default), these parameters revert to their server-wide defaults.
- **dsi_serialization_method** - specifies the method for guaranteeing that the commit order of replicate transactions for parallel DSI is the same as in the primary database, while minimising lock contention between parallel transactions.
  Possible serialization methods are:
  - **'wait_for_commit'** (=default) - a transaction is started once the previous transaction starts to commit. This tends to be the slowest method.
  - **'none'** (in 12.6, this was replaced by **'wait_for_start'**) - a replicate transaction is started once the previous transaction has started. Combined with **dsi_partitioning_rule** = **'origin'**, all transactions from different primary databases use different DSI EXEC threads.
  - **(pre-15.0) 'isolation_level_3'** - same as **'none'/'wait_for_start'**, but uses transaction isolation level 3 (i.e. **holdlock**) for the DSI EXEC threads. In 15.0, replaced by **set dsi_isolation_level** (➢p.34).
  - **'no_wait'** - a transaction is started as soon as a DSI EXEC thread is available.
  - **'single_transaction_per_origin'** - identical to the combination of **'wait_for_start'** and **dsi_partitioning_rule** = **'origin'**.
- **dsi_large_xact_size** - the number of statements in a transaction for it to be considered a 'large' transaction for parallel DSI. Minimum = **4**, default = **100**; no upper limit.
- **dsi_num_large_xact_threads** - the number of DSI threads (default = **0**) reserved for 'large' transactions (defined by **dsi_large_xact_size**) for parallel DSI.
- **dsi_partitioning_rule** - specifies one or more DSI partitioning rules as a comma-separated list; all specified rules are applied. Possible rules are:
  - **'none'** (=default) - each transaction (or transaction group) simply uses the next available DSI EXEC thread.
  - **'time'** - transactions with overlapping start- and end times can be executed in parallel; otherwise they're executed serially.
  - **'user'** - transactions by the same primary user are executed serially.
  - **'name'** - transactions with the same transaction name (but not blank or null) are executed serially. Also see **dsi_ignore_underscore_name**.
  - **'origin'** - transactions from the same primary database are executed serially.

- **'origin_sessid'** - transactions from the same primary database and with the same process ID, are executed serially.
- **'ignore_origin'** - without **'ignore_origin'**, the rules **'time'**, **'user'** and **'name'** apply only to transactions from the same primary database; transactions from different primaries may always execute in parallel. With **'ignore_origin'**, the transaction's primary database is ignored for partitioning purposes. If specified, **'ignore_origin'** must be the first rule; it is ignored otherwise (i.e. **'ignore_origin, name'**, not **'name, ignore_origin'**).

Sybase recommends trying **dsi_partitioning_rule** = **'origin_sessid,time'** when experimenting with partitioning rules. In addition, Sybase recommends not to set **dsi_commit_control** = **'off'** and **dsi_serialization_method** = **'no_wait'** because this may result in transactions not committing in the right order.

- **dsi_ignore_underscore_name** - this setting applies only when **dsi_partitioning_rule** = **'name'**: when **'on'** (=default), parallel DSI ignores transaction names starting with an underscore; when **'off'**, it doesn't.
- **dsi_commit_control** - When **'on'** (=default), parallel DSI commit control is handled internally by RepServer to provide better concurrency and throughput; when **'off'**, commit control is handled through the **rs_threads** table in the replicate database (which is the 'classical', RS pre-12.5 method).
- **dsi_commit_check_locks_intrvl** - (when **dsi_commit_control** = **'on'**) specifies the time (in milliseconds) between executions of the **rs_dsi_check_thread_lock** function string which checks whether a parallel DSI EXEC thread is blocking other sessions while waiting to commit its replicate transaction (➢p.78). Possible values are **0** to **86400000** (=24 hours). Default = **1000** (=1 second). A lower value will detect a blocking situation sooner but also causes additional workload.
- **dsi_commit_check_locks_max** - (when **dsi_commit_control** = **'on'**) specifies the maximum number of times the **rs_dsi_check_thread_lock** function string is executed before the replicate transaction is rolled back and retried by parallel DSI. Possible values are **1** to **1000000**; default = **400**.
- **dsi_commit_check_locks_log** - (when **dsi_commit_control** = **'on'**) specifies the number of times the **rs_dsi_check_thread_lock** function string is executed before a warning is logged by parallel DSI. Possible values are **1** to **1000000**; default = **200**.

Replication System Administration

26 Installation/setup: the rs_init utility

rs_init is a command-line ASCII utility for creating new RepServers and database connections, performing upgrades/downgrades, and enabling password encryption. It is located in **$SYBASE/$SYBASE_REP/install**. Some (but not all) of this functionality can also be performed with the RSP plug-in for Sybase Central (➢p.116).
By default, **rs_init** runs interactively. With the **-r** option, **rs_init** takes its input from a resource file instead. A resource file can be created by hitting **CTRL+w** during the interactive **rs_init** dialog, which writes the user's choices to a file. Alternatively, a resource file can be created with the examples in **$SYBASE/$SYBASE_REP/init/rs**.
Note: It is recommended to always create a resource file with **CTRL+w** before executing the setup: if **rs_init** terminates during execution, all input is lost and without a resource file, you will need to go through the full dialog again. It is also a good idea to create resource file templates if you need to execute certain **rs_init** tasks repeatedly.
Notes:

- The log file of an **rs_init** session is in **$SYBASE/$SYBASE_REP/init/logs**. Check this file when a problem occurs while **rs_init** creates the RepServer.
- On Windows, **rs_init** is a GUI. **CTRL+w** (to create a resource file) doesn't work, but while **rs_init** is executing the user's configuration, you can copy the file **%SYBASE%\%SYBASE_REP%\init\logs\attr.dmp**. This copy can then be edited and used as a resource file on the command line with **rs_init -r**.
- When running **rs_init -r** with a resource file: If, on Unix, a file is used for the stable device, this must exist before starting **rs_init** (use Unix **touch**). When configuring an embedded RSSD, the directory containing the ERSSD files must be created manually first.
- **rs_init** supports the following command-line options (also on Windows):

[**-c** *characterset*]	Specifies the character set to be used
[**-e**]	Dumps the environment settings to the log file, then exits
[**-h**]	Displays **rs_init** command-line options
[**-l** *language*]	Language for this session (for dialog and error messages)
[**-log** *log_file*]	Session log file (dft=**$SYBASE_REP/init/logs/log***mmdd.nnn*)
[**-r** *resource_file*]	Resource file to be executed
[**-a**]	(with **-r**) Validates, but does not execute, the resource file
[**-s** *release_dir*]	Pathname of the RepServer installation directory
[**-v**]	Displays the software version ID

- (Unix only) Hitting '**?**' during the **rs_init** dialog displays on-line help info (note that this information sometimes refers to non-existing menu options).
- Since **rs_init** accesses OS files (like the **.cfg** file), it must be run on the same host as where the RepServer software is installed.
- **rs_init** creates the **RUN_***servername* file in **$SYBASE**. On Windows, the file is named **%SYBASE%\%SYBASE_REP%\install***servername***.bat**.
- When running **rs_init** with a resource file, the undocumented option **-T IGNORE_WARNINGS** suppresses continuation prompts due to warnings.

26.1 Common rs_init problems

- **rs_init** reads the **interfaces** file (Windows: **SQL.INI**) when it starts up; it will not notice any subsequent changes to the **interfaces** file, and the **interfaces** file cannot be modified with **rs_init** (except when creating a new RepServer or ERSSD). Consequently, any server names referenced during the **rs_init** dialog must already exist in the **interfaces** file before starting **rs_init**.
- When setting up a warm standby, the logical connection must be created outside **rs_init**; this cannot be done from **rs_init**.
- When creating a new RepServer, and using OS files for the disk partitions, create these files with the Unix **touch** command before running **rs_init**.
- To avoid run-time permission problems in replicate databases, it is common practice to alias the maintenance user to **dbo** in each replicate ASE database. However, this can cause problems when creating a database connection with **rs_init**, which will complain **'No such user/role...exists'**. To avoid these problems, first drop the **dbo** alias and add the login as a normal database user (in the **public** group); then, run **rs_init**. Once **rs_init** completes, the database user can be dropped and re-aliased to **dbo**.

26.2 Character set & sort order

It is highly recommended that all dataservers, RepServers and RSM servers in a replication system use the same -or a compatible- character set, and the same sort order. For more information about these topics, see the chapter *International Replication Design Considerations* in the *Replication Server Design Guide* (➢p.13).

26.3 Installation tips on Windows

When installing RepServer (or in fact, any other product) on Windows, some Windows environment variables, like **%PATH%**, are modified by the installer. In my experience, it is not uncommon to see that after such an installation, existing programs no longer work correctly due to the additions to those environment variables.
Common issues on Windows are:

- environment variables have become very long, and appear to have been truncated somwhere in the process
- due to changes to **%PATH%**, wrong versions of DLLs are found

To avoid such problems, it's a good idea to manually save the settings for **%PATH%**, **%LIB%**, **%SYBASE*%** and **%SYBROOT%** before installing a new product or a new EBF (Control Panel→System→Advanced→Environment Variables). In case of problems, the previous settings for these variables can then be restored manually.

When ASE and RepServer are installed under the same **%SYBASE%** root directory, it may be a good idea to make a backup copy of the **OCS-***XX_Y* directory, in case problems occur due to connectivity libraries being replaced when a newer release of the other product is installed.

26.4 RepServer environment variables

The following Unix environment variables are used by RepServer. The variables $SYBASE_*xxx* should not contain full pathnames, but only a single directory name which is located below $SYBASE; exceptions are $SYBASE_JRE and $SYBASE_UA. On Windows, read %VARIABLE% instead of $VARIABLE.

Environment variable	Function
$SYBASE	Pathname of installation directory of all Sybase software
$SYBASE_REP	RepServer installation directory, e.g. REP-15_1
$SYBASE_OCS	OpenClient installation directory (with **isql,** libraries etc.)
$SYBASE_SYSAM	License manager installation directory, e.g. SYSAM-2_0
(pre-15.0) $SYBASE_RSM	RepServer Manager installation directory
(pre-15.0) $SYBASE_RSP	RepServer plug-in (for Sybase Central non-Java edition) installation directory
$SYBASE_RMP	RepServer Manager plug-in (for Sybase Central Java edition) installation directory, e.g. RMP-15_0
$SYBASE_JRE	Java run-time environment (for Java-based tools), e.g. $SYBASE/_jvm or $SYBASE/_jvmrep
(15.0) $SYBASE_UA	Unified Agent Framework directory, e.g. UAF-2_0
$PATH	Points to $SYBASE, .../$SYBASE_REP/bin, .../$SYBASE_REP/install, .../$SYBASE_OCS/bin and .../$SYBASE_UA/bin; on Windows, also points to .../$SYBASE_OCS/dll
$LD_LIBRARY_PATH	(Linux, and all Unix flavours except AIX and HP-UX) Points to .../$SYBASE_OCS/lib and .../$SYBASE_OCS /lib3p; with an embedded RSSD, also to .../$SYBASE_REP/ASA9/lib (or ASA8/lib)
$LIBPATH	(AIX only) Same as $LD_LIBRARY_PATH
$SHLIB_PATH	(HP-UX only) Same as $LD_LIBRARY_PATH
%LIB%	(Windows only) Points to ...\%SYBASE_OCS%\lib
$DSQUERY (optional)	Default server name used by client utilities (like **isql**)
(pre-15.0) $LM_LICENSE_FILE	License file pathname (used by the license manager)
$INSTALL_ALL_PATCH	When set to **1**, the installer will not check the to-be-installed EBF to be later than the installed version
(15.0) $SCROOT	Directory where SybaseCentral is installed
(15.0) $SYBROOT	Parent of $SCROOT; typically the same as $SYBASE
(15.1) $DDLGENLOC	Used by **rs_subcmp**; points to the location of **ddlgen** (usually $SYBASE/ASEP/bin/ddlgen)

27 Startup & shutdown

On Unix, a RepServer (or a pre-15.0 RSM server) is started by kicking off the **RUN_***servername* file (typically located in **$SYBASE/$SYBASE_REP/install**) in the background. When ASE is also installed, the **RUN_***servername* can also be started with the **startserver** utility (in **$SYBASE/$SYBASE_ASE/install**).

On Windows, RepServer is installed as a service, named **SYBREP_***servername* (**SYBRSM_***servername* for pre-15.0 RSM servers). The service can be started (or stopped) with the service manager, with the non-Java version of Sybase Central, or from a DOS box with the DOS command **net { start | stop } SYBREP_***servername*. Services on remote hosts can be started and stopped with Windows tools like **sc** or **netsvc**.
When a server is started as a service, its command-line startup parameters are stored in the registry, and can be modified only by editing this registry key directly:
HKEY_LOCAL_MACHINE\SOFTWARE\SYBASE\Server*servername***\Parameters**
On Windows, the server can also be started through the **RUN_***servername* file, but it will run in the foreground in a DOS box (which cannot be closed).

repserver (Windows: **repsrvr.exe**) - the RepServer executable, located in **$SYBASE/ $SYBASE_ REP/bin**. Command-line options:

[**-C** *config_file*]	The RepServer config (**.cfg**) file pathname
[**-E** *errorlog_file*]	The errorlog file pathname (default = **repserver.log**)
[**-S** *repserver_name*]	The name of this RepServer
[**-M**]	Starts RepServer in standalone (a.k.a. 'single-user') mode
[**-I** *interfaces_file*]	The **interfaces** file pathname (default = **$SYBASE/interfaces**)
[**-i** *id_servername*]	Overrides the ID Server name in the **.cfg** file
[**-K** *keytab_file*]	Filename of DCE keytab file (only when using DCE).
[**-v**]	Displays the software version ID

repserver.diag (Windows: **drepsrvr.exe**) - a diagnostic version of the RepServer executable. Some RepServer traceflags work only with the diagnostic RepServer. Otherwise, it is functionally identical to **repserver**. The version string (shown by **admin version**) contains the string .../**DEBUG**/... when running **repserver.diag**.

shutdown [**with nowait**]
(RepServer command) Shuts down the RepServer. The option **with nowait** is un-documented and does not have any additional effect.

28 RepServer traceflags (undocumented)

trace { **'on'** | **'off'** }, **'***module***'**, **'***traceflag_name***'**
(Undocumented) Enables or disables a particular traceflag. Some traceflags can be used with the normal **repserver** executable, others require the RepServer to be started with **repserver.diag** (➢p.100). Traceflags are not maintained after a RepServer restart. *module* and *traceflag_name* must be specified together.
Some traceflags are:

- **'dsi', 'dsi_buf_dump'**
  Logs all replicate SQL commands for all DSIs into the RepServer errorlog (note: when the replicate database is ASE 12.5.0.3+, the same information may also be obtained from the ASE monitoring table **master..monSysSQLText**; see **www.sypron.nl/mda** for more information).
- **'dsi', 'dsi_cmd_dump'**
  Similar to **dsi_buf_dump**, but requires **repserver.diag**.
- **'cm', 'cm_user_pass'**
  (Requires **repserver.diag**) Logs outgoing connection attempts by RepServer for databases (not for routes) into the RepServer errorlog, including the password used for the connection (with encrypted passwords, this is a way to find the plaintext password; this can be handy for troubleshooting connectivity problems).
- **'cm', 'cm_show_connect_disconnect'**
  (Requires **repserver.diag**) Similar to **'cm_user_pass'**, but without passwords.
- **'exec', 'exec_connections'**
  (Requires **repserver.diag**) Logs all incoming connection attempts to RepServer, as well as corresponding disconnects, into the RepServer errorlog. Does not show the password, nor the hostname of the client trying to connect.
- **'sts', 'sts_print_dbproc'**
  (Requires **repserver.diag**) Logs all queries against the RSSD into the Rep-Server errorlog.

- **'*xxx*', 'print_rs_ticket'**
  When an **rs_ticket** marker (➢p.132) passes through a specific RepServer module, prints the information collected by the ticket to the RepServer errorlog.
  '*xxx*' can be **'exec'** (Executor, or REP AGENT thread, where RepServer receives the LTL from the RepAgent), **'dist'** (Distributor) or **'dsi'** (connection to the replicate database). In 15.1, also **'rsi'** for routes.
  The connection parameter **dsi_rs_ticket_report** does not need to be enabled for these traceflags to be used.

29 Disk space & RepServer devices/disk partitions

RepServer stores transactions in stable queues (➢section 30), which are located on 'disk partitions', also referred to as 'stable devices'. A partition consists of 1Mb 'segments' of disk space, and must be created by the DBA with **create** (or **add**) **partition**. Make sure the disk partitions of a RepServer are sufficiently large (or sufficient spare disk space is available) to survive a significant period (say 36 hours) of unexpected downtime of one of the replication system's components.

admin disk_space
Displays the state and amount of used space for all disk partitions in this RepServer.

rs_helppartition [*partition_name*]
(RSSD procedure) Displays the current state and the amount of used space for one or all disk partitions in this RepServer.

add partition *partition_name* **on '***pathname***' with size** *N* [**starting at** *vstart*]
(15.0) create partition *partition_name* **on '***pathname***' with size** *N* [**starting at** *vstart*]
Adds a disk partition of size *N* Mb to the RepServer (note: single quotes must be used around *pathname*). **add partition** and **create partition** are functionally identical.
A partition can be created on a raw device or an OS file; when an OS file is used, it must already exist (not necessarily with the final size; using Unix **touch** is sufficient).
For disk partitions on an OS file, the configuration parameter **sqm_write_flush** (➢p.93) determines whether write operations are buffered or direct through O_DSYNC (=default) or, in 15.1, direct through Direct I/O. On Unix, raw devices or Direct I/O are recommended for best performance.
The maximum size of a disk partition is 1 Tb (in pre-15.0, 2040 Mb). An existing partition can be enlarged with **alter partition** (not possible in pre-15.0).
There can be at most 65536 disk partitions during the lifetime of one RepServer. The clause **starting at** *vstart* may be required to mirror disk partitions outside RepServer.
Example: **create partition part_2 on '/opt/sybase/MYREP.part_2.dat' with size 100**

(15.0) alter partition *partition_name* **expand** [**size =** *N*]
Increases the size of a disk partition with *N* Mb; by default, *N*=2. **expand** is optional.

drop partition *partition_name*
Removes a disk partition from the RepServer. It will be dropped immediately when it is completely unused, i.e. when all queues have grown off this partition onto other partitions. In the mean time, **admin disk_space** displays the status of this partition as **ON-LINE/DROPPED/**. When the partition is an OS file, the file is not deleted when the partition is finally dropped.

alter connection to *dataserver.database* **set disk_affinity to** ['*partition_name*' | **'off'**]
Specifies a disk space allocation: additional disk space for queues for the specified database connection will -if possible- be allocated on the specified partition. **'off'** (=default) removes the existing hint. By assigning each connection (or route) to its own partition, performance may be improved.
Without hints, space for all queues is allocated on the next free segment in the current (or next) partition. Consequently, by default queues grow towards to the end of the last disk partition and then wrap around to the start of the first partition.

alter route to *destination_repserver* **set disk_affinity to** ['*partition_name*' | **'off'**]
Specifies a disk space allocation hint for the queue for the route to the specified RepServer. Otherwise identical to **alter connection**...**set disk_affinity**.

29.1 RSSD tables - disk partitions

Information about disk partitions is stored in the RSSD table **rs_diskpartitions**. Space allocation hints are stored in the RSSD table **rs_diskaffinity**. To display the current hints, use one of the RSSD queries from the electronic supplement to this book (➢p.8).

29.2 Estimating disk space requirements

The RSSD procedures **rs_capacity** and **rs_fillcaptable** can be used to estimate the amount of disk space required for the stable queues. First, **rs_fillcaptable** should be run for each repdef, specifying the expected number of inserts, deletes, updates, and transactions for that repdef; this will insert rows into the RSSD table **rs_captable**. Next, use **rs_capacity** to calculate disk space estimates for the specified parameters. See the *Replication Server Reference Manual* for details about these procedures.

rs_capacity *TransactionDuration*, *FailDuration*, *SaveInterval*, *MaterializationRows*
(RSSD procedure) Estimates the disk space required for stable queues for the specified parameters.

rs_fillcaptable *repdef_name*, *inserts_in*, *deletes_in*, *updates_in*, *inserts_out*, *deletes_out*, *updates_out*, *transactions_in*, *transactions_out*, *DelFlag*
(RSSD procedure) Records estimated rates of DML and transactions for a repdef.

30 Queues

RepServer stores transactions in stable queues, which are located on disk partitions (also referred to as 'stable devices'). A partition consists of 1Mb 'segments' of disk space; a segment consists of 64 16Kb blocks; a block contains one or more messages (sometimes called 'rows'). A segment is allocated to only one queue at a time.
Queues 'grow' over the stable device continuously: when RepServer stores new messages in a queue, additional segments are allocated for that queue. Once all messages in a segment have been delivered to their destination, and a period indicated by the corresponding **save_interval** setting has then expired, the segment is deallocated. As long as **save_interval** has not expired, the already-applied messages can be restored with **sysadmin restore_dsi_saved_segments**.
By default, the next available unallocated segment on the current (or next) disk partition is simply allocated; this can be refined with the **disk_affinity** parameter (➢p.101).
Each queue is managed by an SQM thread. For each inbound queue, there is also an SQT thread, which manages the transactions in that queue (there's another SQT for the outbound queue, which runs as part of the DSI thread).

A queue is identified by two numbers, for example **109:0** (as displayed by **admin who**) or **109, 0** (as it must be entered for **sysadmin** commands). The first number indicates the database or route to which the queue applies. The second number is either **0**, indicating an outbound queue (meaning the queue contains data flowing from the current RepServer to a database or to another RepServer), or **1**, indicating an inbound queue (meaning the queue contains primary data flowing from a RepAgent to the current RepServer), or a large negative number (indicating a (de)materialization queue).
Examples:

109:0	outbound queue for replicate database 109
109:1	inbound queue for primary database 109
16777322:0	outbound queue for route to RepServer 16777322
116:-2147483532	(de)materialization queue for a subscription for a replicate table in database 116

30.1 Diagnostic & maintenance commands for queues

admin who, sqm [, no_trunc]
Displays status information about all queues. This information is not stored in the RSSD. Some useful columns are:

- **First Seg.Block** - the first undeleted segment and block in the queue; this is where the oldest messages in the queue are located.
- **Last Seg.Block** - the segment and block last written to the queue for newly arrived messages. When this is equal to **First Seg.Block**, all messages in the queue have been processed.
- **Next.Read** - the segment, block and row to be read next from the queue, indicating the position where RepServer is processing messages in this queue. If **Next.Read** is identical to, or higher than **Last Seg.Block**, all messages have been delivered; if **Next.Read** is significantly lower than **Last Seg.Block**, this indicates that messages for this queue cannot be delivered, or not fast enough (for example, due to inefficient replicate SQL queries in a replicate database, or due to replicate dataservers/RepServers being unavailable). If **Next.Read** is only a little lower than **Last Seg.Block**, this should be considered normal.

- **Save_Int:Seg** - the **save_interval** setting for the queue (in minutes), and the oldest segment to be deleted.
- The undocumented parameter **no_trunc** displays some columns in a longer format.

admin sqm_readers, *queue_number*, *queue_type*
Displays the read/delete points for the threads reading from a queue.

admin who, sqt [**, no_trunc**]
Displays status information about the transactions being processed for each queue. This information is not stored in the RSSD. Some useful columns are:

- **First Trans** (displayed as **st:***x***,cmds:***n***,qid:***seg***:***blk***:***row*) - **st:***x* indicates the status of the first transaction in the queue; *x* can be **O** (open; no commit/rollback has yet been received from the RepAgent), **C** (closed; commit has been received and transaction is being applied to the replicate database), **R** (read; applied to the replicate but not yet deleted), **D** (deleted).
  cmds: indicates the number of commands in the transaction. **qid:** indicates the segment, block and row where the transaction starts in the queue.
- **Removed** - if non-zero, indicates the SQT cache may be too small (usually this applies to DSI SQT rather than to the DIST SQT). If so, consider increasing **dsi_sqt_max_cache_size** for the connection (➢p.33). However, do not make it too large: see page 121 for more info.
- **no_trunc** (undocumented) displays some columns in a longer format.

sysadmin drop_queue, *queue_number*, *queue_type*
Drops a (de)materialization queue.
Example: **sysadmin drop_queue, 116, -2147483532**

sysadmin dump_file [**,** *dump_file_name*]
Specifies a file name for the output of subsequent **sysadmin dump_queue** or **sysadmin sqt_dump_queue** commands, executed from any session. When executed without *dump_file_name*, closes the file previously opened, and reverts the output from a subsequent **sysadmin** command to the RepServer errorlog file.

sysadmin dump_queue, *queue_number*, *queue_type*, *seg*, *blk*, *cnt* [**, rssd** | **client**]
(15.1) sysadmin dump_queue, { *queue_number* | *servername* [**,** *database*] } **,**
queue_type, *seg*, *blk*, *cnt* [**,** *num_cmds*] [**, L0** | **L1** | **L2** | **L3**]
[**, rssd** | **client** | **'log'** | **'***dump_file_name***'**]
(15.1) sysadmin dump_queue, { *queue_number* | *servername* [**,** *database*] } **,**
queue_type, **'next'** [**,** *num_cmds*]
Dumps the contents of a queue. In 15.1, instead of the queue number, the name of the dataserver and database, or the RepServer name, may be specified.
The parameters *seg*, *blk* and *cnt* specify which part of the queue should be dumped:

- *seg* > **0**, *blk* = **1**..**64**: start dumping at the specified segment and block
- *seg* = **-1**, *blk* = **1**: start dumping at the start of the first active segment
- *seg* = **-1**, *blk* = **-1**: start dumping at the first undeleted block in the queue
- *seg* = **-1**, *blk* = **-2**: start dumping at the first unread block in the queue
- *seg* = **-2**, *blk* = **1**: start dumping at the first queue segment (incl. inactive segments still allocated due to a **save_interval** setting) and the specified block
- *cnt* specifies the number of blocks to be dumped. When *cnt* = **-1**, dumps until the end of the segment; when *cnt* = **-2**, dumps until the end of the queue.
- *num_cmds* specifies that commands should be dumped instead of blocks. This overrides *cnt*, though the numbers have the same meaning as for *cnt*.

L*n* defines what to dump: **L0** (=default) dumps the entire queue; **L1** dumps only the begin/end of transactions; **L2** = **L1** plus the first 100 characters of all other commands; **L3** = **L0** but prints everything except SQL commands in comment marks (**L3** can only be used with *dump_file_name*).
By default (without **rssd**, **client**, etc), the output is written to the RepServer errorlog, unless a different file has been specified previously with **sysadmin dump_file**; with **'log'**, the output is always written to RepServer errorlog irrespective of **sysadmin dump_file**. With **rssd**, the output is written into the RSSD tables **rs_queuemsg** and **rs_queuemsgtxt**; with **client**, the output is sent to the client. Specifying *dump_file_name* has the same effect as **sysadmin dump_file**, sending the output, and that of subsequent **sysadmin dump*** commands, to this file.
With **'next'**, dumping continues from where the previous **sysadmin dump_queue** ended for this queue in the current session, using the previously specified values for *seg*, *blk*, *cnt*, *num_cmds*, **L***n* and the output method (if there was no previous **dump_queue** in this session, *seg*, *blk*, *cnt* are taken as **-1**, **-1**, **-2**). Specifying **'next',**

num_cmds overrides the previous value of *cnt* or *num_cmds*.
Note that the output of **sysadmin dump_queue** may be large, so when dumping to the RSSD, it could fill up quickly.

Examples: **sysadmin dump_queue, 109, 1, 1321, 52, 20** -- dump 20 blocks of 109:1
(15.1) sysadmin dump_queue, 109, 1, 1321, 52, 20, 10 -- dump 10 cmds
sysadmin dump_queue, 109, 1, -1, -2, -2 -- dump unread part of 109:1
(15.1) sysadmin dump_queue, PROD, prod_db, 1, -1, -2, -2 -- same

sysadmin dump_file, '/tmp/109_1.out' -- dump all of 109:1 to a file
sysadmin dump_queue, 109, 1, -2, 1, -2
sysadmin dump_file

(15.1) sysadmin dump_queue, 109, 1, -2, 1, -2, '/tmp/109_1.out'

sysadmin sqt_dump_queue, *queue_number*, *queue_type*, *reader* [**, open**]
(15.1) sysadmin sqt_dump_queue, { *queue_number* | *servername* [, *database*] } ,
queue_type, *reader* [**, open** | **closed** | **read**] [, *num_cmds*]
[, **L0** | **L1** | **L2** | **L3**] [**, rssd** | **client** | **'log'** | **'***dump_file_name***'**]
Dumps the contents of the SQT transaction cache for a queue. Unless multiple readers are active (check with **admin sqm_readers**), specify **0** for *reader*. With **open**, dumps uncommitted transactions; with **closed**, dumps committed-but-not-yet-applied transactions; with **read**, dumps applied-but-not-yet-removed transactions.
num_cmds is the number of commands to dump; **-1** (=default) dumps everything.
The output is written to the RepServer errorlog, unless a different file was specified with **sysadmin dump_file**. For the semantics of **L***n* and the output options (**rssd**, **client**, etc), see **sysadmin dump_queue**.

sysadmin sqm_purge_queue, *queue_number*, *queue_type*
In standalone or hibernation mode, deletes all messages from a stable queue.
Warning: Do not run this command unless instructed by Sybase TechSupport: it may put the replication system in jeopardy and/or lead to loss of replicated transactions.

(15.1) sysadmin dump_tran, { *queue_number* | *servername* [, *database*] } ,
queue_type, *seg*, *blk*, *row* [, *num_cmds*] [, **L0** | **L1** | **L2** | **L3**]
[**, rssd** | **client** | **'log'** | **'***dump_file_name***'**]
(15.1) sysadmin dump_tran, 'next' [, *num_cmds*]
Dumps a specifc transaction in a queue. The transaction is identified by *seg*, *blk*, *row*, for segment number, block number and row number, respectively, corresponding to the start of the transaction. This combination is also known as the LQID (local queue ID); queue dump output to a log file (or to the RepServer errorlog) often also shows the LQID as *seg*:*blk*:*row* (e.g. **1321:52:4**). With **'next'**, the next commands of the transaction specified in a previous command in this session, are dumped.
Otherwise this command is similar to **sysadmin dump_queue**.

(15.1) sysadmin sqm_zap_tran, { *queue_number* | *servername* [, *database*] },
queue_type, *seg*, *blk*, *row*
[, **L0** | **L1** | **L2** | **L3**] [**, rssd** | **client** | **'log'** | **'***dump_file_name***'**]
In standalone or hibernation mode (➢p.106), marks a specific transaction in a queue as deleted so that it will be ignored by RepServer. As long as the blocks containing the transaction have not been processed, the transaction can be undeleted again with **sysadmin sqm_unzap_tran**.
The number of deleted commands is printed. In addition, **L***n* defines what part of the deleted transaction is printed: **L0** (=default) dumps the entire deleted transaction; **L1** dumps only the begin/end; **L2** = **L1** plus the first 100 characters of all other commands; **L3** = **L0** but prints everything except SQL commands in comment marks (**L3** can only be used with *dump_file_name*).
For the output options (**rssd**, **client**, etc), see **sysadmin dump_queue**.
Example: **sysadmin sqm_zap_tran, 109, 1, 1321, 52, 0**

(15.1) sysadmin sqm_unzap_tran, { *queue_number* | *servername* [, *database*] },
queue_type, *seg*, *blk*, *row*
[, **L0** | **L1** | **L2** | **L3**] [**, rssd** | **client** | **'log'** | **'***dump_file_name***'**]
In standalone or hibernation mode (➢p.106), undeletes a specific transaction, which was previously marked as deleted by **sysadmin sqm_zap_tran**, from a queue, thus restoring it. The restored transaction is printed; otherwise the parameters are identical to **sysadmin sqm_zap_tran**.

sysadmin sqm_zap_command, *queue_number*, *queue_type*, *seg*, *blk*, *row*
In standalone or hibernation mode (➢p.106), marks the message at the specified segment/block/row as deleted, so that it will be ignored by RepServer. As long as the block has not been processed, the message can be undeleted again with **sysadmin sqm_unzap_command**.

sysadmin sqm_unzap_command, *queue_number*, *queue_type*, *seg*, *blk*, *row*
In standalone or hibernation mode (➢p.106), undeletes the message at the specified segment/block/row, which was previously marked as deleted by **sysadmin sqm_zap_command**, thus restoring it.

sysadmin purge_all_open, *queue_number*, *queue_type*
Deletes all open transactions from an inbound queue. Does not require standalone or hibernation mode.

sysadmin purge_first_open, *queue_number*, *queue_type*
Deletes the first open transaction from an inbound queue. Does not require standalone or hibernation mode.

sysadmin log_first_tran, [**(15.1)** *N*,] *dataserver*, *database*
Without *N*, writes the first transaction in the outbound queue for the DSI to the specified database into the RSSD exceptions log (it can then be viewed using **rs_helpexception**). With *N*, writes the first *N* transactions.
The transactions are not deleted from the queue.

sysadmin restore_dsi_saved_segments, *dataserver*, *database*
For transactions that have already been applied to the replicate database but are still in the DSI queue due to a **save_interval** setting for the queue, restores those transactions into the queue (so they can be re-applied to the database in a recovery scenario). Requires the DSI to be suspended.

rebuild queues
A troubleshooting command; deletes all stable queues and attempts to reconstruct them; ➢p.118.

30.2 Configuration parameters for queues

The configuration parameters below apply to individual queues. Unless specified otherwise, these settings are static (i.e. require a RepServer restart for changes to take effect), and server-wide defaults can be set with **configure replication server**. Queue-specific settings cannot be displayed with **admin config**; use the RSSD procedure **rs_helpcfg** instead (included in the electronic supplement to this book; ➢p.8).

(15.1)
alter queue, *queue_number*, *queue_type*, **set sqm_cache_enable** [**to**] { **'on'** | **'off'** }
Enables (**'on'**, = default) or disables (**'off'**) SQM caching for the specified queue. SQM caching helps to improve performance if RepServer disk I/O is a bottleneck.

(15.1)
alter queue, *queue_number*, *queue_type*, **set sqm_page_size** [**to**] '*size*'
Defines the page size of the SQM cache for the specified queue. The page size is the size of the disk I/O performed by RepServer, defined as *size**16Kb. Range is **1**..**64**; default = **4**, meaning a page size of 4 * 16Kb = 64Kb will be used.

(15.1)
alter queue, *queue_number*, *queue_type*, **set sqm_cache_size** [**to**] '*nr_pages*'
Defines the cache size of the SQM cache for the specified queue, which is the number of pages in the cache. Range is **1**..**512**; default = **16**, which, with the default page size of 64 Kb (see **sqm_page_size**), results in a cache of 16 * 64Kb = 1Mb.

alter queue, *queue_number*, *queue_type*, **set sqm_xact_with_large_msg** [**to**] { **'skip'** | **'shutdown'** }
Specifies what to do when a 'large' message (i.e. greater than 16Kb) is encountered by RepServer: with **'skip'**, skips the message; with **'shutdown'** (=default), stops the queue. This setting does not require a RepServer restart; also, it cannot be set with **configure replication server**.

resume queue, *queue_number*, *queue_type* [, **skip transaction with large message**]
(not a configuration parameter) Restarts a stopped queue (presumably, due to encountering a 'large' message). **skip transaction with large message** skips the first 'large' message (i.e. greater than 16Kb) encountered.

30.3 RSSD tables - queues

The RSSD table **rs_queues** contains one row for each stable queue; **rs_segments** contains information about the allocation of each segment.
The RSSD tables **rs_queuemsg** and **rs_queuemsgtxt** contain the contents of a queue when it's been dumped to the RSSD with **sysadmin dump_queue**.

31 Special maintenance commands

sysadmin dropprs, *repserver_name*
Drops a RepServer from the ID Server. Note that the corresponding RSSD must also be dropped with **sysadmin dropdb** (➢p.31).

sysadmin hibernate_on [, *comment_string*]
Puts the RepServer in 'hibernation mode', suspending most activity (similar to starting RepServer in standalone mode). This is required for executing certain operations, such as some **sysadmin** commands. An arbitrary *comment_string* can be specified to ensure that hibernation is not turned off by someone else (see below).
Example: **sysadmin hibernate_on, waitforme**

sysadmin hibernate_off [, *comment_string*]
Turns off 'hibernation mode' for this RepServer, and resumes all normal activity. If *comment_string* was specified with **sysadmin hibernate_on**, the exact same string must be specified again with **sysadmin hibernate_off**. *comment_string* can be retrieved from the RSSD table **rs_recovery** with the following RSSD query: **select convert(char(255), text) from rs_recovery**

sysadmin dump_thread_stacks [, *module_name*]
Dumps a stack trace for each RepServer thread to the errorlog as well as the RepServer console. *module_name* can be any name shown as **Name** by **admin who**. For diagnostic purposes only; the results are useful for Sybase TechSupport only.

32 Users, logins, passwords and permissions

In a replication system, various users/logins play a role, as described below. Note that in RepServer, 'user' and 'login' are synonyms, unlike in ASE, where they represent different concepts.

32.1 RepServer user

A RepServer user is a username for connecting to a RepServer. RepServer users (and their passwords) are created with the **create user** command and stored in the RSSD table **rs_users**; these usernames are then used by DBAs, RepAgents and other RepServers (for routes, subscription creation, and ID server connections) to connect to the RepServer.
When a RepServer is created, the DBA can log in with username **'sa'** (with no password; this can be changed with **alter user**). Users for RepAgents, routes, the RSSD primary user and (for an ID server only) the ID server user also exist, named '*repserver_name*_**ra**', '*repserver_name*_**rsi**', '*RSSD_name*_**prim**' and '*repserver_name*_**id_user**', respectively, by default. Different names may be specified during the **rs_init** dialog (➢p.98) when creating the RepServer.

32.2 ID server user

The ID server is a normal RepServer, but also has the special task of assigning unique IDs for like databases, routes, RepServers, etc. in a replication domain. The first RepServer created in a domain almost always acts as the ID server. The ID server must be running when other RepServers create or drop a connection, create a route, or when a new RepServer is created in the domain.
The ID server user is a RepServer user existing only in the ID server. It is named '*repserver_name*_**id_user**' by default, and stored in the RSSD table **rs_users**.
For each RepServer, the name of its ID server and the corresponding ID server user and password are specified in its **.cfg** file (➢p.115). In 15.0.1, the name of the ID server can also be found with **admin config, id_server**.

32.3 RepAgent user

The RepAgent user is a RepServer user through which RepAgents connect to RepServer to send primary transactions. The RepAgent user is named '*repserver_name*_**ra**' by default, and stored in the RSSD table **rs_users**. Its password can be changed with **alter user**...**set password** (obviously, the password used by a RepAgent should be changed accordingly; ➢p.20,23).

32.4 Primary user (RSSD)

The primary user is an ASE (or, for an ERSSD, ASA) dataserver login used by a RepServer to read its RSSD and modify it as a result of executing RepServer commands (like creating repdefs, function strings, etc.) at the local RepServer. When the RepServer has an outgoing route, some of these modifications will be replicated to the destination RSSD. Note that the RSSD maintenance user (see below) is only used when an incoming route exists, for applying transactions from the source RSSD.
A RepServer always has one primary user, named '*rs_name*_**RSSD_prim'** by default, since it has one RSSD. Obviously, the RSSD primary user must have sufficient permissions in the RSSD. When a route is created, the username and password for the RSSD primary user of the source RepServer are also inserted in the destination RepServer's RSSD table **rs_users** (the destination RepServer uses this username to create/drop subscriptions to the source RepServer's RSSD).
When connecting to the RSSD, the dataserver username and password for the primary user are taken from the RepServer **.cfg** file (➢p.115); specifically, from the lines **'RSSD_primary_user='** and **'RSSD_primary_pw='** (for encrypted passwords, **'RSSD_primary_pw_enc='**); this information is (obviously) not taken from the RSSD (where it is also stored; see below).
The username and password in the **.cfg** file must match the actual dataserver login in the ASE/ASA RSSD server. When the dataserver password is changed in ASE/ASA, the password in the **.cfg** file must either be edited manually or -when using encrypted passwords- changed with the **rs_init** utility.

The primary user also happens to be stored in the RSSD table **rs_users**, with -by default- the same name and password as in the **.cfg** file. However, the username and the password from **rs_users** don't ever seem to be actually used (as far as I have been able to determine).
Note that the primary user's password should not be changed with **alter user**...**set password**. Although this command will work fine, it only updates the unused password in the RSSD table **rs_users** and not the actual password in the **.cfg** file (that is, for a classic ASE RSSD; for an ERSSD, **alter user** actually updates both passwords; ➢p.111).

32.5 Maintenance user

A maintenance user is a dataserver login used by RepServer for applying replicated transactions and performing subscription (de)materialization in a replicate database. Each database known to RepServer (including the RSSD) has a maintenance user; even when a database is only used as a primary.
The maintenance user must have sufficient permissions for executing SQL DML statements and stored procedures in the replicate database. For an ASE database, a maintenance user must be able to execute certain T-SQL statements and system stored procedures (like **dbcc gettrunc/settrunc**, **set triggers**, **set replication**, **truncate table**, **sp_reptostandby**, **sp_setreptable**, etc.). This requires the maintenance user either to be granted **replication_role** or **sa_role**, and/or **dbo** or object owner permissions. When using the **rs_init** utility to create a connection, be careful when the maintenance user is aliased to **dbo** (➢p.98).
By default, transactions by the maintenance user are ignored by the RepAgent and therefore not replicated (but RepAgent will pick up maintenance user transactions when configured with **'send maint xacts to replicate'** = **true**; ➢p.21). For this reason, the RSSD maintenance user must be different from the RSSD primary user, and maintenance users in primary databases must be different from application users.
Maintenance user passwords for 'normal' replicate databases and for the RSSD are handled differently:

- For maintenance users for 'normal' replicate databases, the username (named '*dbname*_**maint'** by default) and password are specified with **create connection** (or with the **rs_init** utility) and are stored in the RSSD table **rs_maintusers** (and can be displayed with the RSSD procedure **rs_helpuser**).
  The maintenance user password can be changed with **alter connection**...**set password** (➢p.30).
- For the RSSD maintenance user, the user name (by default named '*rs_name*_**RSSD_maint'**) and password are a bit special: although the lines **'RSSD_maint_user='** and **'RSSD_maint_pw='** (or **'RSSD_maint_pw_enc='** for encrypted passwords) must be present in the **.cfg** file, this username and password are in fact not used when connecting to the RSSD: the username and password from the RSSD table **rs_maintusers** are used instead.

32.6 Route user

A route user is a RepServer user for an outgoing route (named '*repserver_name*_**rsi**' by default), and is used by the source RepServer to connect to the destination RepServer. For more information about routes, see page 85.
This user is stored in the source RepServer RSSD table **rs_maintusers**; the username and password can be changed with **alter route**.
The route user and its password must match a RepServer user/password in the destination RepServer, where it is stored in the RSSD table **rs_users** (the password can be changed with **alter user**).

32.7 RepServer subscription user

The RepServer subscription user plays a role when creating or dropping a subscription with automatic (de)materialization: the same username and password of the RepServer session executing the **create subscription** or **drop subscription** command is also used to connect to the primary RepServer and to the primary dataserver. Therefore, this username (and its password) should be identical across all RepServers and dataservers in a replication domain. It is recommended not to use the RepServer **sa** user for this purpose, but to create a dedicated RepServer user instead (named **repadmin**, **ra** or **subscr_user**, for example). See section 18.2 (p.58) for more information. A similar mechanism is used for request functions; ➢p.41.

32.8 Users, passwords, permissions - Commands

create user *repserver_user_name* **set password** { '*new_password*' | **null** }
Creates a new, unprivileged RepServer user with the specified password. The user is stored in the RSSD table **rs_users**.
A password can be 1 to 30 characters long; if it contains non-alphanumeric characters, enclose it in quotes. **null** specifies a blank password.
Examples: **create user repadmin_jim set password BigSecret**
create user repadmin_joe set password 'xYz-A=b'
create user repadmin_sue set password 'ab cd' -- contains 2 spaces

alter user *repserver_user_name* **set password** { '*new_password*' | **null** } [**verify password** '*old_password*']
Changes the password for the specified RepServer user in the RSSD table **rs_users**.
verify password *old_password* needs to be specified only when the executing user does not have RepServer **sa** permission. Note: do not change passwords for a primary-, maintenance-, subscription- or route user while a subscription or a route is being created or dropped.
Only for an embedded RSSD: when changing the RSSD primary user password with **alter user**, the dataserver login password in ASA and the corresponding password in the **.cfg** file are automatically changed as well (➢p.111). In a classic ASE RSSD, the password in the **.cfg** file and the ASE dataserver password for the RSSD primary user must be updated separately by the DBA.
Example: **alter user sa set password BigSecret**

drop user *repserver_user_name*
Drops the specified RepServer user from the RSSD table **rs_users**.

rs_helpuser [*repserver_user_name* | *maintenance_user_name*]
(RSSD procedure) Displays either the permissions granted to the specified RepServer user, or the dataserver/database for the specified maintenance user. Without any parameter, displays this information for all users and maintenance users defined in this RSSD.
rs_helpuser does not display passwords for these users and maintenance users. When passwords are not encrypted, they can be displayed by querying the RSSD tables **rs_users** or **rs_maintusers** directly. Encrypted passwords cannot be decrypted directly, but for database connections, the plaintext passwords can be found with the **cm_user_pass** traceflag (➢p.100).
Note that route users for outgoing routes to other RepServers, although stored in the RSSD table **rs_maintusers**, are not displayed by **rs_helpuser**.

grant *permission* **to** *repserver_user_name*
Assigns a RepServer permission to a RepServer user (note that these permissions have no relation to ASE permissions). Possible RepServer permissions are:

sa	- has all permissions inside RepServer
create object	- can create repdefs, subscriptions etc.
primary subscribe	- can only create subscriptions
connect source	- required for RepAgent users and route users

Unlike the SQL **grant** statement, only one permission can be granted in a RepServer **grant** (or **revoke**) command. The permissions assigned to a RepServer user are displayed by the RSSD procedure **rs_helpuser**.
Example: **grant primary subscribe to jim**
grant create object to jim

revoke *permission* **from** *repserver_user_name*
Revokes a RepServer permission (assigned with **grant**) from a RepServer user.

set proxy [**to**] [*repserver_user_name* [**verify password** *password*]]
Switches the user for current session to the specified RepServer user, inheriting all permissions of the new user and none of the original user. **verify password** *password* must be specified by users who do not have **sa** permission. The new user for the session is displayed. To revert to the original user, run only **set proxy**.
This command is unrelated, but functionally similar, to the ASE **set proxy** statement.

33 RSSD

The RSSD (Replication Server System Database) is one of the three locations where a RepServer stores persistent data (for completeness, the other two are the stable devices and the RepServer **.cfg** file). The RSSD contains vital information in the **rs_*** tables (➢p.112). Without the RSSD, a RepServer cannot operate.
The RSSD tables can be queried with the RSSD **rs_*** stored procedures (like **rs_helprep**); they can also be queried directly. To query the RSSD, connect to the RSSD dataserver with **isql**.

By default, the RSSD is an ASE database. As of RepServer version 12.6, ASA (Adaptive Server Anywhere, a.k.a. SQL Anywhere) can be used for the RSSD instead: this is known as an 'embedded RSSD' or 'ERSSD'. The main advantages of an embedded RSSD is that ASA is simpler to operate, and requires less DBA involvement than ASE. On the other hand, some RepServer functionality (specifically, creating routes) is available only when the RSSD is hosted by ASE.
To determine whether a RepServer is using an embedded RSSD, run **sysadmin erssd**, or check whether the RepServer's **.cfg** file (➢p.115) contains the line **'RSSD_embedded=yes'**.

For reasons of performance and availability, it is recommended that the RSSD server (either ASE or ASA) does not contain other databases, or serves other applications.

RSSD creation
The type and location of the RSSD must be specified through the **rs_init** utility when a RepServer is created.
The RSSD **rs_*** tables are created by the **rs_init** utility, by running a script from **$SYBASE/$SYBASE_REP/scripts**: **rs_install_systables_ase.sql** is used to create a classic ASE RSSD, and **rs_install_systables_asa.sql** for an embedded ASA RSSD.
The RSSD stored procedures (also named **rs_***) are also created by **rs_init**: **rsprocs_ase.sql** is used for a classic ASE RSSD, and **rsprocs_asa.sql** for an embedded ASA RSSD. The RSSD procedures are described at various places in this book.

33.1 Classic RSSD (in ASE)

To host the RSSD, any ASE version later than ASE 11.0 can be used.
The ASE server hosting the RSSD must be started (and stopped) explicitly by the DBA; RepServer does not handle this itself. This ASE server can run on a different host than the RepServer; however, it is recommend to keep the RSSD server on the same host as the RepServer (provided sufficient memory and CPU is available)
The RSSD must be available when RepServer starts. When the RSSD becomes unavailable while RepServer is running, RepServer keeps retrying to connect to the RSSD every few minutes. No further processing is performed until the RSSD is available again.
The RSSD is created by the **rs_init** utility; the ASE server must already exist.

admin rssd_name
Displays the name of the ASE dataserver and database for this RepServer's RSSD. When an embedded RSSD is used, the dataserver and database name are identical (although this could also be the case for an ASE RSSD; run **sysadmin erssd** to determine whether an embedded RSSD is used).

33.2 Embedded RSSD/ERSSD (ASA)

Instead of ASE, RepServer can also use ASA for its RSSD (ASA=Adaptive Server Anywhere, a.k.a. as SQL Anywhere; 'ASA' is used in this book). This feature is referred to as 'embedded RSSD', or 'ERSSD', because no DBA activity is needed to manage the RSSD: RepServer (re)starts the ASA server when it needs to access the RSSD and ASA is not running; when RepServer shuts down, it stops the ASA server (the startup/shutdown commands used are also logged in the RepServer error log file). It is required that the ASA server runs on the same host as the RepServer.
Note that the embedded RSSD may not be available on all platforms. It is currently supported on Linux, HP-UX, AIX, Solaris and Windows.
An embedded RSSD is functionally equivalent to a classic RSSD on ASE, with one exception in 12.6: when using an embedded RSSD in 12.6, it is not possible to create a route at this RepServer. For this functionality, the RSSD must either be hosted by ASE, or RS 15.0 should be used.

The ASA server and embedded RSSD database are created by the **rs_init** utility. The default ASA login/password(**DBA/SQL**) is removed by **rs_init**; the only logins available are the primary RSSD login and the maintenance RSSD login, by default named '*rs_name*_**RSSD_prim**' and '*rs_name*_**RSSD_maint**', respectively. By default, the passwords are identical to the login name, but with an additional **'_ps'** suffix. The primary RSSD login/password can also be found in the RepServer **.cfg** file.
It is recommended to create a separate login to as a solution to locking yourself out (➢p.131); see p.111 for ASA commands. Make sure to store this password in a safe but accessible place.

sysadmin erssd
sysadmin erssd, backup
sysadmin erssd, { **dbfile_dir** | **translog_dir** | **logmirror_dir** }, **'***new_pathname***'**
(15.0) sysadmin erssd, defrag
Applies only when this RepServer uses an embedded RSSD. Without any parameters, displays the current settings for the ERSSD.
With **backup**, performs a one-time backup of the ERSSD files, independent of the automatically scheduled ASA backups (see below).
When specifying **dbfile_dir**, **translog_dir** or **logmirror_dir**, RepServer moves the database files, transaction log files or transaction log mirror files, respectively, to the directory specified by *new_pathname*. Note that this operation may take some time, and the ERSSD will not be available until the move has completed.
With **defrag**, rebuilds and defragments the ERSSD; do not run at busy times.
The ASA software is installed in **$SYBASE/$SYBASE_REP/ASA9** (this is not displayed by **sysadmin erssd**). RS 12.6 uses **ASA8**.

33.3 Configuration parameters for embedded RSSD

The following server-wide configuration parameters only apply to RepServers with an embedded RSSD (ERSSD). These parameters can only be changed (one parameter at a time) with **configure replication server**. All parameters are stored in the RSSD table **rs_config** in the ASA ERSSD (they don't exist in an ASE RSSD); changes take effect immediately. The current settings are displayed by **sysadmin erssd**.

- **erssd_backup_dir** - specifies the directory where backup files for the RSSD data and log are stored. Default = **'$SYBASE/$SYBASE_REP/backup'**.
- **erssd_backup_start_date** - specifies the date when the backup cycle will start, formatted either as **'YYYY-MM-DD'** or **'MM/DD/YYYY'**. Default = date of RepServer creation.
- **erssd_backup_start_time** - specifies the time of day (formatted as **'hh:mm'** (24 hr) or **'hh:mm AM|PM'** (12-hr)) when the backup cycle will start. Default = **'01:00 AM'**.
- **erssd_backup_interval** - specifies the amount of time between backups, specified as **'***nn* **hours'** or **'***nn* **minutes'** where *nn* is an integer number (**'***nn* **seconds'** is also possible, but is not practical). Default = **'24 hours'**.
  Changing this interval has the effect of performing the next ASA backup at the time of the new interval after the most recent backup. The time of the most recent backup can be found by examining the files in the backup directory (as displayed by **sysadmin erssd**).
- **(15.0) erssd_ra** - the name of the RSSD RepAgent for a RepServer with an embedded RSSD; default= '*ERSSD_name*_**rs**'. This name must be in the **interfaces** file (Windows: **SQL.INI**).

Examples: **configure replication server set erssd_backup_start_time to '06:00'**

Notes:

- Technically, the backup scheduling and execution is performed by ASA. When the above configuration parameters are changed, **configure replication server** updates their new values not only in the RSSD table **rs_config** but also in the ASA system tables **SYSEVENT** and **SYSSCHEDULE**; these ASA tables drive the actual backup scheduling. For this reason, updating the ERSSD configuration parameters should be done only with **configure replication server**; updating the RSSD table **rs_config** directly will not propagate the new values to ASA.
- Only the last two generations of an ASA backup are kept in the backup directory; older generations are deleted automatically. Therefore, do not specify a short backup interval unless the backup files are explicitly copied to a different location.

33.4 Embedded RSSD: miscellaneous ASA information

Direct queries against the ASA ERSSD can be performed with **isql** (located in **$SYBASE/$SYBASE_OCS/bin**).

Useful ASA commands

The tables and stored procedures in an ASA ERSSD are identical to an ASE RSSD. However, ASA uses a slightly different SQL dialect than ASE. ASA commands and procedures are quite different from ASE; some useful commands are listed below.

- To change the password of the RSSD primary user or RSSD maintenance user, use the RepServer commands **alter user**...**set password** or **alter connection**...**set password**, respectively. These commands change the passwords in the RSSD tables, in ASA itself, and in the RepServer **.cfg** file (note: in an ASE RSSD, **alter user/alter connection** neither changes the ASE dataserver password, nor updates the **.cfg** file).
- To create a new ASA login named **'repadmin'** with password **'MySecret'** and full ASA permissions, run these commands in ASA (you can connect with **isql**):
  grant connect to repadmin identified by MySecret
  grant DBA to repadmin
- To create a new ASA login named **'repadmin2'** with password **'YourSecret'** and only permissions to access the RSSD tables, run these commands in ASA:
  grant connect to repadmin2 identified by YourSecret
  grant membership in group rs_systabgroup to repadmin2
- To drop the ASA login **'repadmin2'**, run this command in ASA:
  revoke connect from repadmin2
- To change the password for ASA login **'repadmin'**, run this command in ASA:
  grant connect to repadmin identified by MyNewPasswd
- To display all existing ASA logins, run this command in ASA:
  select name from syslogins

ASA startup & shutdown

RepServer starts and stops the ASA server automatically when needed. The OS commands issued by RepServer to start and stop ASA are logged in the RepServer errorlog: **dbping/dbping_r** checks whether the ASA server is running; **dbspawn** and **dbstop** start and stop the ASA server, respectively. The ASA server binary is **dbsrv9** or **dbsrv8** (for ASA 9 / 8).
However, it may sometimes be necessary to start the ASA server independently of RepServer, for example when you need to update data in the RSSD tables while RepServer is down (for example, when renaming a RepServer; ➢p.133).
To start the ASA server manually, run this command at the OS prompt:

dbsrv9 -x "tcpip(port=*tcpip_port_no***)" -o** *asa_errorlog_path asa_dbfile_path*

To stop: **dbstop -c "eng=***ASA_server_name***;uid=***ASA_login_name***;pwd=***password***"**
Notes:

- When starting/stopping ASA manually, the Unix environment variable **$PATH** must include **$SYBASE/$SYBASE_REP/ASA8/bin**; also, the variable **$LD_LIBRARY_PATH** (on HP-UX: **$SHLIB_PATH**; on AIX: **$LIBPATH**) must include **$SYBASE/$SYBASE_REP/ASA8/lib**. On Windows, the environment variable **%PATH%** must include **%SYBASE%\%SYBASE_REP%\ASA8\win32**.
- The location of the ASA errorlog and database file is described below.
- When stopping ASA with **dbstop**, any privileged ASA login can be used as login/password. The ASA login *RSSD_name***_prim**/*RSSD_name***_prim_ps** should work by default (the default ASA login **DBA/SQL** is removed by **rs_init**).

ASA errorlog & database file
By default, the ASA errorlog and database file are .../**errorlog**/*ERSSD_name*.**out** and .../**dbfile**/*ERSSD_name*.**db** (in **$SYBASE/$SYBASE_REP**). These filenames are also indicated in the RepServer errorlog on the **dbspawn** line (behind the **-o** option); the errorlog filename is also stored in the **.cfg** file.

ERSSD/ASA documentation
More information about the ERSSD can be found in the *Replication Server Administration Guide* (➢p.13). In addition, a whitepaper titled *Internals of Embedded Replication Server System Database* is available at **www.sybase.com** (just search for the title). Full ASA documentation can be found at **www.sypron.nl/repqr2/asa**.

33.5 List of RSSD tables

The RSSD tables are created by the **rs_init** utility, by running a script in **$SYBASE/$SYBASE_REP/scripts**.This script is **rs_install_systables_ase.sql** when a classic ASE RSSD is used, or **rs_install_systables_asa.sql** for an embedded ASA RSSD.
For details about columns, see the chapter *Replication Server System Tables* in the *Replication Server Reference Manual* (➢p.13). A poster of the RSSD tables data model can be downloaded (in PDF format) from **www.sypron.nl/repqr2/rsstd**.

Warning: under normal circumstances, it should never be required to update RSSD tables manually. This may be required only when performing certain non-standard maintenance operations (like renaming a RepServer) or for troubleshooting. If RSSD tables need to be updated anyway, be extremely careful, and shut down RepServer first. Note that manually updating the RSSD is not supported by Sybase.

rs_articles
Contains publication articles.

rs_captable
(Undocumented) Used by the RSSD procedures **rs_capacity** and **rs_fillcaptable**.

rs_classes
Contains classes. The **classtype** column indicates the type of class: **'F'** = function string class, **'E'** = error class and **'D'** = date class. When an outgoing route exists for this RepServer, **rs_classes** is replicated to the destination RSSD.

rs_columns
Contains the columns and parameters of table and function repdefs. When an outgoing route exists for this RepServer, **rs_columns** is replicated to the destination RSSD.

rs_config
Contains configuration parameter settings.

rs_databases
Contains all database connections in this RepServer. The **dbid** column identifies a connection; this value starts at 101 and is incremented for each new connection.
When an outgoing route exists for this RepServer, **rs_databases** is replicated to the destination RSSD.

rs_datatype
Contains datatype definitions for datatype classes.

rs_dbreps
Contains database repdefs. When an outgoing route exists for this RepServer, **rs_dbreps** is replicated to the destination RSSD.

rs_dbsubsets
Contains the inclusion/exclusion lists for database repdef filters for tables, procedures and system procedures. When an outgoing route exists for this RepServer, **rs_dbsubsets** is replicated to the destination RSSD.

rs_diskaffinity
Contains disk affinity settings (disk space allocation hints).

rs_diskpartitions
Contains information about the disk partitions holding the stable queues.

rs_erroractions
Contains error actions for dataserver errors encountered by the DSI. When an outgoing route exists for this RepServer, **rs_erroractions** is replicated to the destination RSSD.

rs_exceptshdr
Contains information about transactions written to the RSSD exceptions log.

rs_exceptscmd
For transactions in **rs_exceptshdr**, points to the actual transaction text in **rs_systext**.

rs_exceptslast
Contains information about the last logged transaction written into the RSSD exceptions log, for each primary database (this does not include transactions skipped by **sysadmin log_first_tran**).

rs_funcstrings
Contains function string information; the actual function string text is stored in **rs_systext**. When an outgoing route exists for this RepServer, **rs_funcstrings** is replicated to the destination RSSD.

rs_functions
Contains information about functions. When an outgoing route exists for this RepServer, **rs_functions** is replicated to the destination RSSD.

rs_idnames
Contains the names and IDs of all RepServers and databases known to the ID server. This table is relevant only in the RSSD of the ID server.

rs_ids
For various types of RepServer objects, contains the ID of the last created object.

rs_locater
Contains the last locater value (an OQID value; ➢p.126) for a queue for each primary database, incoming route, warm standby, and others. The locater reflects the point to which data in the primary transaction log or corresponding queue has been received by RepServer. For a primary ASE database, the locater corresponds to the secondary truncation point in the transaction log. For a RepAgent, **rs_locater.type** = **'E'**.

rs_maintusers
Contains usernames and passwords for maintenance users and outgoing routes.

rs_msgs
Contains a small number of RepServer error messages, for all installed languages.

rs_objects
Contains table repdefs (the **objtype** column = **'R'**) and function repdefs (**objtype** = **'F'**). Table repdefs named **rs_*** are internal repdefs for RSSD tables for routes (these repdefs always exist, also without routes).
Database repdefs are stored in **rs_dbreps**. When an outgoing route exists for this RepServer, **rs_objects** is replicated to the destination RSSD.

rs_oqid
For each stable queue, contains the last OQID (➢p.126) received from the source of that queue.

rs_publications
Contains all publications.

rs_queuemsg
When a queue is dumped into the RSSD with **sysadmin dump_queue**, the messages in the queue are written into **rs_queuemsg**. When the data already exists, it is deleted first.

rs_queuemsgtxt
For queue messages in **rs_queuemsg**, contains the message command text, split over multiple rows if needed.

rs_queues
Contains information about stable queues; each stable queue is one row.

rs_recovery
Contains actions to be performed by RepServer when recovering from a failure.

rs_repdbs
Contains all replicate databases with a subscription to one or more repdefs in this primary RepServer.

rs_repobjs
In the replicate RSSD, contains autocorrection settings for table repdefs that have a subscription in this replicate RepServer.

rs_routes
Contains a row for all incoming/outgoing routes for this RepServer. When an outgoing route exists for this RepServer, **rs_routes** is replicated to the destination RSSD.

rs_routeversions
Contains the versions of the RepServers involved in each route.

rs_rules
Contains the **where**-clauses for subscriptions and articles.

rs_segments
Contains allocation details for each stable queue.

rs_sites
Contains all RepServers with a route to or from the current RepServer. The **id** column contains a unique identifier for each RepServer in a replication domain (i.e. with the same ID server). For the RepServer that is also the ID server, its **id** is 16777317; for RepServers subsequently added to the domain, this number is incremented.
When a RepServer has no routes, **rs_sites** contains only one row, with its own name and **id**. This also applies to the ID server, in contrast with the RSSD table **rs_idnames**, which always contains all RepServers in a replication domain, independent of the existence of routes.

rs_statcounters
A static table, containing a description of each monitor counter.

rs_statdetail
Contains actual monitor counter values for each sample period in **rs_statrun**.

rs_statrun
Contains each sample period where monitor counters have been sampled.

(15.1) rs_statreport
Contains monitor counter data.for use by **rs_stat_genreport** (➢p.122).

rs_subscriptions
Contains all subscriptions created in the current RepServer, as well as all subscriptions created in other RepServers for repdefs in the current RepServer. Subscriptions named **rs_*** are subscriptions to RSSD tables for incoming routes.

rs_systext
Contains text for objects stored in other RSSD tables like **rs_funcstrings** (function strings) and **rs_exceptscmd** (transactions in the exceptions log). When an outgoing route exists for this RepServer, **rs_systext** is replicated to the destination RSSD.

rs_translation
Contains datatype translations for date classes (➢p.28) .

rs_tvalues
(Undocumented) Contains display attributes for RSSD procedures (like **master..spt_values** in ASE) and information for the deprecated RSSD procedure **rs_configure**.

rs_users
Contains the name, password and permissions for each RepServer user. In order to connect to RepServer, the login name must exist in **rs_users**.

rs_version
Contains RepServer versions. In the ID server, contains the version of all RepServers; in other RepServers, contains only its own version.

rs_whereclauses
Contains information about **where**-clauses for articles (not for subscriptions). The actual **where**-clause is stored in **rs_rules**.

34 Configuration (.cfg) file

The RepServer configuration file (referred to as **.cfg** file in this book) is an ASCII file read by RepServer during startup to determine the server name, login and password for the ID server and RSSD server. Because the **.cfg** file contains passwords, it should be protected properlyon file-system level.
By default, the **.cfg** file is located in **$SYBASE/$SYBASE_REP/install** and named *repserver_name*.**cfg**. The actual location of the **.cfg** file is passed to RepServer with the **-C** command line parameter in the **RUN_***servername* file (➢p.100).

The **.cfg** file contains some rather self-explanatory keywords. It is not recommended to edit the **.cfg** file manually, unless you understand what you're doing. When the **.cfg** file does not exist or contains invalid keywords, RepServer will not start.
When the **.cfg** file contains encrypted passwords, these passwords can only be modified through **rs_init** (➢p.98).
When a line starts with '**#**', the entire line is a comment.

(15.0) For RepServers with an embedded RSSD that have outgoing routes, the ERSSD RepAgent also has a **.cfg** file, by default located in **$SYBASE** (➢p.86).

35 Replication system monitoring features

RepServer comes with features for monitoring the status of the various servers in the replication system (not to be confused with the monitoring counters in section 40.3, which are about the internal workings of a single RepServer).
The abbreviations of the various features can be confusing, so here's a quick overview; details are in the sections below:

- RMP - Replication Manager Plug-in for Sybase Central, Java version (12.6)
- RMS - Replication Monitoring Services (15.0)
- RSP - RepServer Plug-in for Sybase Central, non-Java version (pre-15.0)
- RSM - Replication Server Manager (pre-15.0)

35.1 Replication Manager Plug-in (RMP) for Sybase Central

As of 12.6, the 'Replication Manager Plug-in' (RMP) for the Java version of Sybase Central can be used to perform most RepServer DBA tasks through the Sybase Central GUI; this runs on all Java-enabled platforms. RMP includes support for creating repdefs, subscriptions, warm standby etc., reverse-engineering these, resuming/ suspending connections, etc. In 12.6, RMP support is limited to a few core RepServer areas, but in 15.0 almost the full range of RepServer functionality is covered.
In 15.0, RMP replaces RSP, the RepServer Plug-in (➢35.3) for the non-Java version of Sybase Central.
RMP is located in **$SYBASE/RMP-***xx_y* (e.g. **RMP-15_0**). If it is not automatically registered with Sybase Central, you can register it manually through Tools → Plug-ins → Register and browse to **$SYBASE/$SYBASE_RMP/lib/RMPlugin.jar**.

35.2 Replication Monitoring Services (RMS) (15.0)

RMS (Replication Monitoring Services) is a 3-tier utility for monitoring replication systems, involving the Unified Agent Framework (UAF) and the Replication Manager Plug-in (RMP; ➢35.1) for Sybase Central. In 15.0, RMS replaces the pre-15.0 RSM server (➢35.4).
RMS monitors the status of RepServers and dataservers, and can automatically execute user-created shell scripts when certain events occur. With the Replication Manager Plug-in, most RepServer DBA tasks can be performed, and errorlog files for RepServers and dataservers can be viewed remotely (in fact, this plug-in can be handy for monitoring errorlogs of remote ASE servers, even without using RepServer at all).
In addition to monitoring RepServers, RMS can also monitor ASE and IQ servers, non-ASE RepAgents, OpenServers, Direct Connect servers, etc.
RMS can be accessed through the Replication Manager Plug-in for Sybase Central, but also through an ASCII command-line interface. To start and stop RMS, the UAF agent must be started/stopped. For more information about using RMS, see the product manual *What's new in Replication Server*.

35.3 RepServer Plug-in (RSP) for Sybase Central (pre-15.0)

(Windows only) In pre-12.6, the RepServer Plug-in (RSP) for the non-Java version of Sybase Central can be used to perform most RepServer DBA tasks through the Sybase Central GUI. RSP does not support database repdefs/-subscriptions in 12.6.
The plug-in is located in **%SYBASE%\RSP-12_*x*\screpsrv.dll**. Note that these plug-ins work only with the corresponding version of RSM server, and are not backwards compatible. Therefore, you may need to change plug-ins dynamically when different versions of RSM server are around (so it may be a good idea to keep a copy of the .dll file for the plug-in for each RSM server version (=same as RepServer versions)).
In 15.0, RSP has been replaced with RMP (➢35.1).

35.4 RSM server (pre-15.0)

RSM (Replication Server Manager) is a client-server utility for monitoring replication systems. RSM server runs in the background as a Sybase OpenServer application. The 'RepServer Plug-in' (RSP) for the non-Java version of Sybase Central is the client application for accessing RSM server.
In 15.0, RSM server has been replaced by RMS (Replication Monitoring Services; ➢35.2).
The RSM server is located in the **$SYBASE/$SYBASE_RSM** directory tree. The RSM server stores its data in various subdirectories. To create a new RSM server, first add the RSM servername to the **interfaces** file (Windows: **SQL.INI** file). Then, run the tool **./install/rsmgen** (Windows: **.\install\rsmsetup.exe**) to create the **RUN_***servername* file for the RSM server. On Windows, the RSM server is also installed as a service (named **SYBRSM_***servername*).
Before an RSM server can monitor a RepServer, some RSM-related stored procedures must be installed in the RepServer's RSSD. These procedures are located in the script **$SYBASE/$SYBASE_RSM/scripts/rsm***xxxx***.sql**, where *xxxx* is the version number of the RSM server (for example, **1250**).

It is usually not necessary to log into RSM server manually since all tasks can be performed through the RSP plug-in. Nevertheless, RSM Server provides an ASCII command-line interface through **isql**. The login name and password (default=**sa**/none) are defined in **./admin/config/***rsm_servername***.users.rsm**.
See the pre-15.0 RepServer documentation for details.

36 Quiescing a replication system

A replication system is said to be 'quiesced' (or 'quiescent') when all RepServers have processed all their incoming messages and delivered all outgoing messages, when there are no open transactions, and when no subscription (de)materialization is in progress. Quiescing a replication system or an individual RepServer is sometimes required, for example to modify the schema of a replicated table, or for troubleshooting.
To determine whether a RepServer is currently quiesced, run **admin quiesce_check**. Unless all log transfer and incoming routes have been suspended, there is no guarantee that a quiesced state will be maintained.

To quiesce a replication system, perform these steps:

1. In all RepServers, run **suspend log transfer from all**.
2. In all RepServers with outgoing routes, run **admin quiesce_force_rsi** (➢p.88), forcing RepServer to send all messages in the queues for its routes. Wait briefly before proceeding with the next step, to allow the messages to be processed.
3. In all RepServers, run **admin quiesce_check** to determine whether the RepServer is quiesced. For those RepServers that are not quiesced, repeat step 2.
4. Finally, run steps 2 and 3 one last time.

Once a quiesced RepServer can return to its normal state, first resume log transfer for the RSSD (if the RSSD is replicated) before resuming log transfer for the other primary databases.

admin quiesce_check
Determines whether the RepServer is currently quiesced.

The **rs_ticket** feature (➢p.132) can be used to determine whether replication is 'quiesced' for an individual table once primary updates on the table are suspended (even though updates on other tables may continue): once the ticket arrives in the replicate database, this implies that all primary updates on the table have been replicated too.

37 Determining latency

In a replication system, 'latency' is defined as the time between the moment a transaction is committed in the primary database and the moment it is committed in the replicate database. Normally, latency should be small (typically seconds rather than minutes). Latency may increase due to workload peaks or temporary unavailability of any component in the replication system.
Latency can be measured in various ways:

- With the RSP plug-in (➢p.116), set up a 'heartbeat' in RSM server.
- Use the **rs_ticket** feature (➢p.132).
- Perhaps the easiest way to measure latency is by querying the **rs_lastcommit** table in the replicate database. The following query displays the latency (in seconds) for each primary database from where data is replicated to the current, replicate database:

```
select PrimaryDBID = origin,
        datediff (ss, origin_time, dest_commit_time) 'Latency(sec)',
        LastXactOriginTime = origin_time
from rs_lastcommit where origin > 0
```

  Note that the values in **origin_time** (the commit time of the primary transaction) and **dest_commit_time** (the commit time of the replicate transaction) were taken from the system clocks on the hosts where the primary and replicate dataserver were running. Any time difference between the system clocks on those hosts directly affects latency measurements.

38 Coordinated dumps

When a primary database must be restored from backups (for example, due to hardware problems or database corruption), the replicate databases should be restored consistently with the primary database. To make this possible, RepServer provides a feature called 'coordinated dumps'. When a database dump or transaction log dump is performed in a primary database, this event itself is replicated so that a corresponding dump is performed in the corresponding replicate databases as well. By restoring these dumps in both the primary and replicate databases, the replication system can be kept consistent.
To enable coordinated dumps, perform these actions for each replicate database:

- Create custom function strings for the functions **rs_dumpdb** and **rs_dumptran** for all function string classed used by the connection to replicate databases (by default no function strings exist for these functions). These function strings should perform a database dump and a transaction log dump, respectively, and update the **rs_lastcommit** table.
  Example for **rs_dumpdb**:

```
create function string rs_dumpdb for rs_sqlserver_function_class
output language
  'dump database ?rs_destination_db!sys_raw? to
     "/opt/dumps/?rs_destination_db!sys_raw?.dbdump";
  execute rs_update_lastcommit
     ?rs_origin!sys?, ?rs_origin_qid!sys?,?rs_secondary_qid!sys?,
     ?rs_origin_commit_time!sys?'
```

  Pay special attention to the name of the dump file: this should probably include an indication of the date/time to avoid subsequent dumps from overwriting each other, and perhaps also the dataserver name (omitted from this example).
  In fact, it may be more practical to perform all necessary actions in a stored procedure, and execute this procedure from the function string.
- Enable coordinated dumps for the replicate database connection by setting the configuration parameter **dump_load** to 'on':

```
alter connection to SALES_DEPT.prod_db set dump_load to 'on'
```

  The new setting for this configuration parameter takes effect once the connection is resumed (so it should probably be suspended first). By setting it to **'off'** (=default), **rs_dumpdb** and **rs_dumptran** will not be executed for this replicate database.

Notes:

- Coordinated dumps can normally only be used reliably with one-way replication. When a database is both a primary database and a replicate database at the same time, coordinated dumps are unlikely to provide a consistent backup of the replication system (unless all primary updates can be suspended for a certain period of time, and a coordinated dump covers all databases in the replication system).

- When a dump is performed in a primary database, a coordinated dump is performed only for those replicate databases containing subscriptions to primary data in that primary database.
- The maintenance user should have sufficient permissions to perform all actions required for implementing **rs_dumpdb** and **rs_dumptran**.
- Note that the RSSD is not dumped by coordinated dumps, and should be backed up separately.

38.1 Restoring coordinated dumps

Coordinated dumps are made for the purpose of restoring them if needed. However, the restore procedure can be quite complex and would not fit in this quick reference guide (also see the section below). Therefore, please refer to the *Replication Server Administration Guide* (➢p.13), chapter *Replication System Recovery* for full details.

39 Replication system recovery

Disasters occur, and if you're unlucky, they occur in your replication system. When the consistency of a replication system is jeopardised, it may or may not be possible, and may or may not be quick or easy, to restore the replication system to a recent and consistent state.
Much depends on the architecture of the replication system: for example, systems with bi-directional replication can be notoriously difficult to recover when things go wrong; things tend to be significantly simpler for one-way-only replication. Therefore, attention should be paid to recoverability aspects when designing a replication system (see the *Replication Server Design Guide* (➢p.13) for more information).

Recovery procedures can be complex and would not fit in this quick reference guide. Also, there is simply too much to say about this rather complex topic, and including a summary would only create a false impression of completeness. Therefore, please refer to the *Replication Server Administration Guide* (➢p.13), chapter *Replication System Recovery* for full details. When recovery is needed, the *Replication Server Troubleshooting Guide* may also provide some useful hints.
Some individual recovery-related commands are described below.

39.1 Recovery-related commands

Note: the commands described below should be used only in certain recovery scenarios. See the RepServer documentation (as mentioned above) for full details how these commands should be used.

set log recovery for *dataserver.database*
Puts RepServer in log recovery mode for the specified primary database whose transaction log will be recovered from offline dumps (backups). RepServer should have been started in standalone mode; **allow connections** should be executed next.

allow connections
Puts RepServer in log recovery mode, accepting connections only from RepAgents started in recovery mode. Before executing **allow connections**, RepServer should have been started in standalone mode, and **set log recovery** should have been executed for each database for which the transaction logs will be replayed.

rebuild queues
Deletes all stable queues, recreates them and attempts to reconstruct their contents by retrieving the transactions from transaction logs in primary databases, or -in case of incoming routes- from upstream RepServers. Alternatively, transactions can be retrieved from offline transaction database/log dumps (backups).
Finally, **rebuild queues** performs loss detection to determine whether any messages may have been lost; check the RepServer errorlog for warnings indicating that messages may indeed have been lost. If necessary, use **ignore loss** (see below).
Note: **rebuild queues** is a troubleshooting command that should only be used to fix serious problems with queues and disk partitions. When used incorrectly, **rebuild queues** can actually cause transactions to be lost. Therefore, use this command only when you understand what you're doing! See the *Replication Server Administration Guide* (➢p.13), chapter *Replication System Recovery* for more information.

ignore loss from *primary_dataserver.primary_database*
to { *replicate_dataserver.replicate_database* | *replicate_repserver_name* }
Allows RepServer to continue after potential message loss has been detected. In this situation, RepServer will stop processing messages from the primary database to the replicate database or replicate RepServer. This will not be visible by **admin who** since all threads will still be up; RepServer only logs a message in the RepServer errorlog (➢p.128 for additional details). The DBA must either replay the proper transaction logs, or run **ignore loss** to allow processing to continue.
Note that loss detection in fact only tries to verify the absence of message loss by confirming that no messages have been lost. If the first message received after rebuilding the queues has been received before, this means that no messages can be lost for that queue. However, if the first message has not been received before, message loss cannot be excluded; consequently, loss will be reported even though not a single message may have been lost in reality.

Miscellaneous Topics

40 Performance tips

Various performance-related features are available to RepServer DBAs. The following is a summary of some main points, listed -but only loosely- in order of practical relevance (please note that this list is not necessarily complete, but only seeks to provide some guidance):

- First, pick up a copy of an excellent whitepaper about RepServer performance tuning, titled *Sybase Replication Server Performance and Tuning*. For the current location of the latest version, see **www.sypron.nl/repqr2/x2**.
- Use the **rs_ticket** feature (➢p.132) to determine which stage of the replication pipeline seems to be the bottleneck -- or, just as important, to determine which stages are not a bottleneck.
- Verify that the replicate SQL queries are executed efficiently in the replicate database. In particular, look for inefficient query plans, and adjust indexes in the replicate database as necessary.
  To investigate these issues in ASE, use the MDA tables **monOpenObjectActivity**, **monSysStatement** and **monSysSQLText**, or use **sp_showplan**, or -in ASE 15.0.2- use application tracing. To get the exact text of the replicate SQL queries, use the traceflag **dsi_buf_dump** (➢p.100), or -in ASE- use **monSysSQLText / monProcessSQLText**, or application tracing.
- Assuming the previous bullet has been covered, various options exist to potentially improve processing of replicate SQL statements. These all aim to eliminate overhead due to parsing and optimising of replicate SQL queries:
  - In RS 15.0.1, consider enabling **dynamic_sql** to speed up application of SQL statements in the replicate database (➢p.34)
  - If you're running RS pre-15.0.1, you cannot use **dynamic_sql**. However, if the replicate dataserver is ASE 15.0.2, consider enabling the ASE statement cache as well as literal autoparametrization (preferably for DSI connections only; this can be achieved with ASE login triggers)
  - If none of the above is possible, another option is to use customized function strings to execute stored procedures in the replicate database instead of regular SQL statements.
- If the ASE RepAgent cannot keep up (i.e. it falls well behind the end of the log; check with **sp_help_rep_agent** or **rs_ticket**), consider one or more of the following:
  - Configure a log-only named cache in ASE, and bind the primary transaction log to it. If a log-only cache already exists, consider making it larger. In ASE, a buffer pool for double-page I/O (e.g. 4Kb for a 2Kb-page server) will automatically be used exclusively for transaction log I/O if an 8-page buffer pool (e.g. 16 Kb for a 2Kb-page server) also exists.
  - Consider giving the ASE RepAgent a higher priority (➢p.22).
  - Consider binding the ASE RepAgent to an engine of its own as much as possible. This can be achieved by binding application sessions to a different engines (with ASE execution classes and engine groups) than the engine RepAgent appears to be running on.
    Depending on the ASE version, the ASE RepAgent can also be bound explicitly to a specific engine with the **'bind to engine'** option (➢p.22).
  - Consider increasing the RepAgent setting for **'scan batch size'** (➢p.21).
  - Examine the '**repagent**' section of the ASE stored proc **sp_sysmon** for additional clues.
- Enable minimal column replication if possible (➢p.49).
- In a warm standby, as well as with database repdefs, consider creating table repdefs (without subscriptions) for better performance (➢p.50; p.18).
- Replication of large primary transactions may be inefficient. Consider creating a primary stored procedure to perform the DML in the primary database, and replicate this stored procedure instead of the DML (for details, ➢p.49).
- If the replicate dataserver is ASE 15.0, consider enabling the 'delayed commit' feature for the replicate database. Depending on activity on the replicate database by other applications, this can be done either on database level with **sp_dboption...'delayed commit'**, or for the maintenance user only with **set delayed_commit on**. Make sure you understand the impact on transaction durability for other applications when using the **sp_dboption** setting (durability is not an issue for transactions by the maintenance user).

To run **set delayed_commit on** for the maintenance user only, either use a custom function string (like **rs_usedb**) to execute **set delayed_commit on** when connecting to the replicate dataserver, or use an ASE login trigger.
When using delayed commit for a replicate ASE database, it is recommended to set the **save_interval** for the corresponding outbound queue to ensure that, in unforeseen circumstances, any committed-but-lost transactions can be re-applied.

- Ensure frequently used RSSD tables are cached (➢section 40.1 below).
- Consider using a larger network packet size for connections (i.e. increase the **db_packet_size** configuration parameter), routes (**rsi_packet_size**) and RepAgents (**'send buffer size'**; ➢p.22).
- Consider parallel DSI (➢p.95) to improve performance on the replicate side. Also, use internal commit control (**dsi_commit_control** = **on**).
  When many parallel transaction failures occur, set **dsi_commit_check_locks_intrvl** to a lower value (default = **1000**) to detect deadlocks sooner (you may even try setting it to **0**). Note this will likey increase the CPU consumption by ASE.
- The size of the SQT cache for the DSI (configured with **sqt_max_cache_size** or **dsi_sqt_max_cache_size**) should often be increased significantly beyond the default of 1Mb. To see whether this may be needed, run **admin who, sqt**: non-zero values for **Removed** indicate a larger SQT cache size may be beneficial (altenatively, run **admin statistics, sqt** and look for non-zero values for monitor counter **TransRemoved**).
  However, beware of configuring unnecessary high values for this SQT cache: contrary to what you might expect, a large SQT cache size may, in some circumstances, adversely impact RepServer throughput.
- In a warm standby for which no subscriptions to other databases exist, the distributor may be shut down permanently to improve performance (➢p.66).
- Multiple CPUs can be used by setting the configuration parameter **smp_enable** to **'on'**. This makes sense only when (i) multiple CPUs are available and (ii) the RepServer uses close to 100% CPU with the current CPU(s) without **smp_enable**. Note that RepServer does not scale across CPUs as linearly as ASE does.
- Use raw devices (instead of file system devices) for disk partitions. In 15.1, if your platform supports Direct I/O, you may also use file system devices with **sqm_write_flush** set to **'dio'** (➢p.93).
  Also, spread the disk partitions over different physical disks to achieve maximum disk I/O bandwith.
- Assign each connection or route to its own disk partition as much as possible (➢p.101).
- In 15.0, use **admin stats, backlog** to identify queues that are lagging behind; use **admin stats** { **tpc** | **cps** | **bps** } to monitor performance. In 15.1, also use the reports generated by **rs_stat_genreport**.
- Use the RepServer monitor counters (➢p.122) to get a better understanding of RepServer resource usage and bottlenecks. Also see the whitepaper mentioned in the first bullet in this section for more information.
- When, in a busy RepServer, the RSSD is a bottleneck, consider setting **sqm_recover_segs** (default=1) to a higher value (e.g. **10**) to reduce interaction with, and load on, the RSSD.

40.1 Caching RSSD tables

Frequently used RSSD tables can be cached completely in RepServer memory by setting configuration parameters named **sts_full_cache_***RSSD_table_name* to **'on'** (with **configure replication server**). For example: **sts_full_cache_rs_objects**, **sts_full_cache_rs_functions**. These are RepServer-wide parameters, taking effect immediately without a RepServer reboot.
Not all RSSD tables can be cached. This is only possible for the following tables:

rs_classes	**rs_columns**	**rs_config**	**rs_datatype**
rs_databases	**rs_objects**	**rs_functions**	**rs_locater**
rs_publications	**rs_queues**	**rs_repdbs**	**rs_repobjs**
rs_diskaffinity	**rs_routes**	**rs_systext**	**rs_sites**
rs_dbreps	**rs_version**	**rs_users**	**rs_translation**
rs_dbsubsets			

It is recommended to cache at least **rs_objects**, **rs_columns** and **rs_functions**; **rs_repobjs** and **rs_users** are always fully cached anyway. It is important to ensure that the **memory_limit** parameter is sufficiently increased to provide enough memory for the data volume of the cached tables.
Note that the RSSD table **rs_config** also contains **sts_full_cache_*** parameters for tables that cannot be cached (these cannot be set to **'on'**).

40.2 Caching RSSD tables (pre-12.1)

In pre-12.1, RSSD tables are cached according to the configuration parameter **sts_cachesize** (➢p.94). In 12.1, this is superseded by the caching described in 40.1. The information about pre-12.1 is included only for completeness.

sysadmin stscache [, **help** | *subcommand*]
(Undocumented) Displays information about RSSD tables cached due to configuration parameter **sts_cachesize**. Command output is written to the RepServer errorlog.

40.3 Monitor counters/statistics (15.0)

RepServer provides a series of monitor counters for performance monitoring purposes. These counters are used and configured with the commands below.
In 15.0, a central counter concept (other than in pre-15.0) is an 'observation', which is the number of times the counter was adjusted because some event occurred that had to be counted. All counters collect the number of observations, which is the cumulative total of the observed values (e.g. total #bytes replicated), as well as the last and maximum value observed. These values appear in counter-related output as **Obs**, **Total**, **Last**, and **Max**.
Counter names may be displayed prefixed with **#** and/or * (e.g. **#*SegsActive**). **#** indicates the counter cannot be reset; * indicates the counter must always be sampled, irrespective of **stats_sampling**. In 15.0, **admin stats** is a synonym for **admin statistics**.
The RSSD table **rs_statcounters** contains a static description of each monitor counter, which can be displayed with the RSSD procedure **rs_helpconfig**. The RSSD table **rs_statrun** contains one row for each period during which monitor counters have been sampled; the RSSD table **rs_statdetail** contains the actual counter values for each sample period.
In 15.1, the RSSD table **rs_statreport** contains data derived from **rs_statdetail** for the purpose of generating reports with **rs_stat_populate** and **rs_stat_genreport**.

Using RepServer Monitor counters in 15.1
In 15.1, using the RepServer monitor counters has become significantly easier with the introduction of **rs_stat_genreport** (see below), which generates a report on important aspects of RepServer performance, thus providing a kind of 'interpreted' version of some of the counters in the most important areas.
In order to create these reports, take these steps:

- run the following script against the RSSD: **$SYBASE/$SYBASE_REP/scripts/ rs_install_statreport_v***nnnn***_as***x***.sql** ; *x* is **a** or **e**, depending on your type of RSSD; *nnnn* indicates the RS version, and is **1510** for RS 15.1.
- ensure the **stats_sampling** config setting is enabled
- run **admin stats**...**save** to save sampled monitor counters into the RSSD tables
- optionally disable **stats_reset_rssd** to avoid the saved counters to be deleted
- run **rs_stat_populate**, followed by **rs_stat_genreport**, and study the report...

Monitor counters commands

The configuration parameters below apply to monitor counters; they can be changed with **configure replication server**. These parameters are dynamic, so changes take effect immediately. The current settings can be displayed with **admin config** (in 15.0.1; ➢p.90) or with the RSSD procedure **rs_helpcfg** (included in the electronic supplement to this book; ➢p.8).

- **stats_sampling** - enables (**'on'** = default in pre-15.0) or disables (**'off'** = default in 15.0) sampling of non-intrusive counters. In pre-15.0 only, intrusive counters must be enabled separately with **admin stats_intrusive_counters**; in 15.0, **stats_sampling** applies to all counters.
- **(15.0) stats_show_zero_counters** - when **'on'** (default = **'off'**), a counter is not reported when the number of observations is zero (i.e. there was nothing to count).
- **(15.0.1) stats_reset_rssd** - when **'on'** (= default), the RSSD tables **rs_statrun** and **rs_statdetail** are cleared when a new **admin stats**...**'save'** command is

started. When **'off'**, the tables are not cleared. In 15.0 (i.e. pre-15.0.1), the behaviour is equivalent to **'on'** and cannot be changed.

admin stats, { **mem** | **mem_in_use** | **md** | **dsi** }
Displays statistics about memory use (**mem**, **mem_in_use**), message delivery (**md**), and DSI activity (**dsi**) by the current.

(15.0) admin stats, backlog
Displays information on the number of transactions in inbound and outbound queues that have not yet been distributed. The most relevant counter is **SQMRBacklogSeg** (=number of unread segments). Ignore **SQMRBacklogBlock**.

(15.0) admin stats, { **tps** | **cps** | **bps** }
Displays the current RepServer throughput in different modules, either in transactions per second (**tps**), commands per second (**cps**) or bytes per second (**bps**).

(15.0) admin stats, *target* [, **'display'** [, *interval*]]
(15.0) admin stats, *target* [, **'save'** [, *sub_interval*] [, *interval*]]
Displays, or saves in the RSSD, monitor counters.
target can be:

- **'sysmon'** - reports a small set of essential counters
- **'all'** - reports all counters
- *module_name* - reports all counters for a specific module. Possible modules are: **cm**, **dist**, **dsi**, **dsiexec**, **rsh**, **rsi**, **rsiuser**, **serv**, **sqm**, **sqmr**, **sqt**, **sts** or **repagent**; also, (but undocumented) **sync** and **syncele**. Modules **sqt** and **sqm** can be followed by **inbound** or **outbound** (without quotes) to report only on that type of queue (default = both).
- for queues, *module_name* may be followed by the name of a specific counter (**rs_helpcounter** provides a list) to show that counter for all queues
- when *module_name* applies to database connections, it may be followed by a dataserver and database name
- when *module_name* applies to routes, it may be followed by a RepServer name

interval specifies the length of the sampling interval; when omitted, 0 is the default.
When *sub_interval* is specified along with *interval* (possible only with **'save'**), the sampling interval is divided into sub-intervals of the specified length; at the end of each sub-interval the sampled data is written to the RSSD. (NB: in 15.0, *sub_interval* is actually an integer defining the number of sub-intervals in the sampling interval; in 15.0.1, this is changed to be the length of the sub-interval as described above). If the sub-interval is less than 15 seconds, the command is not executed.
In 15.0, *interval* must be an integer number of seconds; in 15.0.1, *interval* can also be specified in the form '*hh*:*mm*:*ss*'; *sub_interval* can be specified the same way.

In 15.0, an **admin stats...'save',** *interval* command returns at the end of the interval. In 15.0.1, the command returns immediately and executes asynchronously in the background. **admin stats, status** shows whether an **admin stats** command with *interval* is currently executing. Only one such command can run at a time in a RepServer. With **'display'** (=default), the results are sent to the client. With **'save'**, the results are written into the RSSD tables **rs_statdetail** and **rs_statrun**.
Examples:

```
          admin stats, 'sysmon', 'display', 30
          admin stats, 'all', 'save', 15, 60
          admin stats, 'sqt'
          admin stats, 'sqm', outbound, 124, save, 60
(15.0.1)  admin stats, 'sqm', 124, save, '00:00:30', '00:10:00'
          admin stats, 'sqm', SegsActive
          admin stats, 'dsi', PROD_STBY, prod_db, save, 60
          admin stats, 'rsi', RS_EMEA
```

admin stats, reset
Explicitly resets all resettable counters to 0. In 15.0, all resettable counters are automatically reset when starting an **admin stats** command with a non-zero sampling interval. A resettable counter has **counter_status & 0x010 = 0** in **rs_statcounters**.

(15.0) admin stats, status
Displays the current config settings for monitor counters. Also shows whether an **admin stats** command with *interval* is executing (either asynchronously with **'save'** (in 15.0.1) or interactively with **'display'**) , and how far it has proceeded.

(15.0.1) admin stats, cancel
Cancels the currently running, asynchronously executing **admin stats** command.

(15.1) rs_stat_populate [*starttime*, *endtime*, '*module_name*', *dataserver*, *database*]
(RSSD procedure) Copies ('populates') saved monitor counter data from **rs_statdetail** into **rs_statreport** for the purpose of subsequently creating formatted reports with **rs_stat_genreport**. Data in **rs_statreport** is not truncated as happens by default with **rs_statdetail**.
All parameters are optional and act as filters on the data being copied; **NULL** (=unspecified=default) means: no filtering. *module_name* identifies an area of interest and can be: **netspeed** (network I/O performance), **repagent**, **sqmw** (SQM writers), **sqt**, **dist**, **dsi**, **dsie**, **rsi**, **aobj** (active objects, i.e. user tables and stored procs). *dataserver* can also be the name of a RepServer.
Run the **rs_install_statreport_v***nnnn***_as{a|e}.sql** script to create this proc (➢p.122).

(15.1) rs_stat_genreport [*starttime*, *endtime*, '*module_name*', *dataserver*, *database*, *top-N-tables*, *top-N-procs*]
(RSSD procedure) Generates a report on important aspects of RepServer performance from the data in **rs_statreport** (placed there by **rs_stat_populate**, which must be run first). All parameters are optional and are the same as for **rs_stat_populate**.
By default, the top-20 active tables and top-20 active stored procedures are included in the report, unless different numbers are specified for the last two parameters.
Run the **rs_install_statreport_v***nnnn***_as{a|e}.sql** script to create this proc (➢p.122).

(15.1) rs_perf_listruns [*starttime*, *endtime*]
(RSSD procedure) Lists the available sets of saved monitor counters in **rs_statdetail** and **rs_statrun**. The results can optionally be used as *starttime*/*endtime* parameters for **rs_stat_populate** and **rs_stat_genreport**.
Run the **rs_install_statreport_v***nnnn***_as{a|e}.sql** script to create this proc (➢p.122).

rs_helpcounter
rs_helpcounter *module_name* | *keyword_substring* [, { **'short'** | **'long'** }]
rs_helpcounter { **'sysmon'** | **'duration'** | **'observer'** | **'monitor'** | **'must_sample'** | **'no_reset'** | **'keep_old'** }
(RSSD procedure) Displays descriptions of monitor counters, as stored in the static RSSD table **rs_statcounters**. Does not display counter values (for this, use **admin stats** or query the RSSD table **rs_statdetail** directly). Without parameters, displays syntax help info and a list of modules names. The other arguments (**'sysmon'**...**'keep_old'**) display all counters in a particular category.
With *module_name*, displays all counters for that module; with *keyword_substring*, displays all counters with that string (case-sensitive) in their display name (i.e. **rs_statcounters.display_name**). The optional **short** or **long** determine how much detail is displayed about each counter.

(15.0) rs_dump_stats ['*comment*']
(RSSD procedure) Formats all data in the RSSD table **rs_statdetail** in comma-separated format (CSV) to allow importing into analysis tools. The *comment* appears on the first line.

40.4 Monitor counters/statistics (pre-15.0)

In pre-15.0, the monitor counters are handled differently than in 15.0 and later.
The configuration parameters below apply to monitor counters; they can be changed with **configure replication server**. These parameters are dynamic, so changes take effect immediately. The current settings can be displayed with the RSSD procedure **rs_helpcfg** (included in the electronic supplement to this book; ➢p.8):

- **stats_sampling** - enables (**'on'** = default in pre-15.0) or disables (**'off'** = default in 15.0) sampling of non-intrusive counters. In pre-15.0 only, intrusive counters must be enabled separately with **admin stats_intrusive_counters**; in 15.0, **stats_sampling** applies to all counters.
- **(pre-15.0) stats_flush_rssd** - enables (**'on'**) or disables (**'off'**; = default) automatic flushing (writing) of counter values to the RSSD table **rs_statdetail**. When enabled, no flushing will take place until it has been enabled on module level with the **admin stats_config_*** commands.
- **(pre-15.0) stats_reset_afterflush** - when **'on'** (= default), the counters are reset after their values are flushed (written) to the RSSD table **rs_statdetail**; when **'off'**, counters are not reset.
- **(pre-15.0) stats_daemon_sleep_time** - the number of seconds after which counter values are flushed (written) automatically to the RSSD table **rs_statdetail**. Possible values are **10** - **1814400** (= 3 weeks) (default = **600** = 10 minutes). Don't set this value too low, or the RSSD might fill up quickly. Note that this value must be enclosed in quotes in **configure replication server**.

admin statistics, { **mem** | **mem_in_use** | **md** | **dsi** }
See previous section.

admin statistics, reset
Explicitly resets all resettable counters to 0. In pre-15.0, all resettable counters are automatically reset when starting an **admin statistics, sysmon** command.
A resettable counter has **counter_status & 0x010 = 0** in **rs_statcounters**.

(pre-15.0) admin statistics, flush_status
Displays the current status for automatic flushing of counter values to the RSSD. In 15.0, this is replaced by **admin stats**...**'save'** (see previous section).

(pre-15.0) admin stats_intrusive_counter, { **'on'** | **'off'** }
Enables (**'on'**) or disables (**'off'** = default) the potentially intrusive counters (i.e. those that may have a negative impact on RepServer performance). To list these counters, run **rs_helpcounter 'intrusive'** in the RSSD.
In 15.0, intrusive counters are no longer distinguished separately.

(pre-15.0) admin stats_config_module, { *module_name*| **all_modules** },{ **'on'**| **'off'** }
(pre-15.0) admin stats_config_connection,
{ *dataserver*, *database* | **all_connections** }, { *module_name* | **all_modules** },
[**'inbound'** | **'outbound'** ,] { **'on'** | **'off'** }
(pre-15.0) admin stats_config_route,
{ *destination_repserver_name*| **all_routes** },{ **rsi** | **sqm** | **all_modules** },{ **'on'**| **'off'** }
Enables (**'on'**) or disables (**'off'** = default) automatic flushing to the RSSD table **rs_statdetail** of counter values for specific modules, and/or specific connections or routes. **'inbound'**/**'outbound'** apply only to inbound/outbound connections only (default = both). The current status is displayed with **admin statistics, flush_status**.
In 15.0, this is replaced by **admin stats** (see previous section).

(pre-15.0) admin statistics , *module_name* [, *display_name*]
(pre-15.0) admin statistics, { **all_modules | sysmon** [, *nr_of_seconds*] }
Displays monitor counter values for one or more RepServer threads. With *module_name*, displays all active counters, and their current value, for that module; with *display_name* (= the column name used in the output of **admin statistics**), displays only that counter. With **all_modules**, displays all active counters. With **sysmon**, displays only the active counters for **dsi**, **dsiexec**, **rsi** and **repagent**; without *nr_of_seconds* or with *nr_of_seconds* = 0, displays the current counter values; with *nr_of_seconds* > 0, waits the specified number of seconds and displays the counter value increase during that period.
In 15.0, this is replaced by **admin stats** (see previous section).

rs_helpcounter
rs_helpcounter *module_name* | *keyword_substring* [, { **'type'** | **'short'** | **'long'** }]
rs_helpcounter { **'intrusive'** | **'sysmon'** | **'rate'** | **'duration'** | **'internal'** |
'must_sample' | **'no_reset'** | **'keep_old'** | **'configure'** }
(RSSD procedure) Displays descriptions of monitor counters, as stored in the static RSSD table **rs_statcounters**. Does not display counter values (for this, use **admin statistics** or query the RSSD table **rs_statdetail** directly). Without parameters, displays syntax help info and a list of modules names .
With *module_name*, displays all counters for that module; with *keyword_substring*, displays all counters with that string (case-sensitive) in their display name (i.e. **rs_statcounters.display_name**). The optional **type**, **short** or **long** determine how much detail is displayed about each counter. With one of the counter status types **'intrusive'** ... **'configure'**, displays all counters of that type.

41 Generation numbers

In RepServer, so-called 'generation numbers' play a role in recovery scenarios when databases are restored from earlier database dumps. Depending on the actual recovery scenario, the function of generation numbers is either to avoid transactions from being applied to the replicate database more than once, or to force transactions to be replicated normally, even when they were already replicated before.
Note that this is a complex topic that is not relevant when everything is working normally. For more information about recovery scenarios and generation numbers, please refer to the *Replication Server Administration Guide* (➢p.13), chapter *Replication System Recovery* and to the *Replication Server Troubleshooting Guide.*
Here, only the two types of generation numbers are described briefly. But first, here's a ***Warning:*** do not change any generation numbers unless you understand what you are doing: it may jeopardise your replication system and cause transactions to be lost!

- Each primary database has a database generation number, which is initially 0, but can be changed with **dbcc settrunc('ltm', 'gen_id',** *new_generaton_no*). This number is part of the OQID (the first two bytes; ➢p.126) of all replicated data.
  When a primary database is restored from a dump, the database generation number should normally be incremented to avoid transactions from the restored dumps being discarded as duplicates. When primary transactions are discarded as duplicates by RepServer, this is shown in the output of **admin who, sqm**: the **Duplicates** column for the inbound queue will increase.
- A DSI generation number is maintained for the combination of a replicate database (more precisely, for each DSI) and each primary database from which it receives replicated data. The DSI generation number (initially 0, but can be changed with **sysadmin set_dsi_generation**) is compared with transactions from the corresponding primary database when they arrive at the DSI: if a transaction has a database generation number in its OQID that is lower than the DSI generation number (or lower than the generation number in **rs_lastcommit.origin_qid** for that primary database), it is discarded by the DSI (this is counted in the **Xacts_ignored** column of **admin who, dsi**); if the database generation number is higher than or equal to the DSI generation number, the transaction is applied to the replicate database normally.

Under normal circumstances, the DSI generation number is set to the same value as the database generation number of the primary database. Don't set the DSI generation number higher than the primary database generation number, since this would cause all primary transactions to be discarded by the DSI!

dbcc settrunc ('ltm', 'gen_id', *db_generation_no* **)**
(ASE command) Sets the database generation number for the current primary database to the specified value. The database generation number should be incremented after restoring database dumps and/or log dumps in a primary database to prevent RepServer from rejecting new transactions as duplicates. After changing the database generation number, stop the RepAgent, disable the secondary truncation point, re-enable it again, run **rs_zeroltm** in the RSSD, and restart the RepAgent.

rs_zeroltm *primary_dataserver*, *primary_database*
(RSSD procedure) Resets the locater for the primary database. See p.20 for details.

admin get_generation, *primary_dataserver*, *primary_database*
Returns the current database generation number for the specified primary database.

sysadmin set_dsi_generation, *dsi_generation_no*, *primary_dataserver*, *primary_database*, *replicate_dataserver*, *replicate_database*
Sets the DSI generation number to *dsi_generation_no*. This number is compared with transactions from the specified primary database when they arrive at the DSI for the specified replicate database (see above for details).
The new DSI generation number takes effect once the connection to the replicate database is resumed (so it should probably be suspended first). The current DSI generation number for the combination of a primary and replicate database can be retrieved from the RSSD table **rs_exceptslast** with this query:

```
select origin_qid      -- the DSI generation number is in the first two bytes
from rs_exceptslast
where error_db = replicate_dbid  -- specify a dbid value as in rs_databases
  and origin = primary_dbid      -- specify a dbid value as in rs_databases
```

42 OQID layout

An OQID (Origin Queue ID, also called just 'queue ID') is a 36-byte binary value uniquely identifying the originating log record for primary data. The OQID is generated by the RepAgent as a 32-byte value; RepServer appends another 4 bytes. The OQID is guaranteed to be universally increasing for a primary database.
For an ASE primary database, the OQID layout is as follows:

Bytes	Contents for ASE primary databases
1-2	primary database generation number (➢p.125)
3-8	timestamp of the log page
9-14	rowID (log page + record no) of the log record for this primary data
15-20	rowID of the log record for the start of the oldest open transaction
21-28	start date/time of the oldest open transaction
29-30	used by RepAgent for rolling back orphan transactions
31-32	unused
33-36	appended internally by RepServer

The OQID layout for non-ASE primary databases is different, but the primary database generation number is always located in the first two bytes.

OQID values appear in the RSSD tables **rs_oqid** and **rs_locater** (among others), as well as in other places. Some examples:

- In the output of **sysadmin dump_queue** to the client, in the column **'Orgn Qid'**.
- In the output of **sysadmin dump_queue** to the RSSD, in the column **rs_queuemsg.origin_q_id**.
- In the output of **sysadmin dump_queue** to a file, behind the string **'oqid='**.
- In the RSSD exceptions log (in the output of **rs_helpexception** *nnn*,**'v'**, behind the **@origin_qid** parameter of **rs_update_lastcommit**)

43 Troubleshooting tips

When replication isn't working properly, follow the suggestions below to diagnose and resolve the problem.
This section covers some common problems encountered by RepServer DBAs, but is by no means complete. For more troubleshooting tips, see the *Replication Server Troubleshooting Guide* (➢p.13).

43.1 General troubleshooting steps

- Run **admin who** or **admin who_is_down** to determine if any replication threads are down. If threads are down, the RepServer errorlog should contain messages indicating the reason (except for REP AGENT threads; see below). For a warm standby, also run **admin logical_status**.
- Always check the RepServer errorlog for error messages (its location can be found with **admin log_name**). When routes are involved, check the errorlogs of all RepServers in the route.
- For error messages in the RepServer errorlog that aren't self-explanatory, look up the error in the file **error_messages_rs** (Windows: **errmsg.rs**) in the **$SYBASE/ $SYBASE_REP/doc** subdirectory. A few errors are also mentioned in this book; see 'error message number' in the index.
- In case of problems with ASE RepAgents, check the ASE errorlog for error messages; the location can be found by running **select @@errorlog** in ASE. For non-ASE RepAgents, check the RepAgent errorlog (➢p.24).
- Check whether the RSSD transaction log (or the data segment) is full: if so, all RepServer processing will come to a standstill. When the RSSD transaction log is full, the RSSD errorlog may not contain any indication of a problem, since its RSSD connection will be in LOG SUSPEND mode in ASE; therefore, this check must be done in ASE with **sp_who** and **sp_helpdb**.
  The RSSD location can be found with **admin rssd_name**; ➢p.109. To determine if an embedded RSSD is used, run **sysadmin erssd**.
- Check whether the RSSD is accessible via the RSSD dataserver logins. If not, there may be a problem with passwords, locked logins, or the RSSD dataserver may have run out of user connections.
- Check whether the stable devices are full (with **admin disk_space** or the RSSD procedure **rs_helppartition**). If so, see section 43.5.

43.2 Connectivity problems

Since a replication system consists of various client/server components, connectivity problems may occur easily, especially when setting up a new replication system. In this case, the errorlog of RepServer (for outgoing connections) or the errorlog of the dataserver or RepAgent (for incoming RepAgent connections) will contain error messages indicating that a connection could not be made.

- First, check whether the name of the server to which a connection is attempted, is correctly defined in **interfaces** file (Windows: **SQL.INI** file) used by the RepServer or ASE server. Both ASE and RepServer write the pathname of the **interfaces** file used to their errorlog file during startup.
- To check whether usernames and passwords are correct or whether a server is reachable at all, simply connect to the target server manually with **isql**. When using encrypted passwords, the **cm_user_pass** traceflag (➢p.100) can help to find the actual passwords used for database connections.

43.3 Problem: Everything looks OK but it doesn't replicate...

Sooner or later, each RepServer DBA encounters a situation where everything seems to be just fine, but replication still doesn't work. Apart from the things mentioned in the sections above, also check these points:

- When data is not replicating, it is a good idea to use **rs_ticket** (➢p.132), in combination with the **prints_rs_ticket** traceflag (➢p.101) to verify whether basic replication is working correctly. This will help you identify the most common problems (marking primary data for replicaton, existence of repdefs and subscriptions, etc.; see below).
- A common reason why replication isn't working is that the primary data is not marked for replication. Verify this with **sp_setreptable**, **sp_setrepproc** or **sp_reptostandby** (➢p.15).
- Check whether a replication definition exists for the primary table or procedure (**rs_helprep**).
- Check whether a subscription exists, and whether its status is 'Valid' (**check subscription**, **rs_helpsub**, **rs_helppubsub** or **rs_helpdbsub**).
- Make sure replication isn't disabled because **set replication off** (➢p.17) is active in the primary session. To verify this, run **set replication on** in the primary database before starting further primary transactions.
- Check whether the primary transactions are performed by the maintenance user: by default such transactions are not replicated because the RepAgent ignores them (though this can be enabled; ➢p.21).
- When using database repdefs, and DDL replication is not working, use **rs_helpdbrep** to check whether the **replicate ddl** clause is enabled for the repdef: by default this is off, suppressing replication of DDL. Use **alter database replication definition...replicate ddl** to enable it.
  Likewise, when replication of **sp_*** system stored procedures is not working with database repdefs, check whether **replicate system procedures** is enabled for the repdef: by default this is off.
  Obviously, a subscription must also exist for the database repdef.
- Check whether a subscription or article exists which has a **where**-clause (display with **rs_helpsub** or **rs_helppub**) that excludes the data modifications in the primary transactions.
- Check whether the replicate SQL statement runs into an error which has been ignored with **assign action** (check the errorlog of the replicate RepServer).
- When using customized function strings, check if the replicate SQL statements being generated are what you expect them to be (for example, with the traceflag **dsi_buf_dump**; ➢p.100, or -in ASE- with the MDA table **monSysSQLText**).
- Check whether the primary transaction is still open (in ASE, with **select @@trancount**); it won't be replicated until the transaction has committed (although, for 'large' transactions, RepServer may already have replicated the transaction except for the commit).
- Check whether any queues are rejecting messages because message loss has been detected. If this is the case, all threads will be up, but nothing is replicated. In the RSSD, such queues are identified by **rs_exceptslast.status** = **2** or **rs_oqid.valid** = **2** (when loss is detected, RepServer writes a message to the errorlog only once, so it may easily be overlooked). Run **ignore loss** (➢p.119) to continue normal processing.
- Check whether any queues are growing faster than they can be processed, by comparing **Next.Read** and **Last Seg.Block** in the output of **admin who, sqm** (for details, ➢p.102). This could indicate a problem with message delivery for a queue, for example due to performance reasons in the replicate database. Also, this could mean that primary transactions are actually being replicated successfully, but simply have not reached the replicate database yet.

43.4 Problem: Transaction log full in primary ASE database

When the transaction log in the primary ASE database is full, this is often an acute problem since applications cannot make any data modifications anymore. Also, it is usually a follow-up problem rather than the root cause. Things to check:

- Is the RepAgent running (**sp_help_rep_agent**) and successfully connected to RepServer (**admin who**)? If not, the secondary truncation point will not move, and eventually cause the transaction log to fill up.

- Are disk partitions full (**admin disk_space**)? If so, is there a problem with a replicate dataserver that has caused delivery of replicate transactions to stop (**admin who**; RepServer errorlog)? Is a network problem causing RepAgents, replicate RepServers or replicate dataservers to be disconnected for a longer period of time (see errorlog files)?

Possible solutions:

- The fastest, but also most drastic solution is to disable the secondary truncation point in the transaction log with **dbcc settrunc('ltm', 'ignore')** (stop the RepAgent first); the transaction log can then be dumped or truncated. However, all transactions in the truncated part of the log will not be replicated, and may be difficult to recover. Therefore, observe this ***Warning:* *disabling the secondary truncation point is a drastic, last-resort option that will stop all replication from this database, and may cause transactions to be lost. Don't do this unless you fully understand the implications!*** Also, note that some problems (see below) are not solved by removing the secondary truncation point.
  If you have removed the secondary truncation point anyway, re-establish it by running **rs_zeroltm** in the RSSD, running **dbcc settrunc('ltm', 'valid')** in the primary database, and restarting the RepAgent.
- If possible, avoid removing the secondary truncation point. Preferably, allow the RepAgent to move the secondary truncation point by enlarging the transaction log or creating additional RepServer disk partitions.

Note that, for the following ASE-level problems -which are not RepServer-related-, disabling the secondary truncation point is not a solution:

- Are transaction log dumps performed regularly (see the ASE Backup Server errorlog), or is the log automatically truncated (**sp_dboption**)? If neither happens, the transaction log will eventually fill up.
- Is a long-running open transaction in the primary database stopping the log from being dumped or truncated (**select * from master..syslogshold**)? If so, make sure the transaction completes by either letting the owner commit or rollback, or by forcefully killing the session (with the ASE **kill** statement).

43.5 Problem: Disk partitions full due to an open transaction

If the disk partitions are full, but there are no problems with replicate RepServers or replicate databases, there may be an open transaction in an inbound queue. Run **admin who, sqt** and look for **'st:O'** in the output (➢p.103). If an open transaction exists, consider closing (committing or aborting) the transaction in the primary database. Alternatively, create additional disk partitions.

43.6 If nothing else works....

When you've tried all suggestions above and replication is still not working, stop all RepAgents and RepServers, and -optionally- the primary dataserver. Then restart -in this order- the primary dataserver, the RepServers and the RepAgents. Although restarting these components should not make a difference in theory, it sometimes does in practice.

43.7 If replication is slow...

If replication is working, but not fast enough, transactions will accumulate in the stable queues on disk partitions and may eventually even cause the primary transaction log to fill up. See section 40 (➢p.120) for suggestions to improve performance.

44 The rs_subcmp utility

rs_subcmp (Windows: **subcmp.exe**) is a command-line utility (located in **$SYBASE/$SYBASE_REP/bin**) for comparing the contents of a primary table and a replicate table, and optionally removing any differences ('reconciling') by making the replicate data identical to the primary (more formally correct, conceptually **rs_subcmp** aims to compare whether data for a *subscription* is identical in the primary and replicate databases; however, since **rs_subcmp** doesn't know the concept of a RepServer subscription, it is the user's responsibility to provide **select** statements (**-c**, **-C**) that match the subscription data).
Notes:

- **rs_subcmp** reports three types of mismatching rows:
  - *orphaned* row: a primary row that doesn't exist in the replicate
  - *missing* row: a replicate row that doesn't exist in the primary

  - *inconsistent* row: exists in both with identical primary key values but differs in other columns
- **rs_subcmp** does not access the RSSD and therefore has no knowledge of your replication system.
- Make sure that the data is retrieved according to the same key order from both the primary and the replicate database.
- Using the 'reconcile' options **-R** and **-r** will cause **rs_subcmp** to make changes to your replicate data. Be careful to use these options correctly: if not, you risk making a mess of your data!
- Use the **-V** option to verify that any data differences are correctly identified before using **-R** or **-r**. Without **-V**, options **-R** or **-r** will not produce any output.
- Run **rs_subcmp** at a time when the primary data is not changing.
- When the replicate data being compared is not currently changing, specify **-n 1**, or **rs_subcmp** will perform the comparison (and retrieve the data) 10 times by default.
- When using a config file (**-f**), any command-line options (see below) override the contents of the config file. Note that a config file has its own syntax (**-F**).
- In 15.0.1, **rs_subcmp** can also be used to compare schemas (**-x**, **-X**). This requires the environment variable **$DDLGENLOC** to point to **ddlgen**.
- **-t** and **-c** are always required except when using **-x 1** or **-x 2**.
- The return status of **rs_subcmp** is 0 when the tables are identical, and 2 if they are different. If an error occurred, the return status is 1.
- See the *Replication Server Reference Manual* (➢p.13) for full details about **rs_subcmp**.

Options:

[**-v**]	displays **rs_subcmp** version information
-u *user_name*	user name for replicate and primary dataserver
[**-U** *primary_user_name*]	user name for primary (if different from replicate)
[**-p** *password*]	password for replicate and primary dataserver
[**-P** *primary_password*]	password for primary (if different from replicate)
[**-I** *interfaces_file*] **(15.0.1)**	**interfaces** file to be used
-S *primary_dataserver*	primary dataserver
[**-D** *primary_database*]	database in primary dataserver
-s *replicate_dataserver*	replicate dataserver
[**-d** *replicate_database*]	database in replicate dataserver
-t *table_name*	table name in replicate and primary
[**-T** *primary_table_name*]	table name in primary (if different from replicate)
-c *select_cmd*	SQL **select** command to retrieve the subscription data from replicate and primary; this must contain an **order by** clause
[**-C** *select_cmd*]	like **-c**, but for primary (if different from replicate)
[**-V**]	prints the differences found, if any
[**-z1** | **-z2**]	**-z1** (=**-z**) prints basic trace information; **-z2** prints info for every row compared
[**-R**]	modifies the replicate table, making it identical to the primary table; then performs a final comparison
[**-r**]	like **-R**, but without the final comparison
[**-g**] **(15.0.1)**	with **-r** or **-R**, generates a reconciliation file (**reconcile***xxx***.sql**)
[**-n** *iterations*]	number of times (default=**10**) primary and replicate data are compared before the final action (**-R**, **-r** or **-V**) is performed
[**-w** *wait_interval*]	number of seconds (default=**5**) to wait between iterations
[**-i** *identity_col*]	name of the identity column in the replicate table; needed when the identity col values need to be updated (with **-r** or **-R**)
[**-k** *primary_key_col* [**-k**...]]	primary key column(s) (for better performance)
[**-a** *replicate_col primary_col* [**-a**...]]	maps primary columns to replicate columns if named differently
[**-1** *text_image_col* [**-1**...]]	updates to these text/image columns will be minimally logged (default: fully logged)
[**-N** *text_image_col* [**-N**...]]	the replicate text/image column allows **NULL**
[**-L** *text_image_sizeKB*]	max.size (in Kb) for text/image data. Default=**26**; upper limit is 2Gb in 15.0; 32Kb in 12.6.
[**-B** *primary_ini_batch*]	SQL batch to be executed after connecting to the primary dataserver, for example to set session options
[**-b** *replicate_ini_batch*]	like **-B**, but for replicate dataserver
[**-f** *configuration_file*]	configuration file to be used; use **-F** to display syntax
[**-F**]	only when specified on its own, displays syntax for config file
[**-h**] **(RS 15.0.1, ASE 15.0.2)**	uses ASE hash functions for faster comparison
[**-H** ...] **(RS 15.0.1, ASE 15.0.2)**	normalization to use with **-h**; see documentation
[**-e** *float_precision*]	number of decimal places to consider when comparing floating-point values

[**-E** *real_precision*]	like **-e**, but for **real** datatypes
[**-o** sort_order]	sort order used for comparing primary key columns
[**-O** sort_order]	like **-o**, but for comparing all columns
[**-q** unicode_sort_order]	Unicode sort order for comparing primary key cols
[**-Q** unicode_sort_order]	like **-q**, but for comparing all columns
[**-j** *charset*]	character set to be used for comparing data rows; should match the character set of the replicate dataserver
[**-Z** *language*]	language to be used for **rs_subcmp** messages
[**-J** *charset*]	character set to be used for **rs_subcmp** messages
[**-x 0 | 1 | 2**] **(15.0.1)**	**0**: compare data rows(=default); **1**: compare database schemas for all objects; **2**: compare schemas for a specific table
[**-X** *filter*] **(15.0.1)**	with **-x 1** or **-x 2**, specifies schema types and subtypes (see below) to include (prefix with **+**) or exclude (don't prefix, just mention) for the schema comparison

Schema types that can be specified with the **-X** option:

A - alias	**R** - rule
D - default	**T** - user table (incl. indexes, triggers, etc.)
E - user-defined datatype	**U** - user
G - group	**V** - view
P - stored procedure	

Schema subtypes that can be specified with the **-X** option:

c - constraint	**i** - index
b - bind default	**m** - procedure mode
r - bind rule	**g** - grant
f - foreign key	**t** - trigger
p - primary key	

Example to display data differences between **proddb..orders** in two servers:
rs_subcmp -U sa -P mysecret -S PROD -s PROD2 -t proddb..orders -k orderid
-c "select orderid, custid, amount from proddb..orders order by orderid" -V

Example to display schema differences for all tables between two databases:
rs_subcmp -S PROD -U sa -P mysecret -s PROD2 -u sa -p mysecret
-D db1 -d db3 -x1 -X+T

45 Miscellaneous tips & tricks

This section contains some tips & tricks that may useful for a RepServer DBA.

45.1 Reverse-engineering RepServer objects

With the RMP (➢p.115) or RSP (➢p.116) plug-ins for Sybase Central, most RepServer objects can be reverse-engineered. For most object types, this is quite straightforward (right-click and choose 'Generate DDL' or 'Generate RCL').

Various stored procedures and shell scripts for reverse-engineering RepServer objects can also be downloaded from **www.sybase.com**; for the current location, see **www.sypron.nl/repqr2/x3**.

45.2 Accessing a replicate database by multiple RepServers

A design principle of RepServer is that each primary or replicate database is managed by only one RepServer. With multiple RepServers (e.g. routes), this implies that a RepServer cannot create a connection to a replicate database that already has a connection in another RepServer. If this is required anyway, use this workaround:

- Create an alias name for the dataserver. For example, for a database named **PROD.prod_db**, add a server name called **PROD_ALIAS** to the **interfaces** file used by the RepServer (with the same network address as **PROD**).
- In the RepServer, a connection to **PROD_ALIAS.prod_db** can now be created.

45.3 When you've locked yourself out...

If you've lost the password for logging into RepServer, query the RSSD table **rs_users**, column **password** for the **username** in question (like **'sa'**).
To change the RepServer **'sa'** password directly in the RSSD (it is recommended to use **alter user**...**set password** instead), run this query in the RSSD:

update rs_users set password = 'easy2remember'
where username = 'sa' -- assuming we're talking about the **'sa'** login here...

Then, restart RepServer and log in with the password set above. In case password encryption is used, this must be disabled first as described on page 93.

When you've also lost the username/password to log into the RSSD, they're in the Repserver's **.cfg** file (➢p.115) -- as long as you don't use encrypted passwords. To find the RSSD password when it's encrypted, use the **cm_user_pass** traceflag (➢p.100). However, this traceflag requires that you can log into the RepServer in the first place, so this may not work.
If you've lost the username/password for RepServer and for the RSSD, and you're using encrypted passwords, use the following procedure to gain access to the RSSD; then, reset the RepServer password.

- For an ASE RSSD: reboot the ASE server with **-p***XXX* (*XXX*= an ASE login name with **sso_role**, typically **'sa'**). A password will be generated for this login; this is printed to the ASE console (not the ASE errorlog). After logging into ASE, reset the password with **sp_password** (and remove the **-p** option).
- For an ASA ERSSD, there is no supported procedure to forcefully gain access to the ASA server, so ensure preventive action is taken. For example, create a separate ASA login, and store the password in a safe, but accessible place. See p.111 to create ASA logins and change ASA passwords.

45.4 The 'rs_ticket' feature

rs_ticket [**'***string-1***'** [, **'***string-2***'** [, **'***string-3***'** [, **'***string-4***'**]]]]
(15.1) rs_ticket _v1 [**'***string-1***'** [, **'***string-2***'** [, **'***string-3***'** [, **'***string-4***'**]]]]
(Stored procedure) Executed in a primary database, replicates a 'ticket' to all replicate databases subscribed to any object in that primary database (no subscriptions are required for **rs_ticket** itself). Up to 4 arbitrary strings can be supplied for the purpose of identifying the tickets in the RepServer errorlog or **rs_ticket_history**. In 15.1, a new version 2 of the ticket feature was introduced. Use **rs_ticket _v1** if the pre-15.1 version 1 is needed instead.

The **rs_ticket** feature provides capabilities to do things like monitoring replication progress, measure latency, determine performance bottlenecks, set up a heartbeat, determine whether replication is quiesced for an individual table -- and more. **rs_ticket** is very light-weight and using it in a normal way does not cause additional overhead or latency.
When executing the stored procedure **rs_ticket** in a primary database, a 'ticket' marker is written to the transaction log and delivered to the qualifying replicate databases. As it travels through the replication system, the ticket gathers progress information in the form of timestamps. These are recorded at:

- the primary database
- the RepAgent Executor, also known as 'EXEC' (where RepServer receives the LTL from the RepAgent)
- the distributor (DIST thread)
- the DSI
- the replicate database (only when **rs_ticket_rdb.sql** is installed; see below)
- (15.1) the RSI

The information accumulated by a ticket can be viewed in various ways:

- In 15.1, things are easiest: each replicate database has a table **rs_ticket_history** which collects the replicated tickets with their accumulated progress information. Since the configuration setting **dsi_rs_ticket_report** is **'on'** by default in 15.1, this means that no configuration is necessary to use tickets: just execute **rs_ticket** in a primary database and then manually query **rs_ticket_history** in the replicate database(s).
- In pre-15.1 (but this also works in 15.1), the simplest way to use **rs_ticket** is to enable traceflag **print_rs_ticket** (➢p.101; **repserver.diag** not required); this will print the progress information for each ticket to the RepServer errorlog as it passes through the different RepServer modules. This does not require any further installation or configuration except enabling the traceflag.
- In order to determine whether (or how fast) replication is flowing, it is also possible to look at the monitor counters named **RSTicket** for the different modules. These counters will not show the ticket's timestamp information, but are incremented when a ticket passes by.
- To collect the ticket information in a database table in pre-15.1, you must install a downloadable script (details below) in the replicate database. This creates the database tables **ticket_hist**, **ticket_detail** and **ticket_result**; these tables can be examined with the stored procedure **ticket_report**. This requires the configuration setting **dsi_rs_ticket_report** to be **'on'** (default = **'off'** in pre-15.1, **'on'** in 15.1) for the connection to the replicate database, so that the **rs_ticket_report**

function gets delivered to the replicate.
The SQL script, named **rs_ticket_rdb.sql**, must be executed in each replicate database, and creates the **ticket_*** tables and stored procedures **ticket_report** and **rs_ticket_report** (the default version of **rs_ticket_report** does not perform any function).
For the current location of this script, see **www.sypron.nl/repqr2/x4**.

In 15.1, the accumulated ticket information contains counters indicates as **B**, **DSI_T** and **DSI_C**, which are the total number of bytes received from the RepAgent, and total number of commands and transactions sent through the DSI, respectively. These are cumulative totals, allowing the delta between two tickets to be calculated.
When interpreting the timestamps for a ticket, take possible system clock differences in the various dataserver and RepServer into consideration.
This feature is not documented extensively in pre-15.1: the documentation must be downloaded from **www.sybase.com**; see **www.sypron.nl/repqr2/x5** for details.

45.5 Commands for waiting

This section describes RepServer commands that will wait for a certain time or event. While waiting, the client connection is blocked and cannot be used for any other commands.

(15.0) wait for delay, '*hh*:*mm*[[:*xx*].*ccc*]**'**
Waits for the specified interval, up to a maximum of 24 hours. *ccc* = milliseconds.
Example: **wait for delay '00:00:15'** -- wait 15 seconds

(15.0) wait for time, '*hh*:*mm*[[:*xx*].*ccc*] [**am** | **pm**]**'**
Waits until the specified time of day, which can be at most 24 hours away.
Examples: **wait for time '2:30 pm'** -- wait until half past 3
wait for time '14:30' -- wait until half past 3

wait for switch for *logical_dataserver.logical_database*
Waits for the **switch active** for the specified logical connection to complete (➢p.66).

wait for create standby for *logical_dataserver.logical_database*
Waits for the standby database creation process (**create connection**... **as standby for**) to complete (➢p.66).

46 Non-standard maintenance operations

RepServer does not support maintenance operations such as renaming existing RepServers, database connections, etc. Some of these operations are described in this section; more can be found at **www.sybase.com**; see **www.sypron.nl/repqr2/x6** for details.
Note that none of the procedures below is formally supported by Sybase, so use at your own risk.

46.1 Renaming a RepServer

To rename a RepServer from *old_rs_name* to *new_rs_name*, follow these steps (note that manual RSSD updates are not supported by Sybase). Please use a transaction for all modifications to **rs_*** tables, and commit only after verifying the results are correct.

1. Shut down all RepServers in the replication domain (i.e. those RepServers with the same ID RepServer as the RepServer being renamed).
2. In the RSSD of the RepServer being renamed, run these queries (each query should hit exactly 1 row):
   update rs_config set charvalue = '*new_rs_name***'**
   where optionname = 'oserver'
3. If the RepServer being renamed is the ID RepServer, run this query in the RSSDs of all RepServers, including the RepServer being renamed and the ID RepServer, (it should hit exactly 1 row in each RSSD):
   update rs_config set charvalue = '*new_rs_name***'**
   where optionname = 'id_server'
4. In the RSSD of the ID RepServer, run this query (it should hit exactly 1 row):
   update rs_idnames set name1 = '*new_rs_name***'**
   where name1 = '*old_rs_name***' and type = 8**

5. In the RSSDs of all RepServers, including the RepServer being renamed and the ID RepServer, run this query (it should either hit exactly 1 row, or 0 rows):

   update rs_sites set name = '*new_rs_name***' where name = '***old_rs_name***'**

6. (Optional) Rename the RSSD of the RepServer being renamed as described in section 46.2. This is not strictly needed, but may be useful if the names of the RepServer and its RSSD are expected to be similar.
7. Change the name of the RepServer being renamed in the **interfaces** file.
8. For the RepServer being renamed, rename its **.cfg** and **RUN_***servername* files.
9. If the RepServer being renamed is the ID RepServer, edit the **.cfg** file of all RepServers and change the ID RepServer's name on the line **'ID_server='**.
10. (Optional) In all primary databases that are handled by the RepServer being renamed, modify the RepServer name in the configuration of the RepAgent as well as the **interfaces** file. This is not strictly needed, but it is generally a good idea to use the same servername in all systems.
11. Restart all RepServers.

46.2 Renaming a database connection

To rename a database from *old_dsname.old_dbname* to *new_dsname.new_dbname*, follow these steps (note that manual RSSD updates are not supported by Sybase). Please use a transaction for all modifications to **rs_*** tables, and commit only after verifying the results are correct.

1. Shut down all RepServers in the replication domain (i.e. those RepServers with the same ID RepServer as the RepServer being renamed).
2. Rename the database in the dataserver (in ASE, with **sp_renamedb**).
3. In the RSSDs of all RepServers, run these queries (each query should either hit exactly 1 row, or 0 rows):

   update rs_databases set dsname = '*new_dsname***', dbname = '***new_dbname***'**
   where dsname = '*old_dsname***' and dbname = '***old_dbname***' and ltype = 'P'**

   update rs_repdbs set dsname = '*new_dsname***', dbname = '***new_dbname***'**
   where dsname = '*old_dsname***' and dbname = '***old_dbname***'**

4. In the RSSD of the ID RepServer, run this query (it should hit exactly 1 row):

   update rs_idnames set name1 = '*new_dsname***', name2 = '***new_dbname***'**
   where name1 = '*old_dsname***' and name2 = '***old_dbname***'**
   and type = 9 and ltype = 'P'

5. If the database being renamed is a primary database, reconfigure the RepAgent if necessary (this is not required for an ASE RepAgent).

Steps 6 and 7 apply only when the database being renamed is an RSSD (note that this procedure has only been tested for an ASE RSSD (i.e. not for an ASA ERSSD)):

6. Edit the **.cfg** file of the RepServer whose RSSD is being renamed and change the lines **RSSD_server='** and **'RSSD_database='**.
7. (Optional) If the names of RepServer users and maintenance users should be changed accordingly, run similar updates as above for the column **username** of the RSSD tables **rs_users** and **rs_maintusers**; also, edit the **.cfg** file of the RepServer whose RSSD is being renamed and change the lines **'RSSD_primary_user='** and **'RSSD_maint_user='**.
8. Restart all RepServers.

46.3 Changing the maintenance user for a database

The maintenance user for a database connection is first defined with **create connection**. Unlike other connection attributes, it cannot be changed with **alter connection**. Instead, this can only be accomplished by directly modifying the RSSD as described below (note that this procedure is undocumented and not supported by Sybase):

1. Shutdown RepServer
2. (Only when the RSSD maintenance user is changed) Edit the RepServer **.cfg** file and modify the username (on the line starting with **'RSSD_maint_user='**) as needed. Without encrypted passwords, also modify the password (**'RSSD_maint_pw='**); with encrypted passwords, use **rs_init** to modify the RSSD maintenance user password. Although the RSSD maintenance user information in the **.cfg** file does not seem to be used (➢p.107), it may be best to keep this identical to **rs_maintusers** anyway.

3. In the RSSD, run this query (it should hit exactly 1 row; please use a transaction and commit only after verifying the results are correct):

   update rs_maintusers
   set username = '*new_maintuser_name***'**
   where username = '*old_maintuser_name***'**
   and destid = '*db_id***'**

4. Restart RepServer

5. When encrypted passwords are used, RepServer will most likely be unable to connect to the database as the new maintenance user. In this case, use **alter connection**...**set password** to set the right password; then suspend and resume the connection.

Warning: this procedure usually works perfectly, but watch out for the following problem. In case the database is also replicated, its transaction log could potentially contain transactions by the old or new maintenance user, which have not yet been read by the RepAgent: these transactions would not be replicated properly. Therefore, ensure the primary transaction log has been fully processed by the RepAgent before making this change.

46.4 Removing a database from the replication system

Removing a database from the replication system is surprisingly simple (though **rs_init** does not provide a function for it). Simply drop all repdefs and subscriptions involving the database, stop the RepAgent if it's running (and optionally disable its configuration), and disable the secondary truncation point in the transaction log. Finally, run **drop connection**. The database itself is not affected by this procedure (except for the RepAgent/truncation point).
If you want to remove the RepServer-related tables and procedures that were created from this database, drop the tables **rs_lastcommit** and **rs_threads**, and in 15.1, also **rs_ticket_history**, as well as the following stored procedures: **rs_check_repl_stat**, **rs_{get|update}_lastcommit, rs_{update|initialize}_threads**, **rs_ticket***, **rs_marker**. In addition, you may want to remove the database user that was create for the RepServer maintenance user, as well as the corresponding dataserver login (unless these are still in use for other purposes).

46.5 Moving a RepServer to another host

Moving RepServer to a physically different host is not too difficult, assuming all pathnames and port numbers remain the same. After shutting down RepServer and the RSSD, the RepServer **.cfg** file and the stable devices can simply be copied to the new host. For raw devices, use the Unix '**dd**' command to copy them (through an intermediate file if necessary).
When using an embedded RSSD, its files must be moved along with the RepServer itself. When using a classic ASE RSSD, strictly speaking the RSSD ASE server does not have to be moved, but if it is moved, this can be done independently from moving RepServer.

The only places where a hostname needs to be changed is in the **interfaces** file on the RepServer host (which must be copied too), as well as in all **interfaces** files on hosts from where connections to the RepServer are made (like hosts for dataservers where RepAgents are running).
In addition, when using RS 15.0 with a non-served SySAM license (i.e. a local license file), a new license key should be generated.
This is all under the assumption that the OS remains the same on the new host. If not, this procedure may still work, but you are strongly recommended to carefully test this first.

Index

E

F

G

H

I

L

M

N

O

P

Q

R

S

T

U

V

W

Z

Notes

Notes